We Are Not Alone

A Maimonidean Theology of the Other

Emunot: Jewish Philosophy and Kabbalah

Series Editor
Dov Schwartz (Bar-Ilan University, Ramat Gan)

Editorial Board
Ada Rapoport Albert (University College, London)
Gad Freudenthal (CNRS, Paris)
Gideon Freudenthal (Tel Aviv University, Ramat Aviv)
Moshe Idel (Hebrew University, Jerusalem)
Raphael Jospe (Bar-Ilan University, Ramat Gan)
Ephraim Kanarfogel (Yeshiva University, New York)
Menachem Kellner (Haifa University, Haifa)
Daniel Lasker (Ben Gurion University, Beer Sheva)

We Are Not Alone
A Maimonidean Theology of the Other

Menachem Kellner

BOSTON
2021

Library of Congress Cataloging-in-Publication Data

Names: Kellner, Menachem Marc, 1946- author.
Title: We are not alone: a Maimonidean theology of the other / Menachem Kellner.
Description: Boston: Academic Studies Press, 2021. | Series: Emunot: Jewish Philosophy and Kabbalah | Includes bibliographical references.
Identifiers: LCCN 2021009319 (print) | LCCN 2021009320 (ebook) | ISBN 9781644696132 (hardback) | ISBN 9781644696149 (adobe pdf) | ISBN 9781644696156 (epub)
Subjects: LCSH: Maimonides, Moses, 1135-1204--Teachings. | Judaism--Relations. | Universalism.
Classification: LCC B759.M34 K449 2021 (print) | LCC B759.M34 (ebook) | DDC 296.3/2--dc23
LC record available at https://lccn.loc.gov/2021009319
LC ebook record available at https://lccn.loc.gov/2021009320

Copyright © Academic Studies Press, 2021

ISBN 9781644696132 (hardback)
ISBN 9781644697023 (paperback)
ISBN 9781644696149 (adobe pdf)
ISBN 9781644696156 (epub)

Book design by PHi Business Solutions
Cover design by Ivan Grave

Published by Academic Studies Press
1577 Beacon Street
Brookline, MA 02446, USA
press@academicstudiespress.com
www.academicstudiespress.com

For Jolene—it just keeps getting better

Contents

Acknowledgements	ix
Preface	xi
1. Jewish Voices Rejected; A Jewish Voice Affirmed	1
2. We Are Not Alone	28
3. Election/Chosen People	42
4. The Convert as the Most Jewish of Jews	68
5. Aher—Then, Now, and in the Future: Othering the Other in Judaism	85
6. Tolerance	105
7. Christianity	137
Conclusion	159
Bibliography	167
Index	185

Acknowledgements

Several friends were kind enough to read and comment on the whole manuscript of this book, saving me from error and improving my presentation. I am grateful to Marc Angel, Avi (Seth) Kadish, Eugene Korn, Danny Lasker, Ken Seeskin, and Edwin Slonim. On specific issues I also benefited from the wise counsel of Matanel Bareli, Mordechai Akiva Friedman, Zev Harvey, Yehuda (Jerome) Gellman, David Gillis, Joel Kaminsky, J. J. Kimche, Eric Lawee, Tyra Lieberman, Yizhak Lifshitz, Diana Lobel, Mordy Miller, Avrom Montag, Abraham Rubin, Chaim Waxman, and, of course, Jolene S. Kellner who never ceases to amaze me. I am also grateful to Lenn Evan Goodman and Phillip Lieberman for their kind permission to cite from the *Guide of the Perplexed* in their forthcoming translation.

Several chapters of this book appeared in earlier versions, as follows: chapter 2, "We Are Not Alone," in *Radical Responsibility: Celebrating the Thought of Chief Rabbi Lord Jonathan Sacks*, ed. Michael J. Harris, Daniel Rynhold, and Tamra Wright (Jerusalem: Maggid Books, 2012): 139–154; chapter 4, "The Convert as the Most Jewish of Jews? On the Centrality of Belief (the Opposite of Heresy) in Maimonidean Judaism," *Jewish Thought/Mahshevet Yisrael* (Ben Gurion University Annual) 1 (2019): 33–52; chapter 5, "Aher—Then and Now and in the Future: Otherizing the Other in Judaism," commissioned for *Oxford Handbook of Jewish Philosophy*, ed. Yizhak Melamed (Oxford: Oxford University Press, forthcoming 2022); chapter 6, "Tolerance," in *Key Concepts in Interreligious Discourses*, ed. Georges Tamer et al. (Berlin/Boston: Walter de Gruyter, in press); chapter 7, "Thinking Idolatry With/Against Maimonides—The Case of Christianity," *Thinking Idolatry Today*, ed. Alon Goshen-Gottstein (Boston: Academic Studies press, forthcoming 2022).

I am grateful to the editors and publishers of these articles for cheerfully granting permission to include my revisions of them in this book.

Preface

I would like to explain why I wrote this book, and how I came to write it. In order to do so, I shall tell a story.

I am what may be called an evolved and evolving feminist. When asked to exemplify changes in the world in which I used to live and the world in which I now live, I show people the *bentscher* distributed at the "wedding reception of Mr. and Mrs. Menachem Kellner" a bit more than fifty years ago. I can hardly imagine agreeing to such language today.

As an evolved and evolving feminist, I was very pleased when a group of younger people in my community, led by a halakhically serious young woman, decided to hold a "partnership" *minyan* once a month, on the eve of the Sabbath when the new moon is announced (*Shabbat mevorkhim*). In this service, complete with *mechitzah* (separation between men and women) and male *hazzanim* (cantors), the only feminist innovation was that women would lead that part of the service (from their side of the *mechitzah*) which has no halakhic standing—known as *kabbalat Shabbat*.

The reaction of several rabbis in the community (individuals who serve informally and with great dedication) was immediate and vociferous. The leaders of the feminist initiative then decided to invite Israel Prize Winner Rabbi Professor Daniel Sperber of Bar-Ilan University, a distinguished rabbi and professor with impeccable Orthodox credentials, to come and speak to the community. Rabbi Sperber came and gave a lecture to a large and supportive crowd. His main point was that indeed almost all contemporary Orthodox rabbis (especially in Israel) oppose "partnership" *minyanim* on both halakhic and policy grounds. However, if, despite that opposition, one was interested in finding rabbinic warrant for the initiative, it could be found. Rabbi Sperber showed that halakhah and tradition are not as monolithic as the rabbinic opponents of the "partnership" *minyan* claimed. He further showed that several of the "innovations" to which they objected were not actually as innovative as they thought.

One of the local rabbis (an IDF reserve officer and holder of a PhD in Jewish thought from an Israeli university), a particularly fine individual, attended the lecture, spoke in response to it the following Sabbath, and took the trouble of visiting many of the families (such as ours) to explain his opposition to the initiative and his response to Rabbi Sperber. I thought then and think now that our rabbi, a family friend and someone whom I admire, largely misunderstood what Rabbi Sperber said.

Our rabbi's response was that while Rabbi Sperber might have a point in strictly historical terms, halakhah should be determined by leading authorities (in Haredi-speak, *gedolim*) and not by "outliers." In my eyes, this boils down to an argument for conservatism in religious affairs. (The fact that several of the rabbis he cited are individuals about whom I have serious reservations did not help his cause.) This conservatism may or may not be a good policy (I personally do not think that it is) but it is not a policy that can be refuted as such (since it expresses values, not facts). However, in my eyes, it is conservatism in this case which drives halakhah and policy, not the other way around. (I should point out that my rabbi friend sees the entire story very differently and that the "partnership minyan" continues—the debate about it died down.)

How is this story relevant to this book? I fully admit—sadly, not cheerfully—that in the eyes of many Orthodox and certainly Haredi rabbis, gentiles have no worth and purpose in and of themselves; they are, in effect, only static, background noise to the real business of the universe. For Haredim the business of the universe is the study of (a narrow aspect of) Torah. For many of those rabbis who identify as religious Zionists, the business of the universe often appears to be the study of Torah (somewhat more broadly construed) and the settlement of the whole biblical land of Israel. While these views are widely held by leading rabbinic authorities today, they are not the whole story by any means. The Jewish story contains other voices, some of them quite prominent; one of those voices is that of Moses Maimonides, arguably the most prominent rabbinic authority since the Talmudic era.

It is my *use* of Maimonides that explains what I am trying to do in this book. A reader content with the Judaism ordinarily presented these days in most traditionalist Jewish circles should not read this book—she or he will not like it one bit. However, a reader who wishes to remain within the traditionalist Jewish world—widely or narrowly construed—and who also affirms that all humans are fully created in the image of God, and have intrinsic worth in God's eyes, will find a measure of support for her or his views. Just as Rabbi Sperber pointed us to voices that provide halakhic warrant for our feminist initiative,

I hope to show that a modified Maimonideanism provides a warrant for the Judaism expressed in these pages.[1]

Let me further explain what I am attempting to do. R. Sa'adia Gaon (882–942) wrote his *Beliefs and Doctrines* for those Jews whose faith was troubled by apparent conflicts between that faith and contemporary science. He also addressed fellow Jews who desired to turn their beliefs into reasoned doctrines. He did not address his book to people who had no such problems; persons content with their received faith did not need his book. Similarly, this book is not addressed to people who are content in their Judaism. It is definitely addressed to those Jews made uncomfortable, or even occasionally embarrassed, by so much of what passes for "Torah-true" Judaism today.

I hasten to point out that while Maimonides appears in every chapter of this book, I do not for a moment pretend that the historical Maimonides would be happy with all the conclusions which I reach. However, I would like to think that were he among us *today*, and knew what we know today, he would be willing to sign off on many of my conclusions. Of course, I am not alone in that view. From the Rabbi of Lubavitch to the "Rabbi of Leibowitz" and in between, all contemporary Orthodox spokespersons (well, almost all) claim Maimonides for their own (this even includes the authors of the scandalous *Torat ha-Melekh*, on which see chapter 1 below).

That said, one of the issues addressed tangentially in this book is one with which I am confident the historical Maimonides would agree: that all human

---

1 Concerning my use of the term "Judaism," I realize that historically Jews have not understood themselves as a religion similar in structure to Christianity and Islam. Leora Batnitzky maintains that arguing over the issue is a mark of Jewish modernity. See her *How Judaism Became a Religion* (Princeton: Princeton University Press, 2011). Avraham Melamed has shown that *dat* (religion) is a term applied by Jews to what came to be called "Judaism" from at least the fifteenth century. See Abraham Melamed, *Dat: Me-Hok le-Emunah—Korotav shel Minu'ah Mekhonen* (Tel Aviv: Ha-Kibbutz Ha-Me'uhad, 2014). A quick check of the Bar Ilan Global Data Base confirms this (ibn Ezra's usages appear to be ambiguous in this regard). The implications of this are vast, but not our point right now. I have argued that Maimonides may have been the first Jew to use the term *dat* in a way similar to the way in which we use the term "religion" and that he certainly had a notion of what we today would call "Judaism" even if it never occurred to him to use the term. See below, chapter 4 and my other studies cited there. Daniel Boyarin's recent *Judaism: The Genealogy of a Modern Notion* (New Brunswick: Rutgers University Press, 2018) is relevant and has a long discussion of Judah Halevi but ignores the much more relevant Maimonides. For an important corrective to Boyarin, see Melamed, *Dat*, esp. 41–51. See also Howard Kreisel, "Maimonides on Divine Religion," in *Maimonides after 800 Years: Essays on Maimonides and His Influence*, ed. Jay Harris (Cambridge: Harvard University Press, 2007), 151–166.

beings are actually and fully created in the image of God. I have addressed that subject in a number of works, among them: *Maimonides on Judaism and the Jewish People* and *Gam Hem Keruyim Adam: ha-Nokhri be-Einei ha-Rambam*. This issue is of crucial importance. Hermann Cohen often pointed out that the doctrine that all human beings are made in the image of God, have a common source in God, makes the notion of *humanity* necessary. No longer are humans defined essentially in terms of tribal affiliation. Translating this ideal into reality is an unfinished project, but an ideal that we must surely pursue.

There are two further and interrelated issues in Maimonides's thought that are not directly addressed in this book, despite their relevance. My friend and colleague David Gillis and I have written a book which addresses two topics, which might well be included in the present volume had we not already written that book. That book is called *Maimonides the Universalist: The Ethical Horizons of Mishneh Torah* (London: The Littman Library of Jewish Civilization, 2020). In the context of the book's chapters that analyze the closing paragraphs of each of the fourteen volumes of the *Mishneh Torah*, we address the following question: to whom is the Torah ultimately addressed—all humanity (*kol ba'ei olam*) or just Israel? It is our claim that Maimonides follows the school of R. Yishmael, as opposed to the school of R. Akiva, and holds that ultimately the Torah is addressed to all human beings.

This reading of Maimonides and his understanding of Judaism also subserves the second topic that might have been taken up in this book, namely, Maimonides's intellectualist and universalist account of the messianic era, the topic of chapter 14 in *Maimonides the Universalist*. For Maimonides the Torah will indeed become the patrimony of all humanity by the time the messianic era reaches full fruition.

In chapter 1 below, I show that—again for Maimonides (*Guide* iii.32)—ideal Judaism is the intellectualist, ethical, and universalist Judaism of Abraham, not the particularist and ritualistic Judaism of Moses. That Judaism, according to Maimonides, is a concession to human frailty. Human frailty being what it is, we cannot do without the Torah of Moses, but we can live our lives in pursuit of the Abrahamic ideal. This idea will come up in several of the chapters of this book.

Abrahamic Judaism failed with Abraham's great grandchildren (the grandsons of Jacob/Israel, almost all of whom were idolaters in Egypt), and failed again with their descendants after Marah (Exod. 15) and the golden calf. This is the "Abrahamic" nature of the theology outlined in this book. This issue, too, will be taken up in the chapter 1 below.

The Abrahamic component of Judaism, addressed to the whole world, and anticipating a messianic fulfillment also addressed to the whole world, is under assault. This is hardly surprising only two generations after the Holocaust in a world in which Jew hatred (often disguised as "anti-Zionism") is again on the rise, among ruffians and among the denizens of academic lounges alike. Just as renewed Jew hatred must be resisted, so must the resultant Jewish assault on the Abrahamic ideal be resisted.

A word about my own stance. I think of myself as a classic liberal. In today's "woke" and (allegedly) "progressive" environment that would mean that many would see me as conservative. Be that as it may, a central focus of this book is to present a universalist version of Judaism (whatever that might be) that conceives of all human beings as being fully created in the image of God (whatever that might mean). This version of Judaism refuses to condemn as false or immoral other religions or cultures (so long as they do not advocate or practice violations of natural morality). The Judaism I describe and defend in this book is rationalist and hence pre-postmodern: truth does matter. I admit that there is no such thing as "Judaism"—there are only Judaisms; this book presents one of many competing Judaisms and shows its rootedness in the historical traditions of the Jewish people.

Jews to the right of me, religiously and culturally, will say (and have said) that I am trying to force my liberal notions on a Judaism that is itself not at all liberal. I am tempted here to make a series of ad hominem rebuttals: Talmudic law reflects foreign influences, not just in terminology; Judah Halevi's views on the special nature of the Jewish people have been shown to have roots in Shi'ite thought; Kabbalah is a form of (partially) Judaized Neoplatonism; Jewish "orthodoxy" is a response to modernity; contemporary "Kookian" notions of the special nature and mission of the Jews reflect Romantic notions of people (*volk*) and land; Haredi notions of *da'at Torah* are as much Catholic as they are Jewish (some would argue they not Jewish at all). However, to argue in this fashion—as if to say: "You, too!"—is to bring myself down to the level of a politician.

Instead, I take it as a given that the Jewish tradition contains both universalist and particularist elements, rationalist orientations and mystical spirituality, elite religion and folk religion. Notice what I have just done: universalist/rational/elite versus particularist/mystical/folk. I admit my crime: by nature and upbringing, I gravitate to the liberal end of the spectrum. Does that affect the way I understand the Jewish tradition? Undoubtedly. Does it make my positions Jewishly illegitimate? Only if I cannot reasonably ground them in the historical texts of Judaism. It is the point of this book to show that I can do that.

Moreover, reading Jewish texts through specific lenses has a long history. Talmudic rabbis presented biblical figures as if they were themselves Talmudic rabbis, and some of them may even have believed their own aggadah that the patriarchs obeyed all the 613 commandments (including those laws innovated by the rabbis themselves). Maimonides and other medieval Jewish philosophers treated prophets and Talmudic rabbis as if they taught philosophy. Medieval Kabbalists turned the second-century Rabbi Shim'on Bar-Yohai into a Kabbalist, and even made him the author of the *Zohar*. Hasidim turned Moses (and perhaps Adam) into the first Hasidic rebbes. Contemporary Haredim seems to believe that Jews have always been Haredim (and always dressed like Polish gentry). The difference between what I do in this book, and what has always been done in the Jewish tradition, is that I am self-conscious about it.

That, however, is a very big difference. Being self-conscious about what I am doing in our historical epoch is more than simply being self-reflective—after all, seeking to be aware of ourselves and of what we are doing is hardly a new activity. Nevertheless, our reflexivity is a function of historical self-consciousness. After Marx and Freud among others, we are, or at least can be, aware of ourselves in new ways. This new self-awareness means that we look at our own traditions from the inside and the outside simultaneously. This is characteristic of academic scholars of the Jewish tradition, but of course, not only of them.

Once we look at the Jewish tradition both from the inside out and from the outside in, we become aware of the fact that we keep faith with the tradition out of choice. It is common to call converts to Judaism "Jews by choice" but nowadays all Jews are actually Jews by choice. I am not sure that this is altogether unprecedented in Jewish history. Certainly ceasing to be a Jew without actively converting to another religion may have been impossible between the time of Philo (whose nephew was an officer in the Roman army which destroyed the Second Temple) and of Josephus on the one hand, and the time of Spinoza on the other. Thus, for two millennia, Jews have not been Jews by choice in the sense in which those of us lucky enough to live in our world are.

There is another relevant point that must be raised: Jews whose texts I study in this book largely saw themselves as being in direct communication with God. Even on as simple level as that of Sholom Aleichem's Tevye, Jews felt themselves able to talk *to* God, not *about* God. I am not sure how many Jews today, at least those who live both inside and outside, can achieve that level, or even try to achieve it.

In light of all the above, a difficult question must be raised: Is there any issue in which tradition trumps liberalism? It is of no use to turn the question towards Jews whose philosophic and cultural tendency is towards conservatism and ask them, is there any issue in which tradition trumps conservatism? Let Jews of a conservative temper wrestle with that one. Trying to look at the matter honestly, I have a hard time finding some area in which Jewish tradition trumps my liberal sentiments. Of course, I regret cases of intermarriage, but do not feel that I have the right to tell people who love each other not to marry.

That does not worry me: I am convinced that my liberal sentiments reflect my Jewish background and studies. In other words, without subjecting myself to the sort of courageous self-analysis of a Freud (and we all know how successful that was) there is really no way that I can disentangle my Judaism from my liberalism. In what follows I hope to present my understanding of what Judaism ought to be and invite others along for the ride. I do so with no pretensions of being an authoritative voice—but I hope to be a convincing one.

Now, a word on how I came to write this book. I did not intend to write it. Over the last few years, I have been invited to contribute articles to journals and collective volumes. I suppose I should not have been surprised that in many cases the articles that I wrote all had something to do with a subject that is often at the front of my mind, and always at the back of it. I refer to the fact that so many Jews—despite all the evidence to the contrary—believe that Jews simply by virtue of their birth are in some intrinsic fashion distinct from and superior to non-Jews. To my mind, this view borders on the irrational, and is fundamentally immoral, not to mention that it contradicts the opening chapters of the Torah. However, it was only while writing the last of these articles (chapter 3 below, on the notion of the chosen people) that I realized that all these articles dealt with aspects of the same issue: how Jews should see themselves and see others.

This book is more than simply a collection of related articles, but less than a book written from scratch, as it were, with a beginning, a middle, and an end. The chapters cohere (and I have worked hard to make them do so) but they can also stand alone (after all, several of them began their lives as independent essays). Together they do make one argument: we the Jews are not alone in God's universe.

CHAPTER 1

Jewish Voices Rejected; A Jewish Voice Affirmed

1. JEWISH VOICES REJECTED

By way of introducing the issues raised in this chapter, I shall quote a close friend who recently wrote to me (about the subject matter of this book). He wrote: "I'm also put in mind of the rabbi whose lessons I have attended for many years, whom I greatly like and respect and who can be truly eye-opening on bible, prayer, Talmud, and anything else, but who has a blind spot about non-Jews, whom he thinks God doesn't care about."

Another telling incident demonstrates this point. When a friend of mine was a scholar in residence at a prominent modern Orthodox American synagogue years ago, he taught the passage at end of "Laws of Slaves" in *Mishneh Torah* in which Maimonides emphasizes that Jews and gentiles are all created equal by God and formed "in the same womb," that is, there is no essential difference between Jews and gentiles.[1] In the synagogue, there was a sophisticated Torah scholar in his twenties who was also the son of a prominent yeshiva head. He protested this purported equality, and stayed with my friend for almost an hour after the Sabbath arguing that Maimonides did not say this because he could not have said it. The belief in Jewish superiority was an essential part of the young scholar's personal sense of Jewish identity. He had formed this identity under the influence of his parents, their peers, and his peers. The text was merely secondary and after the fact. When he saw the text, he was forced either to distort it or to deny its importance. After my friend proved to the young Torah scholar that the universalistic interpretation was correct by citing numerous other Maimonidean texts in the *Mishneh Torah* and in the *Guide of the Perplexed*, this product of the best modern Orthodox

---

1 On this passage, see Menachem Kellner and David Gillis, *Maimonides the Universalist: The Ethical Horizons of Mishneh Torah* (Liverpool: Littman Library of Jewish Civilization, 2020), chapter 12.

education gave up on Maimonides and said it really didn't matter what Maimonides said because he (and presumably "the Torah world") had decided in accordance with the views of Judah Halevi anyway. His prejudice was so deep that he preferred the opinion of the non-halakhist Halevi to that of the greatest halakhist in Jewish history!

One need not adopt the extreme views to be discussed below to believe, in effect, that we Jews are alone in the eyes of God.[2] It is my point in this book to show that texts and traditions offer us a more universalist alternative.

The voice of Rabbi Shlomo Aviner is heard loudly and clearly in the world of contemporary Orthodox Zionism in Israel (*dati-leumi*), the community in which I live. This is thanks to his many books, lectures, internet activities, and especially the multitude of "Sabbath leaflets" (*alonei Shabbat*) to which he contributes.[3] Although considered a political hawk, R. Aviner broke with many of his rabbinic colleagues, and counseled soldiers to obey orders in connection with the Gaza withdrawal of 2005. This independent stand aroused considerable controversy in the world of Orthodox Zionism, earning R. Aviner many enemies.[4] Aviner's voice is not the only voice heard in the dati-leumi community (for which I am grateful), but it is a voice that echoed widely around the world.

One of the issues to which R. Avner often returns is the special nature of the Jewish people. Thus in the pamphlet *Itturei Kohanim* 174 (Sivan, 5759) we find him writing:

> We are the chosen people, not because we received the Torah, but, rather, we received the Torah because we are the chosen people.[5] This is so since the Torah is so apt to our inner nature. Each nation has a special nature, character, public psychology, unique divine character, and the Master of the Universe formed this special nation, *This people which I formed for*

---

2   It is no comfort, and in my eyes wholly irrelevant, to point out that many Christians and Muslims believe that they are alone in the eyes of God. But there are some good jokes on the subject.

3   Rabbi Aviner was born in France in 1943 and made aliyah in 1966. He earned degrees in math and engineering and is an officer in the IDF reserves. After his aliyah, Aviner studied at Yeshivat Merkaz Ha-Rav Kook in Jerusalem and is a disciple of the late Rabbi Zvi Yehudah Kook (1891–1982). R. Aviner is the rabbi of the West Bank settlement Bet El and head of the yeshiva Ateret Kohanim in the Muslim quarter of the Old City.

4   On Aviner, see Motti Inbari, *Messianic Religious Zionism Confronts Israeli Territorial Compromises* (Cambridge: Cambridge University Press, 2012), esp. 59–64.

5   Here R. Aviner reflects Judah Halevi's *Kuzari* ii. 56.

Myself, they will tell My praise (Is. 43:21). There are ... those who claim against us that we are 'racist'. Our answer to them is ... if racism means that we are different from and superior to other nations, and by this bring blessings to other nations,[6] then indeed we admit that we differ from every nation, not by virtue of skin color, but from the aspect of the nature of our souls [ha-teva ha-nishmati shelanu], the Torah describing our inner contents.[7]

In this typical passage, Rabbi Aviner presents his position in the clearest possible fashion and takes issue with his opponents. Let us look more closely at his words. The people of Israel are the chosen people (*am segulah*).[8] Why and how? R. Aviner relates to two possibilities: the descendants of Abraham, Isaac, and Jacob received the Torah and in consequence became the chosen people, or, the descendants of Abraham, Isaac, and Jacob were they only humans capable (*mesugalim*) of receiving the Torah. Receiving the Torah was a consequence of their already having been the chosen people (*am segulah*). In so doing R. Aviner accomplishes several ends: he admits (barely, it seems to me) that there is controversy on the issue (as indeed there is—we shall see below that his view is that of R. Judah Halevi [1075–1141], as opposed to the view of Maimonides [1138–1204]); takes a stand on this controversy; and hints that the opposing view ought not to be taken seriously, since he does not deign to argue against it.

R. Aviner continues and insists that the Torah is appropriate for the inner nature of the Jewish people—"Each nation has a special nature, character, public psychology, unique divine character, and the Master of the Universe formed this special nation—*This people which I formed for Myself, they will tell My praise* (Is. 43:21)." In making this claim he reifies the notion "nation" and establishes that there are nations defined and demarcated one from the other

---

6 How does Israel bring blessings to other nations? In his commentary on Halevi's *Kuzari* 4 vols. (Bet El: Sifriyat Hava, n.d.), 1:108, R. Aviner writes: "The Torah is the greatest divine light, and it belongs only to Israel, and from Israel drops of sanctity drip to each and every nation, according to its stature and state [*inyano*]." See also his response to a question on the internet "Why should we be a nation?" See: http://www.havabooks.co.il/article_ID.asp?id=632.

7 My thanks to Rabbi Dr. Ronen Lubitch for bringing this source to my attention. For the Kabbalistic background to this passage, see below, note 18.

8 Based on the Bar Ilan Responsa Project, this expression shows up only 113 times in the entire body of Jewish literature covered by the database. Most date from in the Middle Ages. The term literally means "treasured nation."

by their inner natures.[9] In so doing, he adopts the views of nineteenth-century German Romanticism and foists this ideology on Judaism.[10] The Jewish people, he teaches, have an inner nature unique to it, a nature to which the Torah is particularly appropriate.[11] A number of things follow from this: R. Aviner takes a position in a tannaitic debate over whether the Torah was ultimately intended for all human beings (*kol ba'ei olam*) or just for Israel.[12] He further raises a metaphysical problem with the conversion of Gentiles to Judaism: How can a person whose inner nature is not Jewish receive the

---

9   It is not surprising that individuals who can be considered part of Aviner's circle are attracted to what used to be known as *voelkerpsychologie*—understood as inquiry into the (so-called) psychological makeup of nations. See, for example, Haggai Stammler, "Psychology of Nations: A Forgotten Field," *Moreshet* 15 (2015): 209–224 (Hebrew).

10 In this, R. Aviner follows in the footsteps of his teacher, R. Zvi Yehudah Kook; R. Zvi Yehudah follows in the footsteps of his father, R. Abraham Isaac Kook (to a great degree), and Rav Kook in turn appears to follow in the footsteps of his teachers, Hegel and other Romantic thinkers. On this intellectual pedigree, see Shlomo Fischer, "Self-Expression and Democracy in Radical Religious Zionist Ideology" (PhD diss., Hebrew University of Jerusalem, 2007), esp. 66–126, 217–234. For a recent and very useful English-language study of the elder R. Kook, see Yehudah Mirsky, *Rav Kook: Mystic in a Time of Revolution* (New Haven: Yale University Press, 2014). On Rabbi Z. Y. Kook, see Gideon Aran, "The Father, the Son, and the Holy Land: The Spiritual Authorities of Jewish-Zionist Fundamentalism in Israel," in *Spokesmen for the Despised: Fundamentalist Leaders of the Middle East*, ed. R. S. Appleby (Chicago: University of Chicago Press, 1997), 294–327; Shai Held, "What Zvi Yehudah Kook Wrought: The Theopolitical Radicalization of Religious Zionism," in *Rethinking the Messianic Idea in Judaism*, ed. Michael Morgan and Steven Weitzman (Bloomington: Indiana University Press, 2015), 229–55; Motti Inbari, *Messianic Religious Zionism Confronts Israeli Territorial Compromises* (Cambridge: Cambridge University Press, 2012), 15–36; Dov Schwartz, *Challenge and Crisis in Rabbi Kook's Circle* (Tel Aviv: Am Oved, 2001; Hebrew); Don Seeman, "God's Honor, Violence and the State," in *From Swords into Plowshares? Reflections on Religion and Violence*, ed. Robert W. Jenson and Eugene Korn (https://www.amazon.com/Plowshares-into-Swords-Reflections-Religion-ebook/dp/B00P11EGOE 2014), Kindle ed.; and Don Seeman, "Violence, Ethics, and Divine Honor in Modern Jewish Thought," *JAAR* 73, no. 4 (2004): 1015–1048. Rabbi Abraham Isaac Kook (1865–1935) founded what became the Israel Chief Rabbinate and is to this day the revered, dominant figure in Orthodox Religious Zionism, especially that branch which continues to see the creation of the State of Israel as "the first flowering" of messianic redemption.

11 I tried to translate Rabbi Aviner's usages back into rabbinic Hebrew with no success. His ideas, I submit, largely come from outside the Jewish tradition and cannot easily be traced to rabbinic texts.

12 On this debate, see Menachem Hirshman, *Torah Lekhol Ba'ei Olam: Zerem Universali Be-Sifrut Ha-Tana'im Ve-Yahaso Le-Hokhmat He-Amim* (Tel Aviv: Ha-Kibbutz ha-Meuhad, 1999) and "Rabbinic Universalism in the Second and Third Centuries," *Harvard Theological Review* 93 (2000), 101–115.

Torah?¹³ He also forces himself to adopt a particularist stance concerning the messianic era: if the Torah is appropriate only for those whose inner nature is Jewish, then the essential difference between Jew and Gentile must be preserved in the days of the messiah. R. Aviner thus once again takes a stand in a controversial matter, without even admitting that there is a controversy on the issue.¹⁴

Aviner's view here is that of Halevi, but it is not clear that he realizes Halevi's view is not the only one in the tradition.¹⁵

Rabbi Aviner is not only the rabbi of a settlement in Samaria, and not only the founder and head of a yeshiva deeply identified with the hopes for the actual construction of a third Temple, he is also a man of the wider world. Born (during the Holocaust), raised, and educated in France, he holds academic degrees, and served as an officer in the IDF. He knows what sort of an outcry his words are likely to arouse, and hence hastens to assure us that he is not a racist, at least not in the accepted sense of the word. His self-confessed racism is not biological—Jews come in all skin shades. No, his racism is spiritual. Jews are indeed superior to other nations, but their superiority is

---

13 I am aware of the many solutions offered for this problem. For Rabbi Aviner (and before him Halevi, not to mention the authors of the *Zohar*), conversion presents a problem. For Maimonides, in contrast, conversion is not a problem that needs to be solved. Once, while teaching an introductory course in Judaism at a leading university in the US, I mentioned the possibility of conversion to Judaism. Two of the students, both of them daughters of Baptist ministers, were surprised and asked, "How is it possible to choose to be chosen?" Apparently, it is Halevi, and not Maimonides, who is taught in Baptist Sunday Schools in the USA.

14 See Menachem Kellner, *Maimonides on Judaism and the Jewish People* (Albany: SUNY Press, 1991); *Maimonides' Confrontation with Mysticism* (Oxford: Littman Library of Jewish Civilization, 2006), chapter 7 (henceforth: *Confrontation*) and "Maimonides' True Religion—for Jews, or All Humanity?" *Me'orot* 7, no. 1 (2008), http://www.yctorah.org/content/view/436/10/. I wonder how R. Aviner would react if he heard me pointing out to my students that the patriarchs and even Moses (before Sinai) were, at most, Noahides, not Jews. It may be that sensitivity to that point stands behind the rabbinic aggadah—apparently rejected by Maimonides—that the patriarchs fulfilled all the commandments. On the patriarchs not observing the commandments of the Torah, see Kellner, *Confrontation*, 76–77. See further, Gerald Blidstein, "R. Menahem Ha-Me'iri: Aspects of an Intellectual Profile," *Journal of Jewish Thought & Philosophy* 5 (1995): 65–66 and (rather surprisingly), R. Yehudah Amital at https://www.etzion.org.il/en/yaakov-was-reciting-shema. Compare further *Commentary on the Mishnah, Hullin* 7:6 and the discussion in Kellner and Gillis, *Maimonides the Universalist*, 58.

15 On Halevi on proselytes in the messianic era, see Daniel J. Lasker, "Proselyte Judaism, Christianity, and Islam in the Thought of Judah Halevi," *Jewish Quarterly Review* 81 (1990): 75–91.

connected to their unique Jewish souls, souls whose "operating instructions" are written in the Torah. This superiority brings nothing but blessings to all other nations.

I think fairness demands that we point out that Aviner is doing himself a disservice here. There is no doubt that he accepts the possibility of conversion to Judaism.[16] Thus, despite what he says about himself, he cannot be a racist in any contemporary sense of the term. He seems to be using "racism" here as shorthand for essentialism.[17]

R. Aviner is willing to accept the consequences of his position on Jewish superiority. In a book aimed at soldiers in the Israeli army, he writes:

> Death is ritual impurity [*tum'ah*] since its essence is the diminishment of the divine vitality in created entities. The measure of ritual impurity matches the measure of the departure of this divine vitality. Gentile graves in an enclosure do not cause ritual impurity according to the basic law [*ikkar ha-din*] since their souls are not so holy and the difference between their bodies without a soul and their bodies with a soul is not all that great. Therefore the departure of the soul in their case does not constitute so terrible a crisis. … Jewish graves do impart ritual impurity since their souls are holy; however, their bodies without a soul are not holy and, therefore, the departure of the soul is the terrible crisis of the departure of the divine vitality from the body—and this constitutes the ritual impurity of death.[18]

According to this horrifying text, the difference between a live Jew and a dead Jew is immense; the difference between a live Gentile and a dead Gentile is much smaller.[19] Rabbi Aviner neither says nor even implies that the killing of

---

16 See, for example, http://www.havabooks.co.il/article_ID.asp?id=1185.
17 Further on this, see Kellner, *Confrontation*, 26–31.
18 Aviner, *Me-Hayil el Hayil* (5759), 230, cited by Yosef Ahituv, "State and Army According to the Torah: Realism and Mysticism in the Circles of Merkaz Ha-Rav," in Aviezer Ravitzky, ed., *Dat u-Medinah ba-Hagut ha-Yehudit be-Me'ah ha-Esrim* (Jerusalem: Israel Democracy Institute, 2005), 466 (Hebrew). For a view similar to that of R. Aviner, see R. Hayyim ibn Attar (c. 1696–1743)'s popular *Or Ha-Hayyim* on Lev. 20:26 and Numbers 19:2. For Zoharic sources see Zohar, Genesis, *Hayyei Sarah*, 131a and *Genesis Va-Yehi*, 220a.
19 Compare R. Aviner's words in his commentary on the *Kuzari* (part 1, 136): "In that we are the *segulah* of humanity, we are also the heart of humanity. We are more human than the others." See also p. 302. For others who hold this view that Jews are "more human" then Gentiles, see below, note 28.

a Gentile is a light matter, but will all his readers understand that?[20] It is not my intention here to protest rabbinic irresponsibility, but, rather, to illustrate a certain, unfortunately widespread, view concerning the inner nature of the Jewish people.[21]

Further, a propos R. Aviner, one of the very many weekly newsletters distributed in Israeli Orthodox synagogues (at least in the non-haredi world) is *Ma'ayanei ha-Yeshuah* (Wellsprings of Salvation—Is. 12:3) whose very title betrays its messianic orientation. The leaflet (at sixteen glossy pages per week, one of the biggest of such pamphlets) is associated with the late Chief Rabbi Mordecai Eliyahu, his son R. Shmuel Eliyahu of Safed, R. Shlomo Aviner and R. Yaakov Ariel of Ramat-Gan. Not untypical of *Ma'ayanei ha-Yeshuah*'s editorial stance is a statement that created a certain uproar in Israel. In its edition of 18 Tevet 5771, an editorial was printed responding to criticism leveled against Rabbi Shmuel Eliyahu—who had issued a ruling forbidding Jews to rent or sell property to Arabs. The editorial asked rhetorically if those rabbis who had criticized Rabbi Eliyahu would also refuse to participate in the concentration (*rikkuz*) of Amalekites in death camps (*mahanot hashmadah*). Given that the unsigned editorial also takes an (irrelevant) swipe at the "primitive religion which has strangled the world for 2010 years," it is fair to assume that the author of the editorial is Rabbi Shlomo Aviner, whose obsession with Christianity is well known and well attested.[22]

---

20 Bear in mind that this text is addressed to teenaged inductees into the Israeli army. Aviner himself rejects this implication of his writings, in a criticism of the book *Torat Ha-Melekh*. See further in Tessa Satherley, "'The Simple Jew': The 'Price Tag' Phenomenon, Vigilantism, and Rabbi Yitzchak Ginsburgh's Political Kabbalah," *Melilah* 10 (2013): 67

21 See Shabbat 86b for the view that non-Jews are rendered gross by the fact that they eat gross things. (One wonders about non-Jewish vegans or Jews who eat nonkosher food.) One is tempted to see this rabbinic statement as support for a "nurture" as opposed to "nature" approach. See below, note 28, for sources that emphasize the ontological inferiority of non-Jews.

22 R. Aviner was a close disciple of the late R. Zvi Yehudah Kook, and is an associate of R. Tzvi Thau (born 1937). All three of these highly influential rabbis are strong believers in the doctrine of innate Jewish superiority. Aviner is a man revered by thousands of disciples and reviled by hundreds of enemies. His obsession with Christianity is well known and well documented (see below in chapter 7). For a good example of his obsession with Christianity, see his article on an alleged "secret Vatican document" concerning Catholic support for the final solution in, not surprisingly, *Ma'ayanei Ha-Yeshuah*, no. 403, 28 Sivan, 5769. When I sent a letter of protest to the editors of the leaflet, R. Aviner replied to me that the "document" was an example of "literary license" on his part.

R. Aviner is by far not the most extreme exponent of the view that Jews are by their very nature different from and superior to non-Jews. With respect to shockingly extremist views, let us examine one notorious example: *Torat ha-Melekh* purports to be a disinterested and entirely theoretical halakhic discussion of the circumstances under which it is permissible to kill Gentiles. The authors, Yizhak Shapira and Yosef Elitzur of Yeshivat Od Yosef Hai in the West Bank village of Yizhar, start their discussion from the (largely uncontested in the halakhic tradition) assumption that the sixth commandment only outlaws the killing of Jews.[23] They go on from there to the astounding (and wholly unsupported in the halakhic tradition) assumption that the lives of Gentiles who are not "resident aliens" have no meaning and no legitimacy. Having "established" that, they then spend more than 200 pages misusing Maimonides to examine the (for them limited) circumstances under which it is *not* permissible to kill Gentiles. One example of their twisted conclusions: that it is reasonable to assume that it is permitted (and perhaps required) to kill children "if it is clear that they will grow up to harm us."[24] *Torat ha-Melekh* appeared with the approbations (*haskamot*) of four rabbis: R. Yizhak Ginsburgh (author of *Barukh Ha-Gever*, a book memorializing Barukh Goldstein, the murderer of Muslim worshippers in the Cave of Makhpelah Mosque in Hebron on Purim day, 1994),[25] R. Zalman Nehemiah Goldberg (who later withdrew his approbation), the now late R. Ya'akov Yosef, son of R. Ovadiah Yosef (former Israeli chief rabbi and leading light of the Shas Party), and R. Dov Lior, rabbi of Kiryat Arba near Hebron, who explicitly stated that the subject matter of the book is rather relevant (*dai aktuali*) to our day and age.

---

23 Which does not mean, of course, that the murder of Gentiles is permitted! Rather, punishment for such offenses is handed over to God, whose punishment is much surer than that of human courts, given the well-known restrictions on the possibility of capital punishment in Jewish courts. See Maimonides, "Laws of the Murderer," i. 1 and ii. 10.

24 Yizhak Shapira and Yosef Elitzur, *Torat ha-Melekh: Dinei Nefashot bein Yisrael le-Amim* (Yizhar: Yeshivat Od Yosef Hai, 2010), 207. I originally wrote these words under the shadow of the murder of the Fogel family in Itamar (11 March 2011), perpetrated by two Palestinian teenagers who agreed with *Torat Ha-Melekh*'s reasoning, but applied it to Jews.

25 On Ginsburgh, see: Shlomo Fischer, "Radical Religious Zionism from the Collective to the Individual," in *Kabbalah and Contemporary Spiritual* Revival, ed. Boaz Huss (Beersheva: Ben-Gurion University Press, 2011): 285–309; Motti Inbari, *Jewish Fundamentalism and the Temple Mount: Who Will Build the Third Temple?* (Albany: SUNY Press, 2009); Raphael Sagi, *Radikalism Meshihi Be-Medinat Yisrael: Perakim Be-Sod Ha-Tikkun Ha-Meshihi Bi-Haguto Shel Ha-Rav Yizhak Ginsberg* (Tel Aviv: Gevanim, 2015); Satherley, "'The Simple Jew'"; Seeman, "God's Honor, Violence, and the State"; and Seeman, "Violence, Ethics, and Divine Honor in Modern Jewish Thought": 1015–48.

The claim that the book is a disinterested theoretical discussion is given the lie by this approbation.²⁶

The publication of the book created a furor in Israel, leading to the arrest of one of its authors on the charge of "incitement." Rabbi Lior was "invited" by the police to answer questions concerning his approbation of the book, an "invitation" he declined. Rabbi Goldberg withdrew his approbation for the book; he is reported to have said that it contains errors in Jewish law and things which the human intellect cannot accept (*ein lahem makom ba-sekhel ha-enoshi*). In light of the police investigation into the rabbis who wrote approbations for the book, fifty leading rabbis in the "Zionist-Religious" community organized a protest meeting in Jerusalem's Ramada Hotel (18 August 2010). They claimed not to be supporting the book *Torat ha-Melekh* itself, but protesting limitations on the freedom of speech of rabbis implied by the police investigations. Statements for and against *Torat ha-Melekh* continue to show up on blogs and in Israeli newspapers.²⁷

---

26 Some of the "pearls" found in this book include the claim that the existence of a Gentile who is not a "resident alien" (and in this day and age, no Gentiles can achieve that status) "has no legitimacy" (*Torat ha-Melekh* 43); Jews and Gentiles share *nothing* in common, but, in effect, belong to different orders of reality (ibid., 45); a Gentile who violates one of the seven Noachide commandments (stealing, for example, even something of slight value, or, in the eyes of the authors of the book, undermining Jewish sovereignty over any part of the Land of Israel) is to be executed without advance warning or due halakhic process. The Jew who witnesses the act can serve as judge and executioner (ibid., 49–51); and so it goes in depressing and blood-curdling detail. *Torat ha-Melekh*'s views are based on readings of Kabbalistic texts mediated through the teachings of Rabbi Y. Ginsburgh, cited as direct inspiration by the authors of the book. I regret to note that the idea that Jews and Gentiles do not share the same human essence is also found in circles that identify with modernity and enlightenment, far from R. Ginsburgh and his morally twisted views. See, for example, Hershel Schachter, "Women Rabbis?" *Hakirah: The Flatbush Journal of Jewish Law and Thought* 11 (2011): 19–23. On p. 20, R. Schachter, distinguished professor of Talmud and Rosh Kollel at Yeshiva University, writes, as if it is totally uncontroversial: "Hashem [God] created all men *B'Tzelem Elokim* [in the image of God], and *Bnai Yisrael* [Jews] with an even deeper degree of this *Tzelem Elokim*—known as *Banim LaMakom* [Children of the Omnipresent]." I hasten to add that R. Schachter (who bases himself here, apparently, on a [mis-] reading of Avot, iii. 14) would be horrified to have his views connected to *Torat ha-Melekh*. I cite him only as an example of the casual way in which many Jews assume some sort of ontological divide between Jews and Gentiles. Further (and unfortunate) expressions of his views may be heard in the following lecture:
http://www.torahweb.org/audioFrameset.html#audio=rsch_050204.
For the text of Avot iii. 14, see below, chapter 5, note 43.

27 For one of many studies on *Torat ha-Melekh*, see Avinoam Rosenak, *Sedakim* (Tel Aviv: Resling, 2013), 166–174. Shortly after *Torat ha-Melekh*'s appearance, I organized a conference about the book at the University of Haifa. All of the speakers but one were going to

There is much precedent for these views about the nature of the Jewish people in the Jewish tradition, but such views were never made the basis for policy proposals as has happened over the last generation.[28] As important, they are far from the only views to be found. To that we now turn.

2. GOD AND ABRAHAM: WHO CHOSE WHOM?

According to Maimonides, God's choice of the Jews was actually a consequence of Abraham's discovery of God and not an historically necessary event. It is worth paying close attention to Maimonides's description of Abraham's career, as presented in the first chapter of "Laws Concerning Idolatry."[29] In this chapter, Maimonides presents what might be called a natural history of religion. The Bible presents its readers with an implicit problem: Given that Noah and his immediate descendants knew God, how did the world become entirely

---

    criticize the book. The sole exception was one of the book's authors. I thought it only fair to let him respond to the half-dozen critics who were going to speak. Inviting him was enough to arouse such a furor on campus that the then president of the university decided to cancel the event. An early example of "cancel culture."

28 For studies of Judaic particularism, see Moshe Hallamish, "The Kabbalists' Attitude to the Nations of the World," in *"Joseph Baruch Sermonetta Memorial Volume,"* ed. Aviezer Ravitzky, special issue, *Jerusalem Studies in Jewish Thought* 14 (1998): 289–312 (Hebrew); Elliot Wolfson, *Venturing Beyond: Law and Morality in Kabbalistic Mysticism* (Oxford: Oxford University Press, 2006); Jerome Gellman, "Jewish Mysticism and Morality—Kabbalah and its Ontological Dualities," *Archiv fuer Religionsgeschichte* 9 (2008): 23–35; Hanan Balk, "The Soul of a Jew and the Soul of a Non-Jew: An Inconvenient Truth and the Search for an Alternative," *Hakirah—The Flatbush Journal of Jewish Law and Thought* 16 (2013): 47–76; Hartley Lachter, "Israel as a Holy People in Medieval Kabbalah," in *Holiness in Jewish Thought*, ed. Alan Mittleman (Oxford: Oxford University Press, 2018), 137–159; For some particularly hair-raising examples of Jewish particularism run amok in the writings of the Maharal of Prague (Judah Leib ben Bezalel Loewe, 1525–1609), see *Derekh ha-Hayyim* III.14 (end of the chapter), *Gur Aryeh* on Exodus 19:22, *Nezah Yisrael*, chapter 3 and *Tiferet Yisrael*, chapter 32. These studies and texts all deal with Judaic particularism in kabbalistic contexts. For philosophic contexts, see Hannah Kasher, *Elyon Al Kol ha-Goyyim: Tsiyyunei Derekh ba-Philosophiah ha-Yehudit be-Sugiyat ha-Am ha-Nivhar* (Tel Aviv: Idra, 2018); and Menachem Kellner, "On Universalism and Particularism in Judaism," *Da'at* 36 (1996): v–xv. See further, Jonathan Garb, "The Conversion of the Jews: Identity as Ontology in Modern Kabbalah," forthcoming in the *Proceedings of the International Conference on Religious Responses to Modernity* (Israel Academy of Sciences and Humanities/Berlin Brandenburg Academy of Sciences, December 2015).

29 For a helpful discussion of this text, which supports the reading I am about to give it, see Lawrence Kaplan, "Maimonides on the Singularity of the Jewish People," *Da'at* 15 (1985): v–xxvii.

idolatrous by the time of Abraham, ten generations after Noah? Here is Maimonides's explanation:[30]

> In the days of Enosh [Gen. 4:26, 5:7–11] mankind fell into grave error; the wise of that generation turned brutish in counsel; and Enosh himself was among the errant. Their fallacy was to say as follows: "Since God created the stars and spheres to govern the world, set them on high, and granted them honor, and [since] they are ministers who serve Him, they deserve to be praised, extolled and honored. Indeed, it is the will of God (blessed be He) that [we] magnify and honor those whom He has magnified and honored, just as a king wants his servants and attendants to be honored—for this redounds to the honor of the king." Once this notion got into their heads, they began to build temples to the stars, offer them sacrifices, praise and extol them verbally, and bow down toward them, in order to win divine favor, by their corrupt lights. That was the root of alien worship.

Having explained the origin of idolatry,[31] Maimonides turns to describe Abraham's rebellion against it:

> After much time had passed, false prophets arose among the human race [and] … [i]t thus became the universal practice to worship the [various] images with distinct rites, and to sacrifice and bow down to them. With the passage of time, the Honored and Revered Name sank [into oblivion, fading] from the mouths and minds of all beings: they recognized it not. So all the commoners, women, and children, knew nothing but the wood or stone image and fabricated temple that they were brought up from childhood to bow down to, worship, and swear by. The wise among them— priests and the like—imagined there was no deity save the stars and spheres, for which those images had been made as [symbolic] representations. But as to the Eternal Source, none recognized or knew Him save singular individuals like Enoch, Methuselah, Noah, Shem, and Eber. Thus

---

30 I cite the translation of Bernard Septimus from his forthcoming translation of the *Book of Knowledge* for the Yale Judaica Series. I have eliminated almost all of Professor Septimus's extremely learned notes. It is my pleasant duty to thank him here for his kindness in furnishing me with an advance copy of his translation. For a detailed exposition of this passage, see Kellner, *Confrontation*, 77–82.
31 *Avodah Zarah*; Septimus translates this more literally as "alien worship."

was the world was declining by degrees, till the World's Pillar, Our Father Abraham, was born. No sooner this hero weaned than he began to ponder, though but a child, and to meditate day and night, wondering: "How can the Sphere forever follow its course with none to conduct it? Who causes it to rotate? For it cannot possibly cause *itself* to rotate?" He had no one to teach or instruct him in anything, but was immersed in [the culture of] Ur of the Chaldees among the foolish adherents of alien worship. His father, mother and the entire populace worshiped alien deities, and he worshiped along with them, while his mind was searching and seeking to understand—till he grasped the true way and understood the right course of his own sound reason: He realized that: there is a single God, He conducts the Sphere, He created the universe, and, in all that exists, there is no god but He. And he realized that all the people were in error, and [that] what had caused them to err was worshiping the stars and images for so long that the truth [of God's existence] was lost to their minds. It was at age forty[32] that Abraham recognized his Creator.

Maimonides goes on to describe how Abraham then refuted the inhabitants of Ur, argued with them, broke their images, and began instructing them in the truth. After convincing his fellow countrymen (and thus apparently upsetting the traditional order), the king sought to kill him. He was miraculously saved, whereupon he emigrated and "began to call out loudly to all the people, teaching them that the world has [but] one God, who [alone] ought to be worshiped." He travelled from city to city and from kingdom to kingdom, teaching this truth which he had discovered. Arriving in the land of Canaan, he proclaimed his message, instructed the inhabitants, implanted truth in their hearts, composed books on it, and taught it to his son Isaac.[33]

---

32 When he had reached intellectual maturity, and not at age three, as Genesis Rabbah 95 has it. See R. Abraham ben David's gloss here.

33 Compare Maimonides's account in *Guide of the Perplexed* iii. 29: "When Abraham, the pillar of the world, grew up he saw clearly that there exists an incorporeal God, a God who is neither a body or a physical force. All these stars and spheres are His handiwork. He saw how absurd the fables were that he'd been raised with and took to rebutting their doctrine and refuting their views. He publicly opposed them, spreading his message *in the name of the* LORD, *God of the Universe* (Genesis 21:33), preaching the reality of God and His creation of the world." Throughout this book I cite the forthcoming translation of Lenn Evan Goodman and Phillip Lieberman. In the translation of Shlomo Pines (Chicago: University of Chicago Press, 1963), the passage is on p. 516. Since the Pines translation is widely used, I will cite page numbers from that translation as well, as follows: "Pines, 516." For other parallels in

Prominent in these texts is the noteworthy emphasis on the activity of Abraham. God is entirely absent from this account, as anything but the object of philosophical speculation. On this account, God does not even issue the command that opens the Abraham story in the Torah (Gen. 12:1), "Get thee hence." Even the (midrashically based) miracle by which Abraham was saved from the king of Ur is presented without directly and clearly involving God—the text literally says: "a miracle was performed for him" (*na'asah lo nes*).[34] Throughout these passages it is Abraham, and not God, who is the subject of active verbs: Abraham meditated, pondered, wondered, searched, grasped, understood, realized, recognized, refuted, argued, broke images, convinced, emigrated, proclaimed, travelled, taught, instructed, implanted, and composed.[35] God is cognized on this account, *but does not act.*[36]

---

the *Guide*, see ii. 39 (Pines, 379) and iii. 24 (Pines, 502). See also *Book of Commandments*, positive commandment 3. The issue also comes up in Maimonides's famous responsum to R. Ovadiah the Proselyte (discussed below in chapter 4). The slight variations in the text are of great interest. I examine this matter in "'*Farteitsht un Farbessert*': On 'Correcting' Maimonides," *Meorot* 6, no. 2 (2007), http://www.yctorah.org/component/option,com_docman/task,doc_download/gid,448/http://libnet.ac.il/~libnet/pqd/opac_uls.pl?1095066.

34 Pes. 118a. The Talmud here has God insisting on saving Abraham Himself (the angel Gabriel had sought the assignment); Maimonides clearly presents the story in an entirely different light. See also Gen. Rabbah xxxix. 3.

35 My thanks to Zev Harvey for drawing my attention to this point.

36 The God described here is the "God of the philosophers." Compare Howard Kreisel, *Maimonides' Political Thought: Studies in Ethics, Law, and the Human Ideal* (Albany: SUNY Press, 1999), 43: "What is crucial to stress in this context is that Abraham is depicted by Maimonides as an Aristotelian philosopher. His deduction that God "created" everything as depicted in "Laws of Idolatry," i. 3, is in reality the Aristotelian view that God is the First Cause of all existence." Agreeing as I do with Kreisel's interpretation, I think it apposite to quote Judah Halevi's parallel account of Abraham in *Kuzari* iv. 17: "The Sage said: Well, then, by that standard, it was right for Abraham to have undergone all that he did in Ur of the Chaldees, and then in departing from his homeland, and also in accepting circumcision, and again in expelling Ishamel, and even further in his anxiety about slaughtering Isaac, since all that he experienced with respect to the divine order (*al-amr al-ilahi*), he experienced by savoring [*dhawq*], not by reasoning." This passage is found in the context of Halevi's distinction between the philosophic God of Aristotle (and of Abraham, according to Maimonides), known in the tradition as Elohim, and the experienced God of the patriarchs, known in the tradition by the Tetragrammaton. Halevi's Abraham goes beyond the God of the philosophers to the God of experience. Halevi makes this clear in the sequel: "God ordered him to abstain from his scientific studies based on reasoning ... and to take upon himself the duty of obeying the One he had experienced by savoring, just as it says: *Savor and see how good the Lord is* (Ps. 34:9)." On this passage, see the discussion in Diana Lobel, *Between Mysticism and Philosophy: Sufi Language of Religious Experience in Judah Ha-Levi's* Kuzari (Albany: SUNY Press, 2000), 89–93. Compare also Hasdai Crescas's comment (*Or Ha-Shem*, I. iii. 6 [Jerusalem:

The upshot of all this is that Abraham discovered God on his own, so to speak.[37] God did not choose Abraham, God did not seek him out, God did not make Himself known to Abraham. God waited till someone discovered the truth about Him; that someone happened to be Abraham, progenitor of the Jews. It did not have to be Abraham. Had the first human being to discover the truth about God been, say, a Navajo, and had that Navajo philosopher the courage and effectiveness of Abraham, then the Navajos would be the chosen people, the Torah would have been composed in the Navajo language, its narratives would reflect their history, and many of its commandments would reflect that history and the nature of Navajo society at the time of the giving of the Torah to them. The inner meaning of the Torah, its philosophical content and spiritual message would all be equivalent to the inner meaning, philosophical content, and spiritual message of the Torah is it was indeed revealed to Moses at Sinai, but its outer garment would be dramatically different.

Here in its starkest fashion is the profound gulf which separates Maimonides from Halevi and thinkers like him.[38] For Halevi, God chose the Jews because of their antecedent special character, the only people on earth in whom the *inyan elohi* was permanently lodged.[39] For Maimonides, it is Abraham's

---

Sifrei Ramot, 1990], 122; in the English translation of Roslyn Weiss [Oxford: Oxford University Press, 2018], 119) to the effect that while it was Abraham's philosophical reasoning that prepared him for prophecy, this reasoning did not bring him to certain knowledge of God, which is the province of prophets, not philosophers: "even though he desired the truth, he did not escape all doubt until God caused His light to emanate upon him, it [i.e., God's light] being prophecy." This passage is discussed by Warren Zev Harvey, *Physics and Metaphysics in Hasdai Crescas* (Amsterdam: Gieben, 1998), 47–48 and 60–65. Note well Harvey's comment (48) about the Maimonides whom Crescas criticized: "His Abraham is an Aristotelian philosopher, or, if you prefer, his Aristotle was an Abrahamic philosopher." It is noteworthy also that a rabbinic text (Sab. 156a, Ned. 32a), "abandon your astrology [that is, philosophical-scientific research]," used by both Halevi and Crescas in the present context, is nowhere cited by Maimonides.

37 In other words, Abraham discovered God through *hekhre'a ha-da'at*, reasoned conviction. He also brought his contemporaries (Noachides in the most literal sense of the term) to acceptance of monotheism through *hekhre'a ha-da'at*. It is a safe assumption that in Maimonides's view Abraham himself and those whom he brought near to God achieved shares in the world to come; that being the case, the standard reading of "Laws of Kings," viii. 11 cannot be correct. See below in chapter 6.

38 For more on the comparison of Maimonides and Halevi vis-à-vis Abraham, see Aviezer Ravitzky, "On the Image of the Leader in Jewish Thought," in *Aharav: al Manhigut u-Manhigim*, ed. Hannah Amit (Tel Aviv: Ministry of Defense, 2000), 45–57 (Hebrew).

39 Arabic: *amr al-ilahi*. There is no agreed upon translation of this term. It refers to the special quality or relationship adhering in (and only in) the people of Israel. For a recent discussion, see Ehud Krinis, *God's Chosen People: Judah Halevi's 'Kuzari' and the Shi'i Imam Doctrine*

choice of God which makes his descendants special, so long as they remain loyal to that choice.⁴⁰

Our point finds further expression in the continuation of Maimonides's account:

> Our Father Jacob taught all his children; but he singled out Levi, appointing him "head" and installing him in an academy to teach "the way of the Lord" (Gen. 18:19) and keep Abraham's charge. He directed his children that there be an uninterrupted succession of Levite appointees, so that the teaching not be forgotten. This enterprise was gathering strength among Jacob's children and those who joined them, a God-knowing nation was coming into being—till Israel's stay in Egypt became prolonged and they retrogressed, learning [the Egyptian's] deeds and worshiping alien deities like them (the sole exception being the tribe of Levi, which remained steadfast to the Patriarchal charge: never did the tribe of Levi worship in alien deities). The root planted by Abraham was on the verge of being uprooted and Jacob's descendants, of reverting to the error and aberrance of the nations.⁴¹ But because God loved us and stood by [his] oath to Our

---

(Turnhout: Brepols, 2014), 189–210. See also Diana Lobel, "A Dwelling Place for the Shekhinah," *Jewish Quarterly Review* 90 (1999): 103–125, 103. Note, however, that Abraham had to make an effort before he was transferred to the Land of Israel to conjoin with the *amr al-ilahi*. See Kuzari, 2:14.

40 The question asked by two Baptist students (above in this chapter) goes to the heart of the debate between the Judaism of Judah Halevi, *Zohar*, Nahmanides, etc., and the Judaism of Maimonides. Truly, for the former, one cannot choose to be chosen. For Halevi, converts remain unequal to born Jews; for the *Zohar* there really is no such thing as conversion—true proselytes are persons born to gentile parents into whose bodies Jewish souls have been placed. For Maimonides, on the other hand, actually, Jews in the fullest sense of the term are not chosen by God, but, rather, are individuals (whoever their parents might be) who choose God. For Maimonides, as I argued in *Maimonides on Judaism and the Jewish People*, all Jews are in effect converts to Judaism. See the next note.

41 This last point deserves expansion, since it is important for the thesis being developed in this book. Maimonides, following midrashic tradition (Mekhilta, Bo, paragraph 5; ed. Jacob Lauterbach (Philadelphia: Jewish Publication Society, 1933), 2:36; Exodus Rabbah, xix. 5) maintains that the Jews in Egypt (with the exception of the tribe of Levi) had assimilated to the idolatrous norms of the Egyptian culture around them (compare the opposed picture drawn by Halevi in *Kuzari* i. 95). Maimonides repeats this claim in a number of places. See, for example, his responsum to R. Obadiah the Proselyte in Y. Sheilat, *Iggerot ha-Rambam*, 1:235 (on this text, see below, chapter 4) and his "Treatise on Resurrection" (Sheilat, 335–336 for the Arabic text and 369 for a Hebrew translation; for an English translation, see A. S. Halkin and David Hartman, trans. and eds., *Epistles of Maimonides: Crisis and Leadership:* [Philadelphia: Jewish Publication Society, 1985], 230). Those of Abraham's

Father, Abraham, he elected Moses—Our Master and the Master of all the Prophets—and charged him with his [prophetic] mission. When Moses our Master attained to prophecy and God chose Israel as His own, He crowned them with commandments, and taught them: how to worship Him and what rules should govern alien worship and all who stray after it.

Israel thus becomes God's chosen people because of Abraham's antecedent choice of God.[42]

---

descendants who stood at Sinai quite literally converted to Judaism (the new religion expressed in the Torah of Moses). This may be seen from the way in which Maimonides opens his discussion of the laws of conversion in "Laws of Forbidden Intercourse," xiii: "With three things did Israel enter the covenant: circumcision, immersion, and sacrifice." So, Maimonides continues, must converts today undergo circumcision and immersion (sacrifice being no longer possible). See the fuller development of this point in Kellner, *Maimonides on Judaism and the Jewish People*, 85–87 and below in chapter 4.

42 Compare iii. 51 (Pines, 623):

> It is also the plane the Patriarchs reached, coming so close to God that His name was made known to the world through them: *God of Abraham, God of Isaac, and God of Jacob. ... This is My universal name* (Exodus 3:15). One result of the joining of their minds with awareness of Him is His eternal covenant with each of them: *I shall remember My covenant with Jacob [and also My covenant with Isaac and My covenant with Abraham shall I remember]* (Leviticus 26:42). For in these four—the Patriarchs and our Teacher Moses—union with God was manifest, by which I mean love and awareness of Him, as our texts proclaim. So, too, was God's mighty providence over them and their posterity, even as they busied themselves in managing people, making their fortune, and pursuing their economic endeavors.

This idea even finds expression in Maimonides's *Epistle to Yemen*, a text in which he must have been greatly tempted to use a stronger notion of the choice of Israel than the one expressed here. Towards the beginning of the epistle, he emphasizes the importance of the following teaching:

> [O]urs is the true and divine religion, revealed to us through Moses, chief of the former as well as of the later prophets. *By means of it God has distinguished us from the rest of mankind, as He declares: Yet it was to your fathers that Lord was drawn in His love for them, so that He chose you, their lineal descendants, from among all the peoples* (Deut. 10:15). This choice was not made thanks to our merits, but was rather an act of grace, on account of our ancestors who were cognizant of God and obedient to Him, as He states: *It is not because you are the most numerous of peoples, that the Lord set His heart on you and chose you—indeed, you are the smallest of peoples [but it was because the Lord loved you and kept the oath He made to your fathers]* (Deut. 7:7). (My emphasis).

I cite from the translation in Halkin and Hartman, *Crisis and Leadership*, 96–97. This text reads as if it were written in direct opposition to the views of Judah Halevi on the election of Israel (as expressed, for example, in *Kuzari* i. 27, i. 48, i. 95, and i.103); see below, chapter 2.

3. FROM ABRAHAM TO MOSES

Israel becomes God's chosen people because of "the root planted by Abraham." What was that root? Clearly: acceptance of the existence of the one true God. This was a religion without any ritual commandments whatsoever.[43]

We have just seen that Maimonides wrote, "When Moses our Master attained to prophecy and God chose Israel as His own, He crowned them with commandments, and taught them: how to worship Him and what rules should govern alien worship and all who stray after it." With which commandments was Israel crowned? The answer to that question, I propose, is found in the continuation of our story in *Guide of the Perplexed* iii. 32, where Maimonides discusses the events at Marah (Exod. 15:22–26).

The *Guide of the Perplexed* contains many shocking chapters; iii. 32 may be the most provocative of them all. There Maimonides teaches that God behaves with "divine wisdom and grace" (close to what Plato would have called "noble lies"),[44] in effect misleading the People of Israel for their benefit.[45] The point of his extended discussion is to explain why the God of all creation would command the bringing of sacrifices. Maimonides's answer is one toward which the reader "will balk at … first, inevitably, and find … terribly troubling" (Pines, 527). What is that answer which readers will find so troubling? It is that God's original intention after the Exodus was to command a Torah consisting only of the Sabbath (which teaches the creation of the world by God) and of laws governing social relations.[46] However, this Torah, God's primary intention as Maimonides explains in our chapter, turned out to be deficient. The Israelites apparently found this religion too abstract. At the first opportunity, with Moses missing on Mt. Sinai, the Israelites slid back into idolatry, creating and

---

43 It will be immediately objected that there is at least one ritual commandment given to Abraham: circumcision. However, as Hannah Kasher shows in "Maimonides's View of Circumcision as a Factor Uniting the Jewish and Muslim Communities," in *Studies in Muslim-Jewish Relations*, ed. Ronald L. Nettler (Luxembourg: Harwood Academic Publishers, 1995), 103–108, Maimonides held the commandment of circumcision to obligate Muslims as well as Jews. On the rabbinic aggadah that the patriarchs obeyed all the commandments, see above note 14.

44 Ar.: *talattuf*. On this term, see Pines, translator's introduction to *Guide*, lxxii, note 32, and Michael Schwarz's Hebrew translation (Tel Aviv: Tel Aviv University Press, 2002), iii.32, note 2.

45 The clearest examples of such misleading expressions are the many verses in the Torah that lead people to attribute corporeality and personality to God.

46 While Maimonides does not make the point explicitly in *Guide* iii. 32, it is obvious that these are the laws expressed in the Decalogue: God, Sabbath, and social relations.

worshiping the golden calf. Seeing this, God realized that the Torah revealed at Marah was insufficient, and was *forced* to reveal a Torah full of sacrifices and detailed ritual—all this according to what Maimonides calls God's second intention.[47] Since the people of Israel had proved themselves unable to worship God without a concrete focus for their worship (the golden calf), God exercised "divine wisdom and grace" and made the people think that God desired them to offer sacrifices to Him. Sacrifices demand a place in which to bring them (Tabernacle in the Sinai wilderness and then the Temple in Jerusalem), a priesthood to officiate, laws of ritual purity and impurity to guarantee that the Temple be treated with awe, and festivals marked by huge numbers of sacrifices and focused on the Temple.[48] All of these are God's second intention, a clear accommodation to the primitive spirituality of the Israelites leaving Egypt.

In *Guide* iii. 32 Maimonides maintains that the sacrificial cult was not part of God's primary intention, as it were, but represents an accommodation on God's part to the (historically contingent) spiritual weakness of the children of Israel leaving Egypt.[49] The sacrifices, that is, serve no purpose of their own, but were instituted despite God's will, so to speak. On top of that, the *mishkan* in the wilderness and the Temple after it were ordained by God only in order to serve as a venue for sacrifices.

Why does the Torah command the erection of such sanctuaries? Maimonides gives the answer to that question in our chapter of the *Guide of the Perplexed*. In this chapter Maimonides describes God's "divine wisdom and grace"

---

47 The italicized word in this sentence is drawn from Isaac Abravanel's presentation of these ideas in his commentary on Jeremiah 7. Abravanel himself did not like these ideas, but realized that Maimonides held them. Abravanel is famous for having concluded his classes on Maimonides in Lisbon by saying: "These are the views of Rabbi Moses (Maimonides) but not the views of our Master Moses." For details, see Liron Hoch and Menachem Kellner, "'The Voice Is the Voice of Jacob, But the Hands Are the Hands of Esau': Isaac Abravanel between Judah Halevi and Moses Maimonides," *Jewish History* 26 (2012): 61–83.

48 In his commentary on Lev. 1:9, Nahmanides gives every indication of having been personally offended by this account of the sacrifices. No wonder. The clear implication of Maimonides's account is that anyone who thinks that God really *wants* sacrifices, and that sacrifices actually accomplish anything ontological or theurgical (views definitely held by Nahmanides) is marked by a primitive, pagan sensibility. See further, Dov Schwartz, "'From Theurgy to Magic': The Evolution of the Magical-Talismanic Justification of Sacrifice in the Circle of Nahmanides and His Interpreters," *Aleph* 1 (2001): 165–213, Roy Pinchot, "The Deeper Conflict between Maimonides and Ramban Over the Sacrifices," *Tradition* 33 (1999): 24–33, and Menachem Kellner, "Tabernacle, Sacrifices, and Judaism: Maimonides vs. Nahmanides," TheTorah.com, accessed 8 February, 2020, https://www.thetorah.com/article/tabernacle-sacrifices-and-judaism-maimonides-vs-nahmanides. See also, below, note 66.

49 See above, note 41.

(Pines, 525) in accomplishing ends indirectly.⁵⁰ God created the world such that individuals have to move through many stages of growth before they attain their full maturity. "Our own providential Ruler," he then points out (Pines, 525–526), "gave us just such care in many articles of our Law. It's impossible to shift in an instant from extreme to extreme. Human nature cannot suddenly drop all that's familiar." We see here an expression of Maimonidean naturalism, with its aversion to miracles, and also a form of conservatism: changes come about through process, not revolution.⁵¹

As we have seen, Maimonides held that the Israelites in the time of the Exodus had become accustomed to divine worship through sacrifices. "So, with the wisdom and grace evident throughout creation, God did not decree that His Law simply annul, reject, and abolish all such worship." Had God done so, the Israelites coming out of Egypt would not have been able to accept the Torah. In explaining this, Maimonides offers an analogy. Just as the Israelites coming out of Egypt could not relate to worship without sacrifices, so also, Jews of Maimonides's own day could not relate to worship without ritualized prayer.⁵² Demanding of the ancient Israelites that they worship without sacrifices was as impossible then as sending a prophet in Maimonides's time (although we doubt that things have changed much since) who would ask people 'to serve God by announcing: 'God forbids you to pray, fast, or call on Him in times of trouble. You must serve Him only by meditating and doing nothing at all' (Pines, 526). "That is why," Maimonides continues, "God kept these [idolatrous] modes of worship but shifted them to His name, rather than things created or imagined, and charged us to do these things for Him."⁵³

The sacrificial cult is an example of divine accommodation: God accommodates the Torah to the primitive needs of the Jewish people at an early stage of their development (just as a wise parent, Maimonides points out, feeds a

---

50 Pines prefers "wily graciousness and wisdom" here (525).
51 This is not the place to go into it, but this also underlies Maimonides's naturalistic messianism. For details, see Maimonides, "Laws of Kings," xi–xii; and the studies cited below in chapter 3.
52 Maimonides, I suggest, paralleled *piyyut*, ritual poetry, with animal sacrifice. On Maimonides's attitude towards *piyyut*, see *Guide* i. 59 and Kellner, *Confrontation*, index, s.v. "*Piyyut*."
53 It is certainly apposite to note that in *Guide* iii. 28 Maimonides distinguishes between necessary and true beliefs (Pines, 512). In our view, this distinction parallels the distinction drawn in *Guide* iii. 32 between God's primary and secondary intentions. At the end of chapter iii. 28 (Pines, 514) Maimonides presents the idea that God immediately answers prayers uttered in times of distress as a necessary belief.

newborn child milk or soft food).[54] As Maimonides says a few paragraphs further on, in responding to a possible objection to this proposal, the sacrificial cult, in all its myriad impressive and colorful detail, was not intended by God "for their inherent worth but for some extrinsic purpose—as if God had tricked us to reach His real goal?" (Pines, 527).[55]

Returning to the order in which Maimonides himself develops his ideas, a sacrificial cult needs a place in which to be performed. Thus, having commanded the sacrifices, God "charged us to do these things for Him—to build Him a temple: 'Let them make Me a sanctuary' (Exod. 25: 8), with an altar in His name: 'an altar of earth shalt thou make Me' (ibid., 20: 21), where sacrifices were offered up to Him: 'When any of you offereth a sacrifice to the Lord …' (Lev. 1: 2). The bowing would be to Him, and it was before Him that incense would be offered" (Pines, 526).[56] All this (including everything having to do with the priests and Levites) Maimonides calls an "act of God's grace."[57] Thanks to that, "the very memory of paganism was effaced and one great truth was made the anchor of our creed: the existence and unity of God—without alienating or estranging people by abolishing the familiar rituals, to which they knew no alternative" (Pines, 527).

After dealing with a number of objections to his explanation for the sacrificial cult and the establishment of the priesthood, Maimonides points out that the biblical sacrificial cult was in many ways more refined than the idolatrous practices that it replaced. One important difference is that sacrifices could no longer be offered "anywhere and at any time. Temples may not be built just anywhere, nor may just anyone offer sacrifice. … He instituted just one house. … And only those of specified descent may serve as priests. All this, to delimit worship of this sort, preserving only as much as His wisdom determined must not

---

54   On the notion of divine accommodation here, see above, note 44.
55   A passage at the end of "Laws Concerning Trespass with Respect to Sacred Objects" has been taken as an indication that in the *Mishneh Torah*, at least, Maimonides held a more traditional position on the nature of sacrifices. However, this interpretation is based upon a faulty text. See David Henshke, "On the Question of Unity in Maimonides's Thought," *Da'at* 37 (1996): 37–52 (Hebrew), and Kellner and Gillis, *Maimonides the Universalist*, chapter 8.
56   Maimonides is quite explicit about this point; compare the following: "The laws about sacrifices and visiting the Temple served only to cement our core principle: It is only to that end that I shifted those practices to My name—to erase all trace of paganism and establish My Oneness" (Pines, 530). Animal sacrifices are an accommodation to human immaturity, and as such must be restricted as much as possible: only in the Tabernacle in the wilderness and in the Temple in Jerusalem.
57   Pines, 527, prefers "divine ruse."

be left behind entirely." Maimonides contrasts this with other forms of worship, including prayer, fringes, mezuzot, and phylacteries, which may be observed in every place and by all people (Pines, 529–530).[58] All of these restrictions were designed by God to limit and restrict sacrificial worship as much as possible.

The point of interest to us in all this is the connection made by Maimonides between the sacrificial cult and the commandments concerning the sanctuary. Maimonides makes the point yet again: "The laws about sacrifices and visiting the Temple served only to cement our core principle: 'It is only to that end that I shifted those practices to My name—to erase all trace of paganism and establish My Oneness'" (Pines, 530).[59]

At this point in his discussion, Maimonides writes:

> It's because of the concern I've just disclosed to you that the Prophets' books so reprehend people's rushing to make sacrifice. God made it clear to the Prophets that sacrifices were not really meant for their own sake and not needed by Him. Samuel says: "Is the LORD pleased by burnt offerings and sacrifices as He is by heeding the LORD's voice?" (1 Sam. 15: 22). Isaiah says: "What need have I for your many sacrifices?" saith the Lord ..." (ibid., 1: 11).[60] And Jeremiah: "When I spoke to your fathers the day I brought them forth from Egypt, I said nothing and gave no command about burnt offerings and sacrifices. This was My command: 'Hearken to My voice. I shall be your God, and ye shall be My people'" (ibid., 7: 22–23).[61]

---

58   See Maimonides, *Mishneh Torah*, "Laws of Fringes," iii. 13; ibid., "Laws of Tefillin," vi. 13; ibid., iv. 25.

59   Compare Halevi's view of the actual efficacy of sacrifices as expressed in *Kuzari* i. 91, i. 98–99, and ii. 26 (which follows from his general account of the commandments in ibid., iii. 23).

60   Being pleased by, and needing something, are not the same thing. Maimonides speaks of God's alleged need for sacrifices, but Samuel speaks of God being pleased. That, perhaps, is why Maimonides then cites Isaiah who speaks of need.

61   Are God's being Israel's God and Israel being God's people *consequences* of hearkening to God's voice? That is certainly the way in which Maimonides understands these things, as expounded in Menachem Kellner, *Gam Hem Keruyim Adam: Ha-Nokri Be-Einei ha-Rambam* (Ramat Gan: Bar Ilan University Press, 2016). We see here Maimonides teaching that the sacrifices were not commanded as part of God's first intention. The commandment concerning sacrifices belongs to another, secondary, intention. Admittedly, there was a commandment to bring the paschal sacrifice at the time of the Exodus, but that was only to force the Israelites publically to deny the Egyptian religion (iii. 46; Pines, 581) The Israelites did not understand that and thought that the sacrifices related to the first intention. Not surprisingly, Judah Halevi reads the verses cited here from Jeremiah differently. See Halevi, *Kuzari* ii. 48.

Maimonides finds support for his position in the words of Samuel, Isaiah, and Jeremiah. Aware of the fact this approach is far from widely accepted, he admits:

> These words trouble everyone I've seen or heard discuss them. "How can Jeremiah say," they ask, "that God gave us no charge about burnt offerings and sacrifices when most of the mitzvot concern just that?"[62] But the point of Jeremiah's words, as I've shown, is that the prime object of the Torah is "that you know Me and worship no other: 'I shall be your God, and ye shall be My people.'" The laws about sacrifices and visiting the Temple served only to cement our core principle: It is only to that end that I shifted those practices to My name—to erase all trace of paganism and establish My Oneness. But you spurned the end and held fast to the means. You doubted My existence—'they denied the Lord and said, Not so!' (5:12). Yet you practiced pagan worship—"[Will ye rob and murder, commit adultery, swear falsely], burn incense to Baal and go after other gods ... and then come to this House, [that bears My name, and stand before Me, saying 'We are safe.' Safe to commit all these horrors!]" (7:9–10). You still attend the Lord's Temple and offer your sacrifices. But that was not the point!

The prophet Jeremiah, as it were, anticipates Maimonides. The prime object of the Torah is to know God and worship no other (the first two, it needs hardly pointing out, of the Ten Commandments).[63] The laws of sacrifices (and corollary commandments, such as visiting the Temple) are secondary, meant only to erase paganism and "cement" the knowledge of God in the community of Israel. Knowledge is the aim; sacrifices are only a means (and, as we know,

---

62 But counting up all the commandments dealt with in books 8, 9, and 10 of the *Mishneh Torah* (which deal with the Jerusalem temple, sacrifices, and ritual purity and impurity), we only arrive at 162, hardly most of the 613. If we add those parts of the seventh book that deal with tithes, etc., to the Levites and priests, we add only another eighteen commandments.

63 These are the only commandments which the people of Israel heard directly from the mouth of God (*mipi ha-gevurah*), as it were (BT Makkot, 23b). Maimonides explains (*Guide* ii. 33; Pines, 364) that this means that the first two commandments can be known by human speculation alone. Note further Jose Faur, *Homo Mysticus: A Guide to Maimonides' Guide for the Perplexed* (Syracuse: Syracuse University Press, 1999), 152: "The rituals and sacramental sacrifices were not included in the ten commandments. It was after the children of Israel had worshipped the golden calf and retrogressed to idolatry that special commandments and injunctions designed to control the effect of the pagan traces were issued."

not part of God's original intention). But, and this is Jeremiah's complaint, the people of Israel abandoned the aim and held fast to the sacrifices.

At this point Maimonides adds a new wrinkle to his discussion. He writes:

> Text and tradition agree that the earliest laws we were given said nothing at all of sacrifices and burnt offerings.[64] Disregard the Paschal sacrifice performed in Egypt (Exod. 12:3–13). That had a clear and evident purpose, as I'll explain (iii. 46); and it was [only] in Egypt. The laws Jeremiah means were those given after the Exodus. That's why the verse specifies, "the day I brought them forth from Egypt". What was first commanded after the Exodus was the law given at Marah: "If indeed ye hearken to the voice of the Lord your God [and obey His commandments, do what is right in His eyes, and keep all His laws, I will not inflict on you all the illnesses I laid on Egypt. I, the Lord, do heal you]" (Exod. 15: 26). It was there that "He gave them a statute and a rule" (ibid.,15: 25). Our sound tradition specifies, "Shabbat and civil laws were ordained at Marah" (B. Shabbat 87b, Sanhedrin 56b). Shabbat was the statute; the rule was civil law, our laws banning acts of injustice. Here was the prime object, as I've explained: embrace of true beliefs—in the world's creation—for, as you know, our Sabbath laws were given us just to instill this belief, as I've explained in this work (ii. 31)—and, alongside true belief, to curb people's wronging each other.[65]

Here we arrive at what we take to be the most revolutionary aspect of Maimonides discussion in *Guide of the Perplexed* iii. 32. As far as I have been able to discern, this aspect has been unnoticed or ignored by earlier commentators on the chapter. In the second stage of our story, God has rescued the Israelites from Egypt, saved them from the Egyptians at the Red Sea, and brought them to a place called Marah. There God issues commandments, supplementing the one commandment already given to the Israelites in Egypt—to count the month we now call Nisan the first of the months of the year (Exod. 12:2). What then are these additional commandments, which "clearly said nothing

---

64 "Text and tradition" as understood and presented by Maimonides.
65 One assumes that Maimonides would have been happier had the rabbinic statement about Marah talked of belief in God's existence, unity, and incorporeality, as opposed to the Sabbath. But at least the institution of the Sabbath teaches the creation of the world. See *Guide*, ii. 31. Further on Maimonides on the events at Marah, see James Diamond, *Maimonides and the Hermeneutics of Concealment* (Albany: SUNY Press, 2002), 148–149.

of sacrifices and burnt offerings"? They are the institution of the Sabbath and the civil laws.

Maimonides emphasizes his point, concluding his argument dramatically:

> Our first laws, then, clearly said nothing of sacrifices and burnt offerings. Those were secondary, as I said. The Psalms voice the same idea as Jeremiah, reproaching the whole nation for flouting the Law's chief intent and failing to distinguish what's primary from what's secondary: "Hear, My people, and I will speak; I indict thee, Israel. God am I, thy God. Not for thy sacrifices do I blame thee, or thy burnt offerings, ever before Me. I'll take no bullock from thy house, nor any goats from thy folds. [Every beast in the forest is Mine; cattle, in the hills, by the thousand!]" (Ps. 50:7–9). Wherever this theme recurs, that is its thrust. Understand this well and reflect on it.

Combining "Laws of Idolatry," chapter 1, with *Guide* iii. 32 and iii. 47 we arrive at the following account: God's covenant with Abraham involved only "the prime object of the Torah." Abraham's descendants, when tested by Egyptian slavery, proved themselves unable to hold fast to Abraham's teaching. Fulfilling his promises to the patriarchs, God sent Moses to become "our teacher" (*rabbenu*) and lead the Israelites out of Egypt, bringing them to Marah. There God tried again, as it were, ordaining the Sabbath and laws governing social behavior (the rest of the Ten Commandments). Abraham's Torah was, we might say, purely theological.[66]

The Torah of Marah added to that Torah a further element of theology (belief in creation of the world) and, in addition, ethics.[67] However, the Children of Israel, when tested again (by Moses's apparent disappearance on Mt. Sinai), proved themselves unable to hold fast to the minimal Torah of Marah. It was at this point that God was "forced" (as Isaac Abravanel and Ovadia Seforno were later to say) to compass the Children of Israel about with sacrifices and their consequences: *mishkan*/temple, priests and levites, ritual purity and

---

66 Nahmanides (Lev. 1:9) followed by many others (more politely) asked, of course, about the sacrifices offered by Cain and Abel (Gen. 4:3–6), Noah (Gen. 8:20–21), and Abraham (Gen. 22:23). The Talmud (Shabbat 28b and parallels) also maintains that Adam offered a sacrifice. Maimonides would reply that none of these were *commanded*.

67 The two aims of the Torah (*Guide* iii. 27) are the inculcation of ethical and intellectual perfection.

impurity, and pilgrim festivals.⁶⁸ All of these are only means, not ends in themselves. They all relate to God's second intention only, and were not meant to be part of the Torah as originally conceived, as it were, by God.

4. MOSES SUPPORTS ABRAHAM—HE DOES NOT SUPPLANT HIM

The motto of the *Mishneh Torah*, like that of all Maimonides's works, is the verse *in the name of the Lord, God of the world*, Abraham's invocation of God in Gen. 21:33.⁶⁹ Abraham preached monotheism and decent behavior to the whole world. In this respect, and hence with respect to the ultimate aim of the commandments, Jews have no inborn, essential advantage over Gentiles. In my book with David Gillis we suggest that Maimonides may have taken Rabbi Judah the Prince as his model in adding moral and spiritual codas to the halakhic content of *Mishneh torah*. We have reached the point where we can see that no less than Rabbi Judah, his models were Abraham and Moses.

The Abrahamic model involves the creation of a monotheism having almost no ritual aspects (with the obvious exception of circumcision). The Mosaic model involves 613 highly detailed commandments. Maimonides expresses the distinction between the Abrahamic and Mosaic models most clearly in two texts: "Laws Concerning Idolatry," chapter 1 and *Guide of the Perplexed* iii. 32. As we saw above, in "Idolatry" we are taught that the community called together by Abraham, "in the name of the Lord, God of the world" consisted of his family, household, and "the persons they had gotten in Haran" (Gen. 12:5 and *Guide* i. 63; Pines, 154), that is, the individuals whom Abraham and Sarah had brought close to God. This community, held

---

68 Isaac Abravanel reads Maimonides as teaching that God's original intention had been to command only the Sabbath and civil laws, but after the sin of the golden calf God realized, as it were, that the Israelites were too primitive to manage without a full panoply of sacrifices and was "necessitated" (*huzrakh*) to command them. See Abravanel's commentary to Jeremiah 7 (328 in the Avishai Shotland edition [Jerusalem: n.p., 2005). Seforno (d. 1550), in his introduction to Exodus and in his commentary on Exod. 24:18 follows the chronology of Maimonides and Abravanel: the *mishkan* follows the sin of the golden calf. In his comment on Exod. 31:18 he even adopts Abravanel's language—*huzrakh*. For rabbinic sources supporting the claim that the *mishkan* was commanded only after and because of the sin of the golden calf—see Exodus Rabbah 33:3 and Tanhumah Terumah 8 (in the 1875 Warsaw edition; the 1885 Buber edition has a very different text) as presented and interpreted by Nehama Leibowitz, *Studies in Shemot* (Jerusalem: World Zionist Organization, 1976), 459–460.

69 This is the translation according to Maimonides's understanding of the verse. The JPS translation gives "In the name of the Lord, the Everlasting God."

together only by shared (minimalistic) theology, did not survive the descent into Egypt. The community would have disappeared altogether had not God, fulfilling His promise to Abraham, sent Moses to be their teacher. Having "learned" that philosophic theology was not enough to hold the community together, God's next step was to constitute them as a people, and not only as a religious community. The nature of that move is the subject matter of *Guide* iii. 32. There we learn that God, as it were, made two efforts in this direction, with only the second being successful.

Once revealed, however, the Torah became obligatory and remains so. This reflects Maimonides's well-known position that the (often historical) explanation of why a commandment was given in no way affects its normative character.

According to Maimonides, then, the Torah was meant to be Abrahamic—consisting, in effect, of what was later to be called ethical monotheism—while the actual Torah of Moses was divine accommodation to the spiritual weakness of the ancient Israelites. Thus, *Mishneh torah* is Mosaic in content (halakhah) but Abrahamic in its overarching, messianic goal.[70]

The point of the *Mishneh Torah* as a whole, then, is the creation of a society that gives its members the greatest shot at achieving their perfection as *human beings*. In this way, the end of the *Mishneh Torah* comes round to its beginning: just as the beginning of the *Mishneh Torah* deals with matters that relate to all human beings, so do the last chapters. Similarly, the *Guide* opens with an emphasis on intellectual perfection (*Guide* i. 1–2)—again, open in principle to all human beings—and closes (iii. 54) with a focus on the imitation of God through doing "loving-kindness, righteousness and judgment in the earth" (Jer. 9: 22–23).[71] So also, the *Mishneh Torah*'s establishment of a perfected society makes possible the achievement of philosophical perfection, which, in turn, enables highly perfected individuals (Jew or Gentile) to imitate God in the best way possible (and become as consecrated as the holy of holies).[72]

---

70 Isadore Twersky writes: "Messianism may be described as the ultimate triumph of Abraham when true belief will be universally restored" (*Introduction to the Code of Maimonides* [New Haven: Yale University Press, 1980], 451). Each of the endings of the books has its local significance, but each is also part of a general trend of arching all of halakhah towards these universal goals. This the main point of Kellner and Gillis, *Maimonides the Universalist*.

71 See *Guide* iii. 54 and the argument for this interpretation in Kellner, *Maimonides on Human Perfection* (Atlanta: Scholars Press, 1990). The closing verses and (Hebrew) poem of the *Guide of the Perplexed* can also be read in a messianic light. See iii. 54 (Pines, 638).

72 See "Laws Concerning Sabbatical Year and Jubilee," xiii. 13 and Kellner and Gillis, *Maimonides the Universalist*, chapter 7.

That is at the Mosaic level of understanding. There is also another, Abrahamic level. Abraham discovered God through observation of the motions of the heavens, and he too understood God's governance of the world, if less comprehensively than did Moses. From that, he went on to found an ethical community guided by correct ideas.[73] In other words, Abraham knew the physics and metaphysics that Maimonides sets out at the beginning of the *Mishneh Torah*. In the biography of Abraham in "Laws Concerning Idolatry," 1:3, Maimonides describes how Abraham wondered "How is it possible that this (celestial) sphere should continuously be guiding the world and have no one to guide it and cause it to turn round; for it cannot be that it turns round of itself?" This echoes the proof given for God's existence in "Laws Concerning the Foundations of the Torah," 1:5: 'For the Sphere is always revolving; and it is impossible for it to revolve without someone making it revolve. God, blessed be He, it is, who, without hand or body, causes it to revolve." Abraham is portrayed discovering the ideas that form the basis of morality and of a society dedicated to the pursuit of knowledge, unlike the kind of idolatrous state in which he grew up, where general ignorance is a mainstay of monarchical and priestly power, and advocates of truth like him are persecuted. In short, the foundations of the Torah and of the Abrahamic community are the same: appreciation of physics and metaphysics, of the laws of nature, and of God as separate from nature.

There is much more to be said about Maimonides's universalism, which is simply another word for Abrahamism. Like Abraham, and despite his love of the Jewish people and pride in his heritage, Maimonides saw no inherent difference between Jew and Gentile and looked forward to the time when the divine image in all human beings would be recognized as such by all humanity (even by Jews). Sadly, there is also much more to be said about the particularist, non-Abrahamic way in which so much of Judaism has developed over the last millennium. Because of that development this chapter, like *Guide of the Perplexed* iii. 32, may strike some readers as provocative, even outrageous. I am convinced, nevertheless, that I have presented a vision of Maimonides as he understood himself. In the coming chapters of this book, I will take that vision and use it to confront problems of which Maimonides himself may have never dreamed. We, however, not only dream up these problems, we are confronted with them on an almost daily basis. Eight hundred years after his death, Maimonides can still help us with that confrontation.

---

73 Ibid.

CHAPTER 2

We Are Not Alone

1. INTRODUCTION

Each of us lives at the center of his or her universe, but few of us mean that literally. Not too very long ago, however, it was a given that human beings literally lived at the center of the universe, at least in Western culture. From our perspective, that universe was very small. It was a sphere that in today's terms was smaller than our own solar system. It was small in other ways as well: spiritual entities aside, all that was thought to exist (or inferred to exist) could be seen by the naked eye: there was nothing either microscopic or nothing telescopic. The world was small in another sense as well: it had no history because it was uncreated and basically unchanging (as Aristotle taught) or because since creation the natural world (miracles aside) was as it was meant to be, with no evolution. In this world, populated by only a few million human beings, people's lives were often nasty, brutish, and short since so many of their fellows were often nasty and brutish (and often short as well, given available nutrition). In such a world, it made immediate intuitive sense to think that one's own group had been specially chosen by God: all other groups believed in arrant nonsense, behaved outlandishly, and were often thought to be barely human.[1]

---

1   Anthony D. Smith has shown that the notion of chosenness is endemic to Western culture (and not just Western culture)—but, of course, the Jews get blamed for the idea more than do other peoples. See Anthony D. Smith, *Chosen Peoples* (Oxford: Oxford University Press, 2003). See further the various (Hebrew) articles in Shmuel Almog, and Michael Heyd, ed., *Ra'ayon Ha-Behirah Be-Yisrael U-Ve-Amim* (Jerusalem: Merkaz Zalman Shazar, 1991). This collection includes articles on the Bible (Benjamin Uffenheimer, 17–40), Ancient Greece ("Promised Land" by Irad Malkin, 41–58), Talmudic Rabbis (Ya'akov Blidstein, 99–120), Prayer (Meir Bar-Ilan, 121–146), early Islam (Haggai Ben-Shammai, 147–179), Muscovite Autocracy (Joel Raba, 191–206), French Nationalism (Myriam Yardeni, 221–236), and Japan (Ben-Ami Shillony, 299–310). For a recent statement of the Jewish doctrine of election in a nonparticularist vein, see: Jerome Yehuda Gellman, *God's Kindness Has Overwhelmed Us* (Boston: Academic Studies Press, 2013). For another nonparticularist approach, see Eugene Korn, "One God, Many Faiths: A Jewish Theology of Covenantal Pluralism," in *Two Faiths, One Covenant?*, ed. Eugene Korn and

The universe we live in is dramatically larger than that of our forebears. Looking outward, we discover that we orbit the sun, not the other way around, and live on a planet that is only one of many that orbit the sun. The sun itself is a star of no particular distinction, tucked into a galaxy of no particular distinction. The Milky Way is part of a galactic cluster, which itself in turn is part of a super-galactic cluster, and so on, with no end in sight. Zooming back in on ourselves, we discover that we are composed of molecules, atoms, atomic particles, subatomic particles, and so on. When Jews look at the world, we discover that in numerical terms we do not even constitute a statistical error in the Chinese or Indian censuses.

Perceiving the world in this way, it becomes harder and harder to accept at face value Rashi's comment on Genesis 1:1 to the effect that all that exists was created only so that God could reveal the Torah to Moses, and in order that the Jewish people could live according to that Torah in a small patch of real estate on the eastern shores of the Mediterranean Sea. Looking at the billions of human beings who surround us, we discover that a huge percentage of them are no less moral and no less sophisticated than we are.[2]

John Pawlikowsky (Lanham, MD: Rowman and Littlefield, 2005), 147–154. Concerning chosenness, Reuven Kimelman make an interesting comment: "Whereas many peoples deem themselves divinely chosen with a manifest destiny, only the Jews are deemed chosen by others." See Reuven Kimelman, "My Response to Alon Goshen-Gottstein's 'Luther the Anti-Semite': A Contemporary Jewish Perspective," *Contemporary Jewry* 40 (2020): 91.

2   Rashi (1040–1105) opens his commentary on the Torah by paraphrasing *Midrash tanhuma* ("Bereshit," 11) as follows:

> Rabbi Isaac said: It was not necessary to begin the Torah [the main object of which is to teach commandments] with this verse, but from "This month shall be unto you [the first of the months]" [Exod. 12: 2], since this was the first commandment that Israel was commanded to observe. But what is the reason that the Torah begins with "In the beginning"? Because of the verse, "The power of His works He hath declared to His people in giving them the heritage of the nations" [Ps. 111: 6], for if the nations of the world should say to Israel: "You are robbers, because you have seized by force the lands of the seven nations [of Canaan]," Israel could reply to them: "The entire world belongs to the Holy One, blessed be He; He created it, and gave it to whomever it was right in His eyes. Of His own will He gave it to them [the seven Canaanite nations] and of His own will He took it from them and gave it to us."

Rashi here expands on the *Tanhuma* text, but, so far as I can judge, in no way distorts it. Emphasizing what I take to be a central focus of his gloss here, Rashi continues, this time paraphrasing *Genesis Rabbah* 1:1:

The challenge to Jewish self-importance constituted by alternative faiths and cultures is not new, but it does have a beginning point in time. The biblical authors were confident that the idolaters against whom they struggled were barbarians. The talmudic sages seem not to have been overwhelmed with admiration for the cultures of the people among whom they lived. Living in an Islamic world, however, Sa'adiah Gaon (882–942), Judah Halevi (1075–1141), and preeminently Maimonides (1138–1204) realized that they confronted a challenge that could not be brushed aside with a broken reed.[3] Samuel ibn Tibbon (c. 1165–1232) and Menahem Me'iri (1249–1306) each showed that they found much in contemporary Christian culture to admire.[4]

It is against this background that I would like to comment on a challenging observation of Rabbi Jonathan Sacks. He wrote: "Those who are confident in their faith are not threatened but enlarged by the different faith of others."[5] There is much to admire in this statement, although, if it is true, it would appear that very few religious people in the premodern West were confident enough in their faith to feel enlarged, rather than threatened by the faith of others. Such would appear to be the evidence of wars of religion, crusades against "infidels" and "heretics," and the persecution of religious, cultural, and ideological others.

"In the beginning He created": This passage cries out for a midrashic interpretation, as our rabbis have interpreted it: [God created the world] for the sake of the Torah since it is called "the beginning of His way" [Prov. 8: 22] and for the sake of Israel, since they are called "the beginning of His crops" [Jer. 2: 3].

For more on Rashi on creation, see Menachem Kellner, "Rashi and Maimonides on Torah and the Cosmos," in *Between Rashi and Maimonides: Themes in Medieval Jewish Thought, Literature and Exegesis*, ed. Ephraim Kanarfogel and Moshe Sokolow (New York: Yeshiva University Press, 2010): 23–58.

3   An excellent and relatively brief introduction to the life and thought of Maimonides may be found in Moshe Halbertal, *Maimonides* (Princeton: Princeton University Press, 2014). Longer studies include Herbert A. Davidson, *Moses Maimonides: The Man and His Works* (Oxford: Oxford University Press, 2005); and Joel Kraemer, *Maimonides: The Life and World of One of Civilization's Greatest Minds* (New York: Doubleday, 2008).

4   On Samuel ibn Tibbon, translator of the *Guide* into Hebrew, see James Robinson, "Maimonides, Samuel Ibn Tibbon, and the Construction of a Jewish Tradition of Philosophy," in *Maimonides after 800 Years: Essays on Maimonides and His Influence*, ed. Jay Harris (Cambridge, MA: Harvard University Press, 2007): 291–306. On Meiri, see below, chapter 7. One must not confuse respect for aspects of Christian culture with respect for Christianity as such. See Eric Lawee, "The Refined People of Edom—Evolving Jewish Attitudes towards Christian Culture in Spain in the Late Middle Ages," *Jewish studies, an internet Journal* 14 (2018), https://jewish-faculty.biu.ac.il/en/JSIJ/.

5   Jonathan Sacks, *The Dignity of Difference*, rev. ed. (New York: Continuum, 2003), 65–6. I wrote the current chapter originally as a contribution to a festschrift in honor of Rabbi Sacks.

Even in our relatively enlightened age, it would appear that more people are threatened than enlarged by the faith of others.

All this is true, but there is still much to be learned from Rabbi Sacks's observation. I believe that it provides a new angle for understanding an 800-year-old debate in Jewish sources. I want to make the case that attempts to ground Jewish *chosenness* in the claim that Jews are distinguished from others by some sort of innate characteristic, which makes them both different from and superior to other human beings, reflects a lack of religious self-confidence. Not to beat around the bush, the alternative view is that of Maimonides, according to which all human beings are equally made in the image of God. What distinguishes Jews from other human beings is nothing innate, ontological, metaphysical, or however you might want to characterize it, but the truth of the Torah. This view is neither pluralist nor liberal, but it does save Maimonides from the charge of a lack of religious self-confidence, and from the charge of racist particularism.[6]

We do not have to remain bound by Maimonides. He takes us many steps on the way towards enabling us to be enlarged by the faith of others, but certainly does not take us all the way—that we will have to do on our own.

2. THE WORLD OF HALEVI AND THE HALEVIANS

Two facts about the earliest statement that Jews are in some actual sense distinguished from non-Jews are significant. The first is that it dates from the twelfth

---

6   Racism per se is a modern illness and it ill behooves me to charge Halevi with it; the same cannot be said for many of his followers today. Maimonides, like every scientifically oriented thinker of his day, accepted the theory of climatology. According to this theory, individuals born and/or raised far from the equator were humanly deficient. See, for example, his unfortunate comment about Turks (from the far North) and Negroes (from the far South) in *Guide*, iii. 51, 618. On the theory of climatology, see Alexander Altmann, "Judah Halevi's Theory of Climates," *Aleph* 5 (2005): 215–46, Abraham Melamed, "The Land of Israel and the Climatological Theory in Jewish Thought," in *Eretz Yisrael be-Hagut ha-Yehudit Bimei ha-Benayim*, ed. Moshe Hallamish and Aviezer Ravitzky (Jerusalem: Yad Ben-Zvi, 1991), 52–79 (Hebrew), and Abraham Melamed, *The Image of the Black in Jewish Culture: A History of the Other* (London: Routledge, 2003). Melamed, *The Image of the Black in Jewish Culture*, 125, 139–145 shows that Maimonides followed ibn Khaldun in denying what we would call the genetic basis of inferiority; Maimonides also ignores the biblical basis, so prominent in defense of slavery in pre-civil war United States. Individuals from the far North or far South raised in salubrious climes would not be defective. Since Maimonides accepts the racist conclusions of the theory of climes because he accepted that theory as scientific fact, and not because he accepted the biblical curse theory, if he were alive today, he would agree with the most up-to-date science available. See Menachem Kellner, "Maimonides on the Science of the Mishneh Torah—Provisional or Permanent?" *AJS Review* 18 (1993): 169–194.

century, not earlier,[7] and the second is that it occurs in a book titled *The Book of Refutation and Proof on Behalf of the Despised Religion*. Judah Halevi's *Kuzari*, as the book is better known, was written as a defense of rabbinic Judaism in the face of attacks by Karaites, Christians, Muslims, neo-Aristotelian philosophers writing in Arabic, and, I would add, by the kind of Judaism soon to be found in the writings of Moses Maimonides. It is noteworthy that Halevi's defense of *Judaism* involves unprecedented claims about the special nature of the *Jews*.[8]

We have thus a fairly late book, written by a poet-philosopher who was clearly affronted by the disdain he felt on the part of the majority cultures then warring over his homeland (born in Christian Spain, Halevi spent his maturity in the Muslim South). He also lived in a world in which Muslims of pure

---

7 I am more than painfully aware of the rabbinic passages (thankfully a very small number) which could be construed as teaching that Jews are not only God's chosen people, especially beloved being firstborn sons, as it were (Exod. 4: 22), but in some inherent sense truly distinct from and superior to non-Jews. But even such statements as AZ 22b, according to which only non-Jews carry the pollution which the Edenic snake cast into Eve (a statement the outer meaning of which Maimonides (*Guide* ii. 30) says is deeply disgraceful), and the various misanthropic statements attributed to R. Shimon bar Yohai need not be read literally (indeed, that is the general approach to R. Shimon bar Yohai's famous statement in BT Yev. 60b–61a that only Jews are called "human"—see especially Tosafot ad loc.). Even if one in-sists on reading them literally and anachronistically, as if they reflected views that found gen-eral expression only in the Middle Ages, they still remain a tiny and wholly unrepresentative set of texts. See Kellner, *Gam Hem Keruyim Adam: Ha-Nokhri Be-Einei ha-Rambam* (Ramat Gan: Bar Ilan University Press, 2016), 21–38.

8 I am writing on the assumption that the Zohar postdates Halevi and that its doctrines were largely unknown to him. Contemporary scholarship usually ascribes authorship of the Zohar to the thirteenth century Spanish kabbalist R. Moses de Leon (c. 1240–1305) and his circle, even if some scholars see it as the outgrowth of a long mystical tradition that preceded it. For a recent analysis of rabbinic views which qualify or reject the traditional ascription of the Zohar to R. Shimon bar Yohai, see Marc Shapiro, "Is there an Obligation to Believe that R. Shimon bar Yochai Wrote the Zohar?," *Milin havivin* 5 (2010–11), Hebrew section: 1–20. On Zoharic doctrines concerning the special nature of the Jews, see Moshe Hallamish, "The Kabbalists' Attitude to the Nations of the World," in *Joseph Baruch Sermonetta Memorial Volume*, Jerusalem Studies in Jewish Thought 14, ed. Aviezer Ravitzky (Jerusalem: Magnes, 1988): 289–312 (Hebrew). Hallamish's focus is on the image of non-Jews in kabbalah, but a picture of the Jew is made clear along the way. See further above in chapter 1, note 13. A propos Halevi, it is important to note that his own views on the special nature of the Jewish people bear all the hallmarks of Shi'ite influence. See Krinis, *God's Chosen People* and Lobel, *Between Mysticism and Philosophy*, 17 and 38. This is rather amusing given the way figures as disparate as the Gaon of Vilna and Rabbi Shlomo Aviner insist that Halevi is a purely Jewish thinker, unlike, for example, Maimonides, whom they hold to have been overly influenced by Aristotle. For details, see James Diamond and Menachem Kellner, *Reinventing Maimonides in Contemporary Jewish Thought* (London: Littman Library of Jewish Civilization, 2019), 184n42.

Arab descent saw themselves as superior to other Muslims and in which some Christians cast doubt upon the simple humanity of Jews, who had every reason to know better, but stubbornly persisted in rejecting the messiahship of Jesus, despite its "obvious" truth. It is hardly surprising that Halevi chose not only to emphasize the truth and beauty of the Torah, but also the special nature of its recipients.

What did Halevi claim in this regard? In light of later iterations of the claim that Jews are significantly distinguished from and superior to non-Jews, Halevi's claims are restrained, and, as was pointed out to me by Rabbi Daniel Korobkin, perhaps wholly theoretical.[9] The biblical story opens, of course, with the creation of all that is. Abraham, the progenitor of those whom we now call Jews, does not show up until twenty generations have passed. For many traditionally oriented Jews today (influenced by R. Judah Halevi and those who follow him), Abraham was chosen by God: Halevi maintained that in the ten generations from Adam to Noah, and in the ten generations from Noah to Abraham, a line of descent developed (or, perhaps more accurately, was caused to develop by God) of individuals capable of achieving prophecy. This special subset of humanity continued to develop through Abraham (but not through his brother Haran or Haran's son Lot, or the children of his second wife Keturah);[10] through Isaac (but not through his brother Ishmael); and through Jacob (but not through his brother Esau); and finally to all of Jacob's descendants, the children of Israel/Jacob. For Halevi, this special subset of humanity is related to the rest of the human race as the heart is related to the rest of the body: the core organ (and the seat of thinking for medievals, following the Bible), without which the other organs cannot survive and which itself, if we take the analogy further, cannot survive without them.[11]

Halevi's intellectual honesty is such that he accepts the consequences of his position. Flying in the face of received halakhah, he maintains that converts

---

9   The differences are only theoretical since no one achieves prophecy anymore. However, there are those who interpret a late poem of Halevi's as explaining his resolve to reach the land of Israel in order to have a prophetic experience. See Yosef Yahalom, *Shirat Hayav shel Rav Yehudah Halevi* (Jerusalem: Magnes, 2008), 93–106.

10 Gen. 25:1–6; see Rashi on Gen. 25:1. See further, Josef Stern, "Maimonides's Parable of Circumcision," *Sevara* 2 (1991): 35–48 and Kasher, "Maimonides's View of Circumcision." See also Menachem Kellner, "Chosenness, Not Chauvinism: Maimonides on the Chosen People," in *A People Apart: Chosenness and Ritual in Jewish Philosophical Thought*, ed. Daniel H. Frank (Albany: SUNY Press, 1993), 51–75. This article appeared with a response by Norbert Samuelson (77–84) and a reply by Kellner (85–89).

11 See Halevi, *Kuzari*, i. 27–28, 96, 101–03, and 115.

to Judaism remain inferior to born Jews (*Kuzari*, i. 27): "whoever joins us from among the nations especially will share in our good fortune although he will not be equal to us."[12] Halevi's honesty is further evidenced by his apparent admission (*Kuzari* i. 113–15) that Jews in practice all too often fail to live up to their divine potential, and, if given the chance, could be as brutal as the nations among whom they live.

Writers coming after Halevi tended to be more absolute in their claims about the special nature of the Jews, most often rooting their claims in kabbalistic notions. Historically, the various forms of Jewish ontological particularism have been purely theoretical discussions, with no concrete consequences in the lives of their authors, or those who read their works. One hopes that the same will be true for the book *Torat Hamelekh*, discussed in chapter 1 above. I do not mean to blame Halevi or his successors in the Jewish tradition for this book, but do want to insist that it is one possible consequence of their ontological particularism.[13]

The doctrine concerning the special innate ontologically superior nature of the Jews is on the face of it so obviously irrational, so observably false in the real world (as Judah Halevi himself had to admit), and so totally unsupported by the overwhelming majority of biblical and rabbinic texts (and to my mind both immoral and fundamentally un-Jewish) that one is driven to wonder how anyone could take it seriously, and how it could have become so dominant a theme in medieval and contemporary Judaism. Two answers spring to mind, the second of which will bring us back to Rabbi Sacks's observation about confidence in one's faith.

Jewish history may not be exclusively "lachrymose" (as the historian Salo Baron famously pointed out) but the survival of the Jews in the face of exile and persecution is indeed remarkable. Persecuted individuals and peoples often develop a common defense mechanism: they view their persecutors as inferior. Is it any wonder that the Jews adopt that view? All people need to feel special; persecuted individuals and peoples (when they do not succumb and internalize the views of the persecutors—a syndrome that appears particularly widespread today among Jewish enemies of Israel) will often and understandably claim

---

12 See further Lasker, "Proselyte Judaism." The inferiority which Halevi attaches to converts to Judaism relates not to matters of *yihus* (descent; a convert may not become a king of Israel, for example, nor marry a *kohen*), but to their very nature—in effect, they are no longer Gentiles, but not entirely Jewish either. Translations from the *Kuzari* are taken from Barry Kogan's version that is forthcoming from Yale University Press; my thanks to Prof. Kogan for sharing his translation with me.

13 See above, chapter 1, notes 25 and 26.

moral and even innate superiority over their persecutors. This is perhaps one way of understanding how a religious tradition that begins with the insight that all human beings are created in the image of God could spawn a book like *Torat hamelekh*.[14] This matter is so central to Judaism, so fundamental, that I am not familiar with any Jewish thinker, no matter how liberal and universalist in his or her views, who manages without some interpretation or other of the idea of Jewish chosenness. Even Mordecai Kaplan—whose view of God is basically that of George Lucas' Obi-Wan Kenobi, namely, that there is an unselfconscious natural force in the universe—arrives in his last book *The Religion of Ethical Nationhood* at the unexpected conclusion that it is only the special nature of Jewish nationalism which stands between the world and nuclear armageddon. Thus, even those who try to naturalize everything (such as Mordecai Kaplan) end up with some notion of Jewish chosenness.[15]

The issue achieves added urgency in the light of a comment I once heard from the late Emil Fackenheim: Jews were murdered in the Holocaust because their great-grandparents refused to assimilate. From this, it follows, I submit, that the decision to remain Jewish in the face of great assimilatory pressures and inducements is a *moral* choice, and one that might be fraught with unimaginably horrible consequences for one's grandchildren, God forbid. One must have good reasons for remaining Jewish.[16]

Given all this, it is hardly surprising that Jews and Judaism have developed mechanisms for keeping Jews Jewish. One mechanism that appears to have proved effective is the claim that Jews constitute a metaphysical kind, distinct from and superior to other humans. This is certainly one way to encourage loyalty in the face of fierce persecution, and in the face of the blandishments of the contemporary world, which, in the USA, at least, seem to be wiping out the Jewish people through kindness, not murder.

The view that Jews are in some serious way innately different from and superior to Gentiles is deeply rooted in contemporary Judaism.[17] This is so

---

14 This issue is taken up again below, in chapters 5 and 6.
15 See chapter 3 below on the election of Israel. Kaplan's views are taken up there at somewhat greater length.
16 Fackenheim clearly thought that Jews should remain Jewish. He is well known for introducing the "614th commandment": Thou shalt not give Hitler posthumous victories (by assimilating). The emotional weight of that cry has gotten weaker with each passing year, but, beyond that, one would hope that there are positive reasons for remaining Jewish.
17 In my experience, so-called liberal and secularist Jews are no less particularist than are the Orthodox. Indeed, when it comes to the full acceptance of proselytes, Orthodox Jews in Israel are typically much more open than their secularist counterparts.

much the case that after I wrote a book (*Maimonides on Judaism and the Jewish People*) to convince one of the members of my synagogue that for Maimonides there is no inherent difference between Jews and non-Jews, he read it, admitted the cogency of my arguments, and then said that, in consequence, his admiration for Maimonides had diminished. Another member of my synagogue, a lawyer, sought to convince me that when Maimonides used the talmudic expression *kol ba'ei olam* (all human beings), he could not mean to include non-Jews, since the term is found in the liturgical poem "Unetaneh tokef":[18] for him it was a given that God neither judges nor even listens to the prayers of non-Jews. For people like my fellow two synagogue-goers, billions of Gentiles are like static, background noise, of no possible interest to God.

This is certainly not the view of Maimonides and his contemporary followers, as I will argue after making one more point. Biblical authors, and to a great extent the rabbis of the Talmud, appear to have been convinced that idolaters were brutal and corrupt. As much as idolatry was a religious deviation, it was also a cause of profound moral corruption and in that sense was truly a source of *tum'ah*, ritual impurity. But what happened when the Gentiles among whom the Jews lived, and with whom they conducted business, and with whom they often had social ties[19] turned out to be moral individuals, trustworthy in their personal dealings, and sophisticated in their religious beliefs? People confident in their faith would be untroubled by such a situation. But perhaps people not so confident in their faith would seek to bolster their identities by denigrating the others as, in effect, not fully human, not truly made in the image of God to the fullest extent possible, not only different, but also innately inferior? There is no way to perform psychoanalysis on long-dead Jews, but, looking at those Jews among us today who most disdain Gentiles, is it far-fetched to see the results of a persecution complex (as paranoids may really have enemies, so also, as it were, one can acknowledge persecution without justifying a persecution complex), the results of a lack of self-confidence?

Again, there is no way of knowing, but it does help set the stage for a wholly other way of looking at the difference between Jews and Gentiles, one which grows out of untroubled confidence in the truth of Torah.

---

18 A central element in the liturgy of the high holidays. For a recent study, see Reuven Kimelman, "U-N'Taneh Tokef as a Midrashic Poem," in *The Experience of Jewish Liturgy: Studies Dedicated to Menahem Schmelzer*, ed. Debra Reed Blank (Leiden: Brill, 2011), 115–146. See further, Kellner and Gillis *Maimonides the Universalist*, chapter 7.

19 If there were no such social ties, why forbid the consumption of Gentile wine, oil, and bread, for fear that it might lead to intermarriage? See, for example, Shabbat 17b.

3. MAIMONIDES AND THE MAIMONIDEANS

There are many ways of proving that Maimonides rejected the idea that Jews are in some innate sense distinct from and inherently superior to non-Jews.[20] One of the most direct texts is his letter to Ovadiah the Proselyte.[21] In this letter, he writes that Abraham is as much the father of proselytes as he is of born Jews. That this is no rhetorical flourish is evidenced by the fact that Maimonides makes this statement in a halakhic responsum and that he derives halakhic consequences from this claim. Indeed, he goes on to say (as if he were directly controverting Halevi, which is not an impossibility)[22] that the proselyte is actually closer to God than the born Jew.[23] In further contradistinction to Halevi, Maimonides points out that the children of Israel at Sinai were themselves all converts to Judaism: the Jews are a nation constituted by a religious act, not by shared descent. This point was made by a prominent twentieth-century Maimonidean, Rabbi Joseph Kafih, but before turning to his comments, I want to elaborate just a bit on Maimonides's position.

My friend Hayim Shahal pointed out to me that the Hebrew expression *kedoshim tihiyu* (you shall be holy [Lev. 19:2]) can be read in the future tense (as a promise) or in the imperative (as a commandment or challenge). Maimonides read it in the latter sense, Halevi in the former.[24] Another way of putting

---

20 Much of my academic writing has been devoted to this issue. In particular, see *Maimonides on Judaism and the Jewish People* (Albany: SUNY Press, 1991); *Maimonides's Confrontation with Mysticism* (Oxford: Littman Library of Jewish Civilization, 2006); *Science in the Bet Midrash: Studies in Maimonides* (Brighton, MA: Academic Studies Press, 2009) and *Gam Hem Keruyim Adam: Ha-Nokhri be-Eynei ha-Rambam* (Ramat-Gan: Bar-Ilan University Press, 2016). In a review of that last book in *Iyyun* 65 (2016): 400–404 (Hebrew) Hannah Kasher takes Maimonides to task for his sharp intellectual elitism and me for insufficiently emphasizing it. That may be the case with respect to that book; it is certainly not the case with respect to this one. Here I deal as much with the consequences (actual or possible) of the views of Halevi and Maimonides.

21 For an English translation of much of the letter, see Franz Kobler, *Letters of Jews through the Ages*, vol. 1 (New York: East and West Library, 1978), 194–6; for a brilliant discussion, see James Diamond, *Converts, Heretics, and Lepers: Maimonides and the Outsider* (Notre Dame: University of Notre Dame Press, 2007). For discussion, see below, chapter 4.

22 See Howard Kreisel, "Judah Halevi's Influence on Maimonides: A Preliminary Appraisal," *Maimonidean Studies* 2 (1991): 95–122.

23 In a certain sense, converts are more Jewish than born Jews, since born Jews may or may not know truth while converts (at least in a Maimonidean *beit din* (religious court) only become Jewish by virtue of knowing the truth). See chapter 4.

24 By reading the verse that way Maimonides means that verses such as Lev. 19:2 and 11:44 (calling upon the Jews to be holy) are not positive commandments, but "charges to fulfill the whole Torah, as if He were saying: 'Be holy by doing all that I have commanded you

the same point: for Halevi, the Torah was given to the Jews for only the Jews could receive it; for Maimonides, it was receipt of the Torah that created the nation of Israel out of a motley collection of ex-slaves and hangers on. Maimonides's views in this regard are so extreme that I believe that it is fair and correct to say of him that the history recorded in the Torah could have been different (had Abraham been a Navajo, for example, as suggested above in chapter 1) and that the commandments which reflect that history (the festivals, the sacrificial cult, etc.) could also have been different. For Maimonides, in other words, the Torah records what actually happened, not what had to happen. History could have worked out differently (but, of course, it did not).[25]

In 1958, the then prime minister of Israel, David Ben-Gurion, wrote to about fifty Jewish intellectuals asking for help in defining who is a Jew. One of the answers he received was from Rabbi Joseph Kafih (1917–2000), then at the beginning of a magnificent career of translating and explaining Maimonides's works. Rabbi Kafih wrote to Ben-Gurion:

> What is the meaning of the term "Jew"? It must be stated that the term does not denote a certain race. Perhaps it is wrong to use the word "race" so as not to mimic the modern-day racists and their associates, as according to the perception of the Torah, there are no different races in the world. In order to uproot this theory, the Torah felt compelled to provide extensive details of the lineage of all the people in the world so as to attribute them to a single father and a single mother. Thus it might be more proper to say that the term "Jew" does not denote a certain tribe, or in other words, does not indicate the descendants of Abraham, Isaac, and Jacob in the limited sense of the phrase. We know beyond any doubt that throughout the generations, many people of different nations became intermixed with the Israelites.[26]

---

to do" (Maimonides, *Book of Commandments*, 4th principle—in the second volume of the translation by Charles Chavel [London: Soncino, 1967], 2:381). Nahmanides, in his critical glosses on the *Book of Commandments*, criticizes Maimonides for seeing such verses as generalizations of the commandments as opposed to divine promises, as he takes them to be. Further on this, see *Confrontation*, chapter 3 in general, and p. 102 in particular.

25 See Menachem Kellner, "Maimonides's Moses: Torah, History, Cosmos," in *Moshe Avi ha-Nevi'im: Demuto Bere'i he-hagut le-Doroteha*, ed. Moshe Hallamish et al. (Ramat Gan: Bar Ilan University Press, 2011), 151–177 (Hebrew)

26 R. Kafih's letter may be found in Eliezer Ben-Rafael, *Jewish Identities: Fifty Intellectuals Answer Ben-Gurion* (Leiden: Brill, 2002), 247–53.

But Jews are not just followers of a religion, Rabbi Kafih writes, since at their core is a nation; anyone who accepts the religion becomes so deeply interwoven in the nation that he or she becomes indistinguishable from born Jews. Rabbi Kafih also makes the very interesting point that the detailed accounts of the "descent of man" in the book of Genesis were included in the Torah to emphasize that all the nations of the earth are essentially one family, all descended from one source.

Maimonides does not need to posit the superiority of Jews over non-Jews since he is convinced of the truth of the Torah. Since the Torah is true, and since all humans are essentially the same, there is no reason why all humanity will not someday accept the Torah. His messianism, following that of Isaiah and of Amos, is universalist.[27]

We have established that according to Maimonides non-Jews are made in the image of God, just as Jews are. What of non-Jewish religions? Can one find truth in them? Maimonides clearly held that there was some truth in Christianity and Islam, since he tells us that they each have a role to play in making the world ready to accept the messiah.[28]

Christianity teaches the sanctity of the Written Torah, acknowledges that the Torah's commandments were at least once normative, and looks forward to a messianic redemption. Islam professes a no-nonsense version of austere monotheism.

Let us now recast our discussion in terms common to contemporary Jewish discourse: Why be Jewish? For Halevi and his many followers the answer is simple: you are Jewish. Remaining Jewish means remaining what you are; you can fool yourself into thinking that you can cease being Jewish but the attempt means that you are untrue to your innermost essence.[29] For Maimonides the answer is also simple: one should remain Jewish because Judaism is true (a view that Halevi and those in his camp would, of course, heartily endorse). That is enough for Maimonides, but not, it appears for Halevi—it is here that I detect the lack of Jewish theological self-confidence that I suggest is to be found in Halevi, but very clearly not in Maimonides.

---

27 See below, chapter 3 on election, and on Maimonides's messianism, Kellner and Gillis, *Maimonides the Universalist*, chapter 14.
28 For the text, see below in chapters 6 and 7 on Maimonides's insistence that Christianity is still idolatry.
29 One wonders, as Eugene Korn pointed out to me (personal communication), how Halevi would account for the masses of Jews who cheerfully assimilate out, ignoring their (alleged) ontological superiority over non-Jews.

It is because of that self-confidence that Maimonides has no trouble acknowledging the partial truth of Christianity and Islam.[30] That made sense in his world in his day; but does it make sense in ours? Maimonides lived and thought in a world in which truth was one, objective, unchanging, and in principle *accessible*. This made excellent sense in his finite, static universe. While I have no desire to admit to any version of epistemological relativism, it cannot be denied that our confidence in what we can know has been shaken. The appropriate response to this situation is not, it seems to me, relativism, which makes a mockery of truth and of the possibility of actual communication; nor pluralism, which makes a mockery of truth and of revelation; but, rather, the appropriate response to our predicament ought to be modesty.[31] A person who is modest about her claims to truth, as opposed to absolutist about them, is open to the possibility of being inspired, enlarged in Rabbi Sacks's term, by other people whose claims to truth are equally restrained and modest.[32]

4. WE ARE NOT ALONE

While not giving up on the idea that revelation (be it Jewish, Christian, or Muslim) teaches truth in some hard, exclusivist sense, putative addressees of revelation ought to be modest about how much of it they understand, and restrained in the claims they make on behalf of revelation and about adherents of other religions.[33] Admittedly, it may be easier for a Jew to advance this position than for a Christian or a Muslim. This is so for several reasons. First, until the Middle Ages, at least, Jews sought to understand how God instructs them to inject sanctity into their lives, and paid very little attention to the question of how God expects them to think.[34] Given the notion that the Torah contains many levels of meanings, and the profound differences among Jewish thinkers about the nature and content of those meanings, a stance of theological modesty

---

30 See below, chapter 7 on Christianity.
31 My wife and I have argued for this position in "Respectful Disagreement: A Response to Raphael Jospe," in *Jewish Theology and World Religions*, ed. Alon Goshen-Gottstein and Eugene Korn (Oxford: Littman Library of Jewish Civilization, 2012), 123–33. On religious relativism see below, chapter 6 on tolerance.
32 Here I go beyond Maimonides, who was much more optimistic than we can be about accessing truth, both of reason and of revelation. One need not be a postmodernist to admit that access to absolute truth is more problematic than many of our medieval forbears thought.
33 On religious modesty, see below, chapter 6, on tolerance.
34 This is the burden of Menachem Kellner, *Must a Jew Believe Anything?*, 2nd ed. (Oxford: Littman Library of Jewish Civilization, 2006).

ought to be easier for Jews to maintain than for adherents of more clearly theologically based religions. Second, given the nature of Jewish-Gentile relations over the last two millennia, Jews had very little reason to look to Gentiles for spiritual enrichment. We, however, live in a different world, and I thank God for that.[35] Last, Jews have traditionally paid little attention to the beliefs and practices of others. This is so since Judaism has never taught that one must be Jewish in order to achieve a share in the world to come.

Having left the ghetto and the North African mellah, we live in a world very different from that of our forebears. Looking around, we discover admirable Gentiles from whom we can learn much. We are no longer alone.

---

35 The Lord of all the Universe is not too great to have revealed the Torah, but is certainly too great to be captured by our puny understanding of Torah. To claim otherwise is to be guilty of cosmic hubris, and to close ourselves off to the possibility of being enlarged by meetings with others, individuals who also seek God and whom God does *not* ignore.

CHAPTER 3

Election/Chosen People

1. INTRODUCTION

Traditionally, when a Jew reaches the age of majority (twelve for girls, thirteen for boys), the first formal act they do is to be called to the Torah reading.[1] At that point, the following blessing is recited: "Blessed are You, the Lord, our God, Who has chosen us from among all the peoples, and given us His Torah."[2]

This text gives clear expression to the doctrine of the chosen people, but leaves several important issues unclear. Among them:

1. Was the Torah given to Israel in consequence of God's choice or was the giving of the Torah the mechanism of God's choosing? In other words, what is the precise relationship between the choosing of Israel and its receipt of the Torah?
2. Why has God chosen "us" from among all the peoples?
3. Could God have chosen another people to be chosen? (That is, before the choice of Israel all peoples could have been chosen.) Or was Israel chosen because of some antecedent quality or characteristic?
4. Could God "un-choose" the Jews?[3]

---

1 For the moment, it is not yet the case with respect to most expressions of Orthodoxy.
2 On this and related blessings and their connection to the election of Israel, see the discussion in David Novak, *The Election of Israel: The Idea of the Chosen People* (Cambridge: Cambridge University Press, 1995), 10.
3 The following verses from the beginning of Exod. 19 seem to support both possibilities. These verses, as God's first announcement to Israel of its special status, are particularly significant.

> On the third new moon after the Israelites had gone forth from the land of Egypt, on that very day, they entered the wilderness of Sinai. Having journeyed from Rephidim, they entered the wilderness of Sinai and encamped in the wilderness. Israel encamped there in front of the mountain, and Moses went up to God. The Lord called to him from the mountain, saying, "Thus shall you say to the house of Jacob and declare to the children of Israel: 'You have seen what I did to the Egyptians, how I bore you on eagles' wings and brought you to Me. Now then, if you will obey Me

5. Could the choice have been rejected?
6. Furthermore, once chosen, for whatever reason, are the chosen people as such in some significant sense different from and superior to the common run of humanity?

These questions will frame the discussion that follows.

The doctrine of the chosen people, while certainly central to Jewish self-understanding, is not unique to the Jews.[4] The Jews, however, may be the only people to ground their chosenness in a covenant with God. Why did God enter into the covenant with the patriarchs Abraham, Isaac, and Jacob, and their descendants?[5] There is surprisingly little discussion of this point in the Bible itself. We will see that there are many iterations of the idea that God chose the Jews ("How odd of God to choose the Jews; not so odd the goyyim annoyed Him") out of love for their ancestors. But why did God love their ancestors? That is a question that, as we shall see, generated an ongoing debate between Judah Halevi and his followers and Maimonides and his followers.

The Torah teaches that the Jews were God's *am segulah*, treasured (chosen) people. What does it say about the "unchosen," then, the vast run of humanity? Very little. There are clearly "others," first and foremost those who are to be exterminated: the seven Canaanite nations and Amalek.[6] Other others include those with whom Israelites may not marry (Moabites and Amonites). There are other others, of course, about whom the Torah does not have much to say, beyond acknowledging their existence: Edomites and Egyptians primarily. There are also Abraham's other progeny, Ishmael assuredly, but also those born to him after Sarah's death by his wife Keturah. Here it is very useful to bring into

---

faithfully and keep My covenant, you shall be My treasured possession among all the peoples. Indeed, all the earth is Mine, but you shall be to Me a kingdom of priests and a holy nation.' These are the words that you shall speak to the children of Israel."

4 For a study of the surprising number of nations which have seen themselves as "chosen" see Anthony D. Smith, *Chosen Peoples*, above chapter 2, footnote 1.
5 On the so-called Noachide commandments, which are meant to apply to all humanity, see David Novak, *The Image of the Non-Jew in Judaism: An Historical and Constructive Study of the Noahide Laws* (New York: Edwin Mellen Press, 1983).
6 For sources and discussion, see Menachem Kellner, "And Yet, the Texts Remain: The Problem of the Command to Destroy the Canaanites," in *The Gift of the Land and the Fate of the Canaanites in Jewish Thought*, ed. Katell Berthelot, Menachem Hirshman, and Josef David (Oxford: Oxford University Press, 2014): 153–179. On Judaism and its others generally, see below, chapter 5.

play Joel Kaminsky's distinction between the elect (God's chosen people), the "anti-elect" (Amalek and the "Seven Nations"), and the majority of humanity, that Kaminsky calls the "non-elect."[7]

Alexander Altmann put this matter well. Judaism, on the whole,

> is intolerant of Israelites falling away from the God of the Fathers and of the Covenant. It shows no trace of intolerance of heathens following their customs and traditions. Ruth the Moabite is welcomed as a proselyte, but Orpah, her sister-in-law is not reproved because of her return to her native paganism. David and Solomon extended their kingdoms far beyond the Israelite borders but they did not impose their religion on the subjugated peoples.[8]

Altmann also notes (on the following page) that Jonah did not demand that the inhabitants of Nineveh worship the God of Israel, let alone become Jews. This I take to be an important point.

2. ELECTION—THE BIBLE

Let us now repeat the brief biblical account of Jews and their "others" given above (in chapter 2) The story opens, of course, with the creation of the cosmos. Abraham, the progenitor of those whom we now call Jews, makes no appearance until twenty generations have passed. For many Western monotheists today, Abraham was chosen by God. According to R. Judah Halevi and those Jews who follow him, Abraham belonged by descent to the special subset of humanity capable of achieving prophecy. This special division of humanity continued to develop through Abraham (but not through his brother Haran, or his nephew Lot, or the children of his second wife, Keturah),[9] through Isaac

---

[7] See Joel Kaminsky, *Yet I Loved Jacob: Reclaiming the Biblical Concept of Election* (Nashville: Abingdon, 2007) and Kaminsky's following studies: "Did Election Imply the Mistreatment of Non-Israelites?," *Harvard Theological Review* 96 (2003): 397–425 and "A Light to the Nations: Was There Mission or Conversion in the Hebrew Bible?," *Jewish Studies Quarterly* 16 (2009): 6–22. On Kaminsky, see Jon Levenson, "Chosenness and Its Enemies," *Commentary* 126, no. 5 (2008): 25ff. For another important statement by Levenson, see "The Universal Horizon of Biblical Particularism," in *Ethnicity and the Bible*, ed. Mark G. Brett (Leiden: Brill, 1996), 143–169.

[8] Alexander Altmann, "Tolerance and the Jewish Tradition," in *The Robert Waley Cohen Memorial Lecture* (London: The Council of Christians and Jews, 1957): 1–18, 6.

[9] See above, chapter 2, footnote 10.

(but not through his brother Ishmael), and through Jacob (but not through his brother Esau), and finally to all of Jacob's descendants, the children of Israel/Jacob.

The Torah itself seems to support a view later to be held by Maimonides rather than that later to be held by Judah Halevi. The clearest expression of this might be Deuteronomy 7:6–8:

> For you are a people consecrated to the Lord your God: of all the peoples on earth the Lord your God chose you to be His treasured people. It is not because you are the most numerous of peoples that the Lord set His heart on you and chose you—indeed, you are the smallest of peoples; but it was because the Lord favored you and kept the oath He made to your fathers that the Lord freed you with a mighty hand and rescued you from the house of bondage, from the power of Pharaoh king of Egypt.[10]

God chose Israel as a special treasure for no characteristic of theirs, but, rather, to keep a promise made to the patriarchs, their ancestors. This and similar verses can be read differently, but this seems to be the simple sense, and it is certainly the way that Maimonides (but not Halevi!)[11] read them.

It turns out that the Bible (and rabbinic texts) do not offer clear answers to the questions raised above at the beginning of this chapter. This is not surprising: these texts are not overtly theological in nature and rarely address abstract theological issues straightforwardly, if at all. The first question raised above was, was the Torah given to Israel in consequence of God's choice or was the giving of the Torah the mechanism of God's choosing? Deuteronomy (7:6–8) as we just saw appears to answer that question by de-linking God's choice to some quality of the Jewish people.

Zekhut avot (ancestral merit) is explicitly cited in Deuteronomy 10:14–15:

> Mark, the heavens to their uttermost reaches belong to the Lord your God, the earth and all that is on it! [15]Yet it was to your fathers that the Lord was drawn in His love for them, so that He chose you, their lineal descendants, from among all peoples—as is now the case.

---

10 See also Gen. 17:1–4, Deut. 4:31–40, and Deut. 10:14–15.
11 So far as I could determine, Halevi pays no special attention to these verses in the *Kuzari*.

The book of Genesis is largely devoted to the history of God's relationship with the patriarchs, but the reason behind that relationship is never made clear. God chooses Abraham by commanding: "Go forth …" (Gen. 12:1) but no explanation for that choice is found.

The ancestral patrimony is not raised in a third passage from Deuteronomy dealing with what came to be called the election of Israel (14:1–2):

> You are children of the Lord your God. You shall not gash yourselves or shave the front of your heads because of the dead.[2] For you are a people consecrated to the Lord your God: the Lord your God chose you from among all other peoples on earth to be His treasured people.

That these verses teach that God chose Israel from among all the nations is clear. Why? These verses do not tell us.

Similarly, in a further passage in Deuteronomy (26:16–19):

> The Lord your God commands you this day to observe these laws and rules; observe them faithfully with all your heart and soul.[17] You have affirmed this day that the Lord is your God, that you will walk in His ways, that you will observe His laws and commandments and rules, and that you will obey Him.[18] And the Lord has affirmed this day that you are, as He promised you, His treasured people who shall observe all His commandments,[19] and that He will set you, in fame and renown and glory, high above all the nations that He has made; and that you shall be, as He promised, a holy people to the Lord your God.

"High above all the nations (*elyon al kol ha-goyyim*)"—many will want to read that as a claim of Israel's inherent superiority.[12] Nevertheless, the verse itself speaks of superiority in fame, renown, and glory, nothing else. Here the connection between election and obedience to the commandments is made clear.

The prophet Amos seemed to be conflicted about the nature of the election of Israel. On the hand one, he wrote (1:1–2):

> Hear this word, O people of Israel,
> That the Lord has spoken concerning you,

---

12 See Hannah Kasher's exploration of this idea in Jewish philosophical texts *Elyon Al Kol ha-Goyyim*.

> Concerning the whole family that I brought up from the land of Egypt:
> You alone have I singled out
> Of all the families of the earth—
> That is why I will call you to account
> For all your iniquities.

On the other hand, six chapters on, he states (9:7):

> To Me, O Israelites, you are
> Just like the Ethiopians
> —declares the Lord.
> True, I brought Israel up
> From the land of Egypt,
> But also the Philistines from Caphtor
> And the Arameans from Kir.

But the following verse makes clear that unlike the Philistines and Arameans,

> Behold, the Lord God has His eye
> Upon the sinful kingdom:
> I will wipe it off
> The face of the earth!
> But, I will not wholly wipe out
> The House of Jacob
> —declares the Lord.

For Amos, being the apple of God's eye, as it were, can have negative consequences—unique attention and unique punishment—but the House of Jacob will never be wiped out.

One thing is clear from this brief survey: there is no obvious biblical doctrine of election. Given the nature of the Bible itself, this is not surprising, even if it would surprise many Jews today.

3. ELECTION—SOME RABBINIC VIEWS

Continuing with the issue of theological surprises, there is very little doubt that most Jews raised in a traditional context today would be surprised to discover that rabbinic texts contain a variety of positions concerning God's choice of

Israel.[13] Many of them would be even more surprised to discover that many such texts imply the view (later adopted by Maimonides) that God might have chosen other nations, and that the choice of Israel reflects no special qualities found in the Jewish people. This, I submit, is the upshot of the following passage (taken, as are other passages in the Talmud, from the Soncino translation):

> R. Johanan further said in the name of R. Jose: Three things did Moses ask of the Holy One, blessed be He, and they were granted to him. He asked that the Divine Presence should rest upon Israel, and it was granted to him. For it is said: Is it not in that Thou goest with us [so that we are distinguished, I and Thy people, from all the people that are upon the face of the earth] (Exod. 33:16). He asked that the Divine Presence should not rest upon the idolaters, and it was granted to him. For it is said: 'So that we are distinguished, I and Thy people'. He asked that He should show him the ways of the Holy One, blessed be He, and it was granted to him. For it is said: Show me now Thy ways (Exod. 33:13). (Ber. 7a)

If Moses had to ask for the three things mentioned, it means that (a) the divine presence did not *have* to rest upon Israel, (b) that the divine presence *could* have rested upon other nations, even idolatrous nations, and (c) that Moses might not have been vouchsafed an understanding of God's ways. The first two of these interest us here: it would appear from this passage that Moses realized that God in principle could have chosen another nation, not Israel.[14]

---

13 Halevi's tremendous influence might play a role here. Daniel J. Lasker argues that Halevi carefully avoids showing his readers the wide variety of rabbinic opinions on the nature of election. See Daniel J. Lasker, "R. Judah Halevi as Biblical Exegete in the *Kuzari*," in *Davar Davur Al Ofanav: Mehkarim Be-Parshanut Ha-Mikra Ve-Ha-Koran Bimei Ha-Benayim Mugashim Le-Haggai Ben-Shammai*, ed. S. Hopkins et al. (Jerusalem: Makhon Ben-Zvi, 2007), 179–192 (Hebrew).

14 Maimonides does not cite this source in this context, but it could very well underlay his own position, that the choice of Israel was neither preordained (as Halevi would have it) nor necessary. See the discussion in Kellner, *Confrontation* throughout and chapter 7 in particular. Compare Jerome Gellman, "The God of the Jews and the Jewish God," in *The Routledge Companion to Theism*, ed. Victoria S. Harrison et al. (n.p: Routledge Handbooks Online, 2012), 44:

> At most (Maimonides scholars are divided about this), God might intervene to withhold prophecy, but does not *grant* prophetic status. The personal, active relationship between God and the prophet disappears. As a result, the chosenness of the Jewish people, as signifying an intimacy between God and the people, also disappears. ... Maimonides rarely refers to the Jews as the "chosen people." For him the Jews are

This may also be the message of the following oft-cited passage (AZ 2b): "R. Johanan says: This teaches us that the Holy One, blessed be He, offered the Torah to every nation and every tongue, but none accepted it, until He came to Israel who received it." The point of this passage is not to teach history, but to praise the ancient Israelites, who accepted the Torah unconditionally.[15] However, the praise makes no sense had the Torah been predestined for the Jews.

Menachem Hirshman has analyzed in detail the many texts that ask why Torah was given in the Wilderness of Sinai as opposed to the Land of Israel. Hirshman demonstrates that these texts teach that God chose to do so in order that the Torah could have been available to all the nations.[16] It should be no surprise that thinkers who hold such a view expect the Torah to be accepted by all nations in the fullness of time.

These few paragraphs do not do justice to the rich variety of rabbinic opinions on the nature of the election of the Jews. What they do indicate is that the variety of opinions available to the post-rabbinic Jewish tradition is certainly more variegated than many Jews today have become accustomed to think.

4. ELECTION—LITURGY

The Jewish liturgy may be no more interested than the Bible in theological consistency, but it surely emphasizes the election of Israel in the context of God's love for the Jewish people.

A text well known to all Jews who attend traditional services on the three pilgrim festivals and on the High Holy Days states:

> You have chosen us from among all nations, loved us, desired us above all other tongues; You have sanctified us with your commandments and brought us close, our King, to your worship; you have called us by your great and holy name.

---

simply the people of Moses, the prophet who knew God's mind, as it were. ... It is not preposterous to propose that for Maimonides, had Moses been a Hittite, then the Hittites would have been the recipients of his legislation, not the Israelites.

Gellman and I agree about this; he used Hittites for the example and I used Navajos (thanks to Tony Hillerman). See *Confrontation*, 81 and above, chapter 1 after note 37.

15 In contrast to the other nations, each of which inquired what would be required of them before accepting the Torah (Mekhilta d'Rabbi Ishmael, Yitro, Massekhta Hahodesh, v). For a more detailed analysis of this text in its context and other relevant texts, see Kellner, *Gam Hem Ḳeruyim Adam*, 30–37.

16 Hirshman, *Torah Lekhol Ba'ei Olam*.

Here we see God's love for the Jewish people and the election of Israel directly connected. Sanctification by the commandments,[17] the privilege of worshiping God, and having God's name (El) made part of the people's name (Isra-*el*) all appear to be consequences of that election, even if we are not told why God loved the Jews.

The motif of love finds emphatic expression in a central place in the daily liturgy, the blessing preceding the recitation of the Shema:

> With great love have you loved us, our Lord and God, with great and boundless compassion have you been compassionate to us. Our Father and King, because of our ancestors who trusted in you. … Blessed are you, Lord, who chooses his people of Israel in love.

Here the motif of ancestral merit takes pride of place. It should be pointed out that followers of both Halevi and Maimonides accept this idea. For Halevi the patriarchs of the Jewish people were chosen for God's special interest because of their descent—no one else could have been chosen. For Maimonides it was the historically contingent fact that Abraham chose God and raised a son and grandson who followed in his footsteps that gained for them the special merit in light of which God promised to elect their progeny.

We have examined examples from the liturgy expressing God's special love for the Jewish people. Additionally, the liturgy teaches that God is concerned with the well-being of all human beings, apportioning reward and punishment to them all. Thus, for example, in a hymn traditionally given pride of place in the Ashkenazi liturgy of the High Holy Days ("Unetanah Tokef") we find:

> We acclaim this day's pure sanctity, it's awesome power. This day, Lord, Your dominion is deeply felt. Compassion and truth, its foundations, are perceived. In truth do You judge and prosecute, discern motives and bear witness, record and seal, count and measure, remembering all that we have forgotten. You open the Book of Remembrance and it speaks for itself, for every man has signed it with his deeds. The great shofar is sounded. A still, small voice is heard. This day even angels are alarmed, seized with fear

---

17 By which Maimonides means that verses such as Lev. 19:2 and 11:44 (calling upon the Jews to be holy) are not positive commandments, but "charges to fulfill the whole Torah, as if He were saying: 'Be holy by doing all that I have commanded you to do" (Maimonides, *Book of Commandments*, 4th principle). See above, chapter 2, note 24.

and trembling as they declare: "The day of judgment is here!" For even the hosts of heaven are judged. This day all who walk the earth [*kol ba'ei olam*] pass before You as a flock of sheep. And like a shepherd who gathers his flock, bringing them under his staff, You bring everything that lives before You for review. You determine the life and decree the destiny of every creature.[18]

Despite what many traditionalist Jews mistakenly believe,[19] this hymn means what it says: On Rosh ha-Shanah God examines and judges *all* human beings, Jew and non-Jew.

This duality, God's particular love for the Jewish people, allied with concern for all humanity, finds dramatic expression in one of the core elements of the Jewish liturgy, the *aleinu* prayer, the first paragraph of which emphasizes the election of Israel while the second anticipates a universalist messianic era.[20]

5. ELECTION—JUDAH HALEVI AND MAIMONIDES

Judah Halevi and Maimonides essayed answers to the question of why God chose the Jews, answers that reflect very different understandings of what the Jewish religion actually is.[21] For Halevi, God really had no choice, as it were, in the matter of choosing the Jewish people: the choice of the patriarchs and their descendants after them was determined by their special qualities.[22] For

---

18 See Kimelman, "U-N'Taneh Tokef as a Midrashic Poem," 117.
19 See Kellner, "Monotheism as a Continuing Ethical Challenge to Jews," in *Monotheism and Ethics: Historical and Contemporary Intersections among Judaism, Christianity, and Islam*, ed. Y. Tzvi Langermann (Leiden; Brill, 2012), 75–86 for an analysis of this text and an example of learned Jews who refuse to accept it at face value. For another universalist hymn from the liturgy ("Va-ye'etayu") see *Gam Hem*, 37.
20 For recent studies of *aleinu*, see Ruth Langer, "The Censorship of Aleinu in Ashkenaz and Its Aftermath," in *The Experience of Jewish Liturgy: Studies Dedicated to Menachem Schmeltzer*, ed. Debra Reed Blank (Leiden: Brill, 2011), 147–166 and "Jewish Liturgical Memory and the Non-Jew," in Goshen-Gottstein and Korn, *Jewish Theology and World Religions*, 167–186.
21 For an insightful comparison between Halevi and Maimonides, see David Hartman, *Israelis and the Jewish Tradition: An Ancient People Debating its Future* (New Haven: Yale University Press, 2000). The different views of Maimonides and Halevi about the nature of the Jewish religion reflect different views about God. Halevi's God is surely "the God of Abraham, Isaac, and Jacob," while the God of Maimonides is surely that, but also seeks to come as close as possible to "the God of the philosophers." Further on this, see *Confrontation*, 80n.
22 David Novak puts the point succinctly: For Halevi, "God's 'choice' of Israel is not so much a choice as it is an inevitability of creation, the culmination of what began with his primordial and absolute will at the moment of the creation of the world." See Novak, *The Election*

Maimonides God did not choose the Jews; rather, the Jews (or, more precisely, their progenitor, Abraham) chose God. The covenant with Abraham's descendants was both a fulfillment of a divine promise made to Abraham and a reward to him for having chosen God. As we have seen, the Torah itself offers no conclusive support to either view.

Judah Halevi and the many who follow him in the Jewish tradition[23] largely deny that God cherishes all humanity equally—Jews truly are alone. In addition, they also maintain that there is something uniquely special about *Jews* as such.[24] Thus, for them, the question, "Why remain Jewish?," has an obvious answer. Maimonides, by contrast, denies that Jews as such are in any way different from non-Jews as such.[25] In that case, why remain Jewish? His answer is simple: there is something uniquely special about *Judaism* as such.[26] This unique teaching will ultimately be accepted by all of humanity.[27]

As pointed out above (in chapter 1), for Halevi this special subset of humanity is related to the rest of the human race as the heart is related to the rest of the body. The heart is the core organ (and the seat of thinking for medievals, following the Bible), without which the other organs cannot survive and which

---

of Israel, 215–216. Ehud Krinis traces this idea of Halevi's to Shi'ite influence. See above chapter 1, note 39. For Halevi, it would appear, history as it happened had to happen as it happened. For Maimonides, on the other hand, the Torah records the history of the Jewish people as it happened to happen, as it were, not as it had to have happened. See Kellner, "Maimonides's Moses," and my discussion of "Laws of Idolatry," chapter 1 above.

23 For one expression of Halevi's impact on later (Kabbalistically inflected) thinkers, see Isadore Twersky's succinct comment: "In many respects, R. Judah Halevi, Nahmanides, and the Maharal constitute a special strand of Jewish thought—threefold, yet unified." See Isadore Twersky, "Maimonides and Eretz Israel: Halakhic, Philosophic, and Historical Perspectives," in *Perspectives on Maimonides*, ed. Joel Kraemer (Oxford: Littman Library of Jewish Civilization, 1991), 261n. See also: Peter Schaefer, *Mirror of His Beauty: Feminine Images of God from the Bible to the Early Kabbalah* (Princeton: Princeton University Press, 2002), 113–117 and Sara Sviri, "Spiritual Trends in Pre-Kabbalistic Judeo-Spanish Literature: The Cases of Bahya Ibn Paquda and Judah Halevi," *Donaire* 6 (1996): 78–84.

24 For studies of Judaic particularism, see above, chapter 1, footnote 28.

25 See Kellner, *Confrontation* throughout and chapter 7 in particular, and Kellner, *Gam Hem*. Raphael Jospe (personal communication) points to Maimonides's (unique) use of the expression "holy seed" in "Laws of Forbidden Intercourse," xii: 13 as a possible exception to his consistent denial of any inherent difference between Jews as such and non-Jews as such. I plan to address this text in another place.

26 This uniqueness is expressed popularly in Maimonides's "Thirteen Principles," on which, see Kellner, *Must a Jew Believe Anything?*; halakhically in "Laws of the Foundations of the Torah," i–iv; and philosophically in the *Guide of the Perplexed*.

27 For Maimonides's messianic texts, see Kellner and Gillis, *Maimonides the Universalist*, chapter 14.

Election/Chosen People | 53

itself, if we take the analogy further, cannot survive without them.[28] Similarly, the Jewish people are, as it were, the core organ of humanity. Maimonides, on the other hand, taught that it was Abraham who chose God, not the other way round and, in consequence of that choice, God entered into a covenant with Abraham, with his son (Isaac), with his grandson (Jacob), and ultimately with their descendants at Sinai.[29] Maimonides and Halevi et al. all agree that the nation that came to be called Jewish was chosen by God. For Halevi, this is a function of the special nature of the Jewish people, determined from creation. For Maimonides this is basically a function of an historically contingent event—it did not have to be the ancestor of the Jews who rediscovered God.

The Bible is, of course, a complex document, but until the book of Ezra there appear to be no texts which clearly support Halevi over Maimonides, that is, which support the claim that the Jewish people are in some inherent fashion innately superior to non-Jews, to the other.[30] Indeed, Christine Hayes, in an important article,[31] opines that

> [t]he rabbis seem eager to disassociate themselves from Ezran holy seed rhetoric and related Second Temple traditions that denounced even casual interethnic unions as capital crimes, subject to the vengeance of zealots. They rule that those who read a universal prohibition of intermarriage into the Bible are to be severely suppressed (M. Megillah 4:9). The rabbis' failure to take up Ezra's ban on foreign wives and their children—indeed, their very reversal of this program by allowing conversion—is all the more

---

28 See Diana Lobel, *Between Mysticism and Philosophy*, 17 and 38 and Lasker, "Proselyte Judaism." It would be anachronistic to condemn Halevi as a racist. It is certainly not anachronistic to condemn those today who, relying on him (and others), adopt what it is hard not to call racist attitudes towards non-Jews. For a discussion of a prominent and influential contemporary, R. Shlomo Aviner, who follows Halevi in seeing the Jews as innately superior to non-Jews, and denies that this is racism, see in chapter 1 above and Diamond and Kellner, *Reinventing Maimonides*, 181–189.
29 Maimonides, "Laws of Idolatry," chapter 1 (above in chapter 1). For discussion, see *Confrontation*, 77–79 and the studies cited there.
30 A propos Halevi, it is important to recall that his own views on the special nature of the Jewish people bear all the hallmarks of Shi'ite influence. See Krinis, *God's Chosen People* and Lobel, *Between Mysticism and Philosophy*.
31 Christine Hayes, "The 'Other' in Rabbinic Literature," in *The Cambridge Companion to the Talmud and Rabbinic Literature*, ed. C. Fonrobert and M. Jaffee (Cambridge: Cambridge University Pres, 2007), 243–269, 246–247. See further, Christine Hayes, *Gentile Impurities and Jewish Identities: Intermarriage and Conversion from the Bible to the Talmud* (Oxford: Oxford University Press, 2002).

remarkable in light of the rabbis' general perception and presentation of themselves as Ezra's (indirect) successors.

Assuming that Hayes is correct, we might have here an example of a rabbinic attempt to resist the conversion of universalist aspects of the Bible to a hard-edged particularism. We will see below examples of the opposite tendency.

6. ELECTION—SOME SURPRISING CONTEMPORARY THINKERS

Switching gears, we will now look at three twentieth-century Jewish thinkers, not one of them a traditional theist, and all three of whom wrestled with the question of Jewish identity and chosenness. Without apparently meaning to, Mordecai Kaplan, Iaaac Deutscher, and George Steiner all confronted the question of why be Jewish today, and—surprisingly—each answered with a variant of the old notion of the Jews as the chosen people. This discussion will help us to understand how central the notion of Jewish chosenness remains, even in circles where we could hardly expect to find it.

Mordecai Kaplan (1881–1983), the founder of the Reconstructionist movement in Judaism, was a thoroughgoing naturalist who, nonetheless, ended his long career by, in effect, affirming the chosenness of the Jews (even though he held that there is no God to do the choosing). In a guide to his movement that he published in 1951, he wrote:

> When our forefathers declared an idea to be revealed, it was because they were convinced, in light of their faith in God and of their conception of Him, that the idea was somehow related to God's purpose in having created them, and to the fulfillment of their destiny as individuals, as Jews, and as human beings. We today, who look upon God as the Power that prods man to become fully human, must regard as revealed any idea that helps individuals and groups to achieve the full stature of their humanity. Man's discovery of religious truth is God's revelation of it, since the very process of that discovery implies an activity of God.[32]

---

32 Mordecai Kaplan, *Know How to Answer: A Guide to Reconstructionism* (New York: Jewish Reconstructionist Foundation, 1951), 78–79. This book appeared close to two decades after the publication of Kaplan's *Judaism as a Civilization: Towards the Reconstruction of American Jewish Life* (New York: Thomas Yoseloff, 1934), the book for which he is best known. The title of Kaplan's guide, based as it is on a statement in Avot (ii. 14), shows how deeply Kaplan remained connected to the traditional world of his childhood.

Like a force of nature, Kaplan's God is not personal at all. How do we know that it exists? The very fact that human beings behave altruistically proves that the cosmos, as it were, is not indifferent to human flourishing.

Kaplan's last book, published when he was eighty-nine years old, is called *The Religion of Ethical Nationhood: Judaism's Contribution to World Peace* (New York: Macmillan, 1970). What is Judaism's contribution to world peace? After a detailed exposition of how Jews ought to reconstitute (i.e., reconstruct) themselves into "a living, interactive and creative people" (132), Kaplan affirms that

> [u]nless nations voluntarily limit their individuality and absolute sovereignty, the current world situation could lead to the extinction of mankind. By resuming peoplehood as a spiritual dimension, Jews may articulate the need for each nation to regard national individuality as a divine gift rather than demonic power. (135)

Living under the threat of nuclear armageddon, with the actual obliteration of humanity a threatened possibility, Kaplan was acutely aware of the dangers of nationalism. The Jews could save the world (my language, not his) because of their unique transnational status (124). Judaism "as a civilization" participates in Jewish history, culture, and practices, but also encourages full participation in the culture and practices of the host nations in which the Jews find themselves. It is that sense in which Judaism is transnational. How can this transnational Judaism save civilization? Kaplan answers:

> Mankind should live by voluntarism and personal commitment rather than coercion. Why should not Jews set an example as pioneers of that ethical principle? For more than a century Jews throughout the world have carried on, voluntarily and without legal coercion, gigantic undertakings in philanthropy, education, religion and state-building. Why should not these undertakings be formalized through permanent and effective organizational machinery? (134)

Judaism's unique contribution to world peace is a function of the unique status of the Jews as a people, but a spiritual people, not a nation in the dangerous sense of nationalism so prevalent in our world today. Jews are truly "chosen" even without a God to do the choosing.

It is not my intention here to give even a superficial summary of Kaplan's views, nor is it my intention to criticize them. Rather, I want to show that despite his being a thorough-going naturalist (a polite way of saying, in effect, atheist) who certainly did not believe in the existence of a personal god which could bestow election on any human collective, and who denied revelation in any traditionally recognizable sense of the term, even he could not free himself from some sense of Jewish chosenness.

Kaplan's younger contemporary, Isaac Deutscher (1907–1967), lapsed Polish rabbinical prodigy, Marxist (but not of the "vulgar" kind),[33] biographer of Stalin and Trotsky, atheist, and internationalist, coined the widely cited expression, "the non-Jewish Jew" (about which more below).[34] Deutscher thought that nationalism was passé; establishing Israel, the Jewish people returned to the international stage too late:

> The world has compelled the Jew to embrace the nation-state and to make of it his pride and hope, just at a time when there is little or no hope left in it. You cannot blame the Jews for this; you must blame the world. But Jews should at least be aware of the paradox and realize that their intense enthusiasm for "national sovereignty" is historically belated. They did not benefit from the advantages of the nation-state in those centuries when it was a medium of mankind's advance and a great revolutionary and unifying factor in history. They have taken possession of it only after it had become a factor of disunity and social disintegration.[35]

Nevertheless, despite his reservations concerning Jewish enthusiasm for a project that had missed the boat historically (but not morally), Deutscher strongly identified as a Jew: "I am, however, a Jew by force of my unconditional

---

33 Deutscher is still an icon of the left. His *The Non-Jewish Jew and Other Essays* (Oxford: Oxford University Press, 1968), was reprinted by Verso ("the largest independent, radical publishing house in the English-speaking world") in its Radical Thinkers: Jewish Thought series, containing books (so far) by Jacqueline Rose (*The Last Resistance*), Gillian Rose (*Judaism and Modernity: Philosophical Essays*), and Michael Loewy (*Redemption and Utopia: Jewish Libertarian Thought in Central Europe*). One wonders what Deutscher would have thought of the company he is here forced to keep. As recently as 2017 *The Nation* published "The Red Emigrant," an essay by Bruce Robbins, subheaded "For Isaac Deutscher, exile helped him discover his real community—the internationalist left," (https://www.thenation.com/article/archive/the-red-emigrant/). That exile, however, also helped him discover ethnic solidarity with other Jews.

34 On Deutscher, see Susie Linfield, *The Lion's Den: Zionism and the Left from Hannah Arendt to Noam Chomsky* (New Haven: Yale University Press, 2019), 140–164.

35 Deutscher, *Non-Jewish Jew*, 41

solidarity with the persecuted and exterminated. I am a Jew because I feel the Jewish tragedy as my own tragedy; because I feel the pulse of Jewish history; because I should like to do all I can to assure the real, not spurious, security and self-respect of the Jews" (51). Deutscher identified as a Jew, not only because of his "solidarity with the persecuted and exterminated," not only but because the Jewish tragedy is his own,[36] and not only because he personally feels the pulse of Jewish history, but because he wants to do all he can "to assure the real, not spurious, security and self-respect of the Jews." Seeing the security granted to Jews by the State of Israel as spurious in no way weakens his concern for the "security and self-respect of the Jews."

Deutscher was thus no Zionist, but he certainly was no anti-Zionist either. Deutscher did not believe that antisemitism is a spent force (56). It is perhaps for this reason that Deutscher had a warm spot for the State of Israel (91): "In Israel the oldest people in the world have formed the youngest nation-state; and they are emotionally anxious to make good the time lost. To nearly all the Jews here the ideal of individual and collective happiness is to grow a solid, protective national shell."[37]

Attracted to Marxists in Israel, Deutscher feels no closer to them than to "like-minded people in France, Italy, Britain, and Japan." But then what makes up the Jewish community? Surely not racial ties—that would be another triumph for Hitler. But then what makes him a Jew? As we saw above, he answers:

> Religion? I am an atheist. Jewish nationalism? I am an internationalist. In neither sense am I, therefore, a Jew. I am, however, a Jew by force of my unconditional solidarity with the persecuted and exterminated. I am a Jew because I feel the Jewish tragedy as my own tragedy; because I feel the pulse of Jewish history; because I should like to do all I can to assure the real, not spurious, security and self-respect of the Jews.[38]

---

36 Literally, not metaphorically: he lost his entire family in Holocaust.
37 The historian Tony Judt in effect echoes Deutscher's claim that Jews have missed the boat, becoming nationalists too late—the nationalist moment in history is passed. See the essays in part 2 of his *When the Facts Change* (London: William Heinemann, 2014). Judt himself appears to have been so invested in his position that he paid no attention to the final chapters (20–24) of his remarkable book *Postwar: A History of Europe since 1945* (London: William Heinemann, 2005). Apparently, for Judt, every national group in the world can have its own nation state, only not the Jews. Judt's investment in his position perhaps explains his otherwise inconceivable support for Shlomo Sand's historically ignorant book *The Invention of the Jewish People* (London: Verso, 2014), to which Judt contributed an enthusiastic blurb.
38 Deutscher, *Non-Jewish Jew*, 51.

What sets the Jews apart? Why remain Jewish? The Jews have a message for the wider world: "unconditional solidarity with the persecuted and exterminated."[39] In her study of Deutscher, Susie Linfield explains (146):

> If figures such as Trotsky and Luxemburg were, in Deutscher's phrase, "very Jewish indeed"—a description they would have indignantly protested—so too is Deutscher's essay. It is imbued with a view of the Jewish people, or at least some Jewish people, as chosen; and imbued, too, with a deep albeit secular messianism. Deutscher essentially posited: If the Jews can only reclaim, or sustain, their adherence to universalist emancipation, the world might be redeemed. This is a grand, indeed grandiose proposition, and a stirring one, which traces its lineage to the Hebrew prophets. What makes this essay so poignant is the way that Deutscher grapples, as must we, with the knowledge that this universalism—this rootless transnationalism—was in part what made the Jews so vulnerable, so hated, and led to the black smoke that we still inhale.

Redemption of the world depends upon Jewish adherence to universalist emancipation. In what way? "The Jewish heretic who transcends Jewry belongs to a Jewish tradition" (26). Non-Jewish Jews are determinists, rejected moral absolutism, agreed that "knowledge to be real must be active," and believed in "the ultimate solidarity of man" (36). One can quibble with these characterizations (especially given the Marxist terms in which Deutscher develops these ideas), but they help us to understand Linfield's characterization of Deutscher as seeing the Jews as "chosen" (without, of course, a God to choose).

The youngest of our three thinkers, George Steiner (1929–2020), was an extraordinarily prominent literary critic on both sides of the Atlantic, a non-Zionist supporter of Israel's right and need to exist, an agnostic, and a Jewish chauvinist. Ordinarily, people who reject the notion of a personal God also reject the notion of Jewish chosenness, since there is no One to do the choosing. But despite being a profound thinker who has made important contributions to Western culture, and one who is at home in all aspects of Western literature and philosophy, George Steiner the agnostic comes very close to affirming that in some nontrivial sense Jews are special and crucial for the well-being of the world. He certainly denies the divine election of the Jewish people, but fails to

---

39 In an as yet unpublished article, Kenneth Seeskin suggests that the Jewish culture of dissent is a reason to preserve Jews and Judaism. I wrestle with the issue generally in chapter 5 below.

free himself from the idea that without the Jews not only would the (Western) world be much the poorer, it might not even survive. In effect, even without a God to do the choosing, the Jews again turn out to be the Chosen People.[40]

The following essay title says it all: "We Are the Guests of Life and of Truth: Concerning the Capriciousness of Existence, the Wonder of the State of Israel and the Lost Nobility of the Jewish People (a Grateful Response of Acceptance to the Borne Prize)."[41] To repeat: we, the Jews, says Steiner, are the guests of life and truth. That, it turns out, will be a crucial statement since it is their status as guests everywhere, at home nowhere, that makes the Jews special, and crucial. Jews are not only the guests of life, but *guests of truth*. For a philosopher, there can hardly be a higher nobility. As guests, never at home, the Jews should not have a nation-state of their own, but that they do have one is a "wonder." Steiner's ambivalence about that "wonder" explains how and why the Jews have lost their "nobility"—by ceasing to be guests, the Jews lose their special status and undermine their special contribution to humanity.

That contribution finds expression in the following (wildly exaggerated) statement (87): "I am convinced that this quasi-absurd survival and the continuance of living on of the Jews has a meaning or, perhaps, it possesses an ontological purpose." I am not sure what an "ontological purpose" is, but it sure sounds important. What is the meaning and ontological purpose of Jewish existence? Steiner continues: "Because the Jew was always driven away, because he was nowhere at home, because his only true home was a text: the Torah, the Jew per definition is a guest upon this earth, a guest among all the people. It is his task to serve humanity as an example, as a model of this situation. It is his duty to show that other people, no matter how firmly they seem to be rooted, are guests to one another and guests of life."

Unlike many of his contemporaries, Steiner never underestimated or forgot the horrors of the Holocaust and the attempt of the Nazis and their many collaborators to eradicate every last Jew from the face of the earth.[42] The Jews

---

40 Steiner's agnostic theology finds moving expression at the very end of his autobiographical *Errata: An Examined Life* (New Haven: Yale University Press, 1998), 175–190, esp. 185.
41 George Steiner, "We Are the Guests of Life and of Truth: Concerning the Capriciousness of Existence, the Wonder of the State of Israel and the Lost Nobility of the Jewish People (a Grateful Response of Acceptance to the Borne Prize)," *European Judaism* 36, no. 2 (2003): 84–90.
42 Note Deutscher in 1968: "It is an indubitable fact that the Nazi massacre of six million European Jews has not made any deep impression on the nations of Europe." See Deutscher, *Non-Jewish Jew*, 37. In our day, the constant, ignorant, and morally corrupt claim that Israel behaves in a Nazi-like fashion, might have surprised even Deutscher.

were not only the objects of Nazi wrath they are, Steiner maintains, the only people who can prevent another, and perhaps greater, holocaust. How? By teaching all human beings to see themselves and others as guests on this earth. Thus, he states:

> I cannot shake off the conviction that the torment and the mystery of resilience in Judaism exemplify, enact, an arduous truth: that human beings must learn to be each other's guests on this small planet, even as they must learn to be guests of being itself and of the natural world. This is a truth humbly immediate, to our breath, to our skin, to the passing shadow we cast on a ground inconceivably more ancient than our visitation, and it is also a terribly abstract, morally and psychologically exigent truth. Man will have to learn it or he will be made extinct in suicidal waste and violence.[43]

Not only have the Jews shown the way to be guests, as such, they have also created contemporary civilization. I personally am proud of Jewish contributions to Western culture, but would be hard-pressed to write a sentence such as the following:

> Prague, Budapest, Vienna, Leningrad, Frankfurt and New York have been the Jewish capitals of our age, but also the capitals tout court. In them, the clerks,[44] the addicts of the word and of the theorem, the exact dreamers after Einstein, have led, have danced the life of the mind; for that motion of the dance before the ark in which the text of the Law is housed, lies at the ancient core of Jewish consciousness.[45]

---

43 George Steiner, "Our Homeland, the Text," *Salmagundi* 66 (1985): 4–25, 23.
44 By "clerks," it is safe to assume that Steiner means "intellectuals." I have no doubt that Steiner was familiar with Julien Benda's *La Trahison des Clercs* (Paris: B. Grasset, 1927)—often translated as *The Treason of the Intellectuals*.
45 Steiner, "Our Homeland, the Text": 18, 20. J. J. Kimche comments (unpublished paper): "Steiner's theories of Jewish textual excellence has implications for his understanding of European intellectual history as a whole. Steiner is a determined advocate of what I would call the 'coiled spring' theory of modern intellectual history; the assertion that the intellectual climate of modernity is the result of Jewish conceptual creativity exploding outwards, as a coiled spring, finally emancipated from prior constraints of discrimination and hatred. The contributions of Spinoza, Marx, Freud, Levi-Strauss, Benjamin, Kafka, Wittgenstein, Einstein, and the entire Frankfurt School are presented by Steiner as a 'secular deployment of the long schooling in abstract, speculative commentary and clerkship in the [Jewish] exegetical legacy (while at the same time a psychological-sociological revolt against it).'" The Steiner quote is from "Our Homeland": 20. See also, J. J. Kimche, "The Judaism of George

It is sentences such as these that justify my claim above that Steiner is a Jewish chauvinist. Not only is he a Jewish chauvinist, he also writes as if he believed that the Jewish people are, in effect, chosen. The following paragraph is found in the long chapter that Steiner devotes to his Jewish identity in his autobiography:

> Of course, there is a Jewish question. Only cant or a self-deluding investment in normalcy could deny that. The political map, the plethora of ethnic-historical legacies, the patchwork of societies, faiths, communal identifications across our globe teems with unresolved conflicts, with religious-racial enmities, with non-negotiable claims to an empowering past, to sacred grounds. Nonetheless, the Jewish condition differs. Irreducibly, maddeningly, it embodies what modern physics calls a "singularity," a construct or happening outside the norms, extraterritorial to probability and the findings of common reason. Judaism pulses and radiates energy like some black hole in the historical galaxy. Its parameters are those of "strangeness," another key-notion in current theoretical physics and cosmology.[46]

Remarkable writing, but once we reduce the overblown metaphors to the hard ground of reality, we once again find Steiner affirming the irreducible uniqueness of the Jewish people. Even hyper-particularist Kabbalists could sign off on this statement (if we add God to the equation).

Let us close with a Steinerian statement close to the very end of the chapter on Jewish identity in his autobiography (68–69):

> The vocation of the "guest," the aspiration of the messianic, the function of the moral irritant and insomniac among men, does strike me as an honor beyond honors. Wherever, whenever they are present or prosper, bestiality, stupidity, intolerance will choose the Jew for their target. Truly, a chosen people and a club I would not resign from (even if this was feasible).[47]

Steiner," *First Things*, December, 2020, https://www.firstthings.com/article/2020/12/the-judaism-of-george-steiner.

46 *Errata*, 53. My friend and colleague Eli Schonfeld points out that the Jewish question is not a *Jewish* question.

47 Steiner reiterates many of themes mentioned here in an interview: https://forward.com/culture/366594/he-may-be-our-greatest-jewish-thinker-but-what-does-he-think-about-jewish-t/. Assaf Sagiv criticizes Steiner's views about Jews and Judaism in "George Steiner's Jewish Problem," *Azure* 15 (2003). Steiner's brief "Reply" appeared in *Azure* 16 (2004).

Being a guest is a vocation (hardly a secular term), an expression of a messianic aspiration, and an honor beyond honors. It is the task of the Jew to be a moral irritant and hence a target of bestiality, stupidity and intolerance. Is it a surprise that many Jews today say, "Ich bin moychel toyves" (thanks, but no thanks), and affirm that at long last it is right and proper for Jews to "want to be happy"?[48]

7. ELECTION TOMORROW—A MODIFIED MAIMONIDEANISM

According to the twelfth of Maimonides's "Thirteen Principles," Jews are bid to anticipate the coming of the messiah, "even though he tarries," (as the popular "Ani Ma'amin" poem puts it) and pray for his coming.[49] Why? Not in order to enjoy power and dominion, or this-worldly pleasures, but in order to be free to devote themselves to the Torah *and its wisdom*.[50] Such devotion will make those wise enough to engage in it "worthy of life in the world to come." In such a well-organized and enlightened world, in which its natural riches are shared among human beings rationally as opposed to selfishly, not only will war disappear, but delicacies will be as common as dust. This is not a function of miracles, but of proper organization and the self-restraint of a population focused on important matters. Is it any wonder that in such a world human beings (not

---

Sagiv's article was reprinted in *The Jewish Divide Over Israel: Accusers and Defenders*, ed. Edward Alexander and Paul Bogdanor (New Brunswick: Transaction, 2006), 47–63. It was reprinted again in *Wounds of Possibility: Essays on George Steiner*, ed. Ricardo Soeiro (Cambridge Scholars Publishing, 2012), along with Steiner's reply on 213. I was first introduced to Steiner's views on Judaism in an excellent term paper submitted at Shalem College (Jerusalem) by J. J. Kimche.

48 On Hermann Cohen's alleged criticism of Zionism on these grounds, see Franz Rosenzweig's introduction to *Jüdische Schriften*, vol. 1, by H. Cohen, ed. B. Strauss (Berlin: publisher, 1924), xl. My thanks to George Kohler for tracking down the actual source of this well-known anecdote. Steven Schwarzschild has argued that there is much reason to doubt the accuracy of Rosenzweig's anecdotes about Cohen. See Steven S. Schwarzschild, "Franz Rosenzweig's Anecdotes about Hermann Cohen," in *Gegenwart in Rueblick*, ed. Herbert Strauss and Kurt Grossman (Heidelberg: Stiehm, 1970), 209–218, reprinted in *The Tragedy of Optimism: Writings* [by Steven Schwarzschild] *on Hermann Cohen*, ed. George Kohler (Albany: SUNY Press, 2018), 35–42.

49 On Maimonides's principles of faith, see Menachem Kellner, *Dogma in Medieval Jewish Thought* (Oxford: Oxford University Press, 1986), 10–65, and Kellner, *Must a Jew Believe Anything?* On the poem "Ani Ma'amin," see Joshua Berman, *Ani Maamin: Biblical Criticism, Historical Truth, and the Thirteen Principles of Faith* (Jerusalem: Magid, 2020).

50 I purposefully ignore Maimonides's strict intellectual elitism; the Maimonideanism I propose here is modified.

just Jews) will achieve great wisdom? The point of the messiah's coming is thus to help human beings bring about a peaceful society enjoying the just allocation of resources and devoted to the cultivation of the intellect.[51]

Maimonides brings his most extensive discussion of the messiah to a dramatic summation in "Laws of Kings," xii. 4. With this text, he ends the entire *Mishneh Torah*:

> The Sages and Prophets did not long for the days of the Messiah that they might exercise dominion over the world, or rule over the nations, or be exalted by the peoples, and not in order to eat and drink and rejoice, but so that they be free to devote themselves to the Torah and *its wisdom*, with no one to oppress or disturb them, and thus be worthy of life in the world to come, as we explained in "Laws Concerning Repentance". [52] Then there will be neither famine nor war, neither jealousy nor strife. Good things will be abundant, and delicacies as common as dust. The one preoccupation of the whole world will be only to know the Lord. Hence they[53] will be very wise, knowing things now unknown and will apprehend knowledge of their Creator to the utmost capacity of the human mind, as it is written: *For the land shall be full of the knowledge (de'ah) of the Lord, as the waters cover the sea* (Is. 11:9) [emphasis added].[54]

Maimonides provides a parallel description of the messianic world in a very short chapter of the *Guide of the Perplexed* (iii. 11; Pines, 440–441).

---

51 On this, Eugene Korn (personal communication) comments: "Interesting: The godless Jews wind up more pessimistic than Kohelet, while the antiquated traditional theists wind up the historical optimists. The divide between theistic/atheistic existentialists yields the same results: hope vs pessimism."

52 "Laws Concerning Repentance," ix. 2.

53 Presumably the inhabitants "of the whole world," the *ba'ei olam* who, Maimonides says, can achieve the highest possible level of sanctity even in this dispensation (see Kellner and Gillis, *Maimonides the Universalist*, chapter 7 and Hirshman, *Torah Lekhol Ba'ei Olam*). On the textual issues here see: Simon-Raymond Schwarzfuchs, "Les lois royales de Maimonide," *Revue des etudes juives* 111 (1951–52): 63–86. On 81–82, Schwarzfuchs shows that many printed editions and manuscripts add the word "Israel" here. On literary grounds alone it appears clear that the word is an emendation since the proof-text from Isaiah speaks of the entire earth. See Kellner, "*Farteitcht un Farbessert* (On 'Correcting' Maimonides)," *Me'orot* 6, no. 2 (2007), http://library.yctorah.org/files/2016/07/Kellner-on-Rambam-FINAL.pdf. See also the next note.

54 For detailed glosses on this passage see Kellner and Gillis, *Maimonides the Universalist*, chapter 14.

Zev Harvey has pointed out that this chapter of the *Guide* is a kind of poetic and philosophical rendition of the last paragraph of the *Mishneh Torah*, glossing it in the way Maimonides meant it to be read.[55] Here is the chapter in its entirety:

> These great evils that come about because the human individuals who inflict them upon one another because of purposes, desires, opinions, and beliefs, are all of them likewise consequent upon privation. For all of them derive from ignorance, I mean from a privation of knowledge. Just as a blind man, because of absence of sight, does not cease stumbling, being wounded and also wounding others, because he has nobody to guide him on the way, the various sects of men—every individual according to the extent of his ignorance—does to himself and to others great evils from which individuals of the species suffer. If there were knowledge, whose relation to the human form is like that of the faculty of sight to the eye, they would refrain from doing any harm to themselves and to others. For through cognition of the truth, enmity and hatred are removed and the inflicting of harm by people on one another is abolished. It holds out this promise, saying: *And the wolf shall dwell with the lamb, and the leopard shall lie down with the kid, and so on. And the cow and the bear shall feed, and so on* (Is. 11:6–8). Then it gives the reason for this, saying that the cause of the abolition of these enmities, these discords, and these tyrannies, will be the knowledge that men will have then concerning the true reality of the deity. For it says: *They shall not hurt nor destroy in all My holy mountain; for the earth shall be full of the knowledge of the Lord, as the waters cover the sea* (Is. 11:9). Know this.

There is, of course, much more to be said about Maimonides's view of the messiah and of the messianic era, but the texts cited here should be enough for me to be able to conclude this chapter with the following argument. I assert, following what I learned from Steven Schwarzschild (who always insisted that he was only following Hermann Cohen), if not necessarily from Maimonides himself, that ends should determine means.[56] That being the case, if we can show

---

55 See Zev Harvey, "Averroes, Maimonides, and the Virtuous State" (Hebrew), in *Iyyunim Bi-Sugyot Filosofiyot Likhvod Shelomoh Pines* (Jerusalem, 1992), 19–31.
56 For Schwarzschild on Maimonides's Cohenian messianism, or Maimonidean Cohenianism, see the references below in footnote 59.

that Maimonides anticipated a messianic era characterized by enlightenment[57] and (therefore) peace, we can then point out to him (whatever he himself may have thought in the midst of the crusades) that war and discrimination among human beings will never achieve that end. This position is Maimonidean, if not necessarily that of Maimonides himself.[58]

Judaism, Maimonides would insist, has something important and valuable to teach the whole world even for those who deny the truth of the Torah as adumbrated in the rabbinic tradition. I refer to aspects of the messianic hope as expressed by Maimonides, especially as that hope was understood by Hermann Cohen and by Steven Schwarzschild after him.[59]

Two aspects of Maimonides's messianic teaching are relevant to us here are: universalism and naturalism. This is not the place to defend an interpretation of Maimonides according to which by the time the messianic process reaches its completion all human beings will worship God from a stance of religious equality.[60] In Maimonides's view, the point of the messianic era is to bring the Torah *lekhol ba'ei olam*, to all human beings. One can easily derive

---

57 There is an interesting debate between Hermann Cohen and his followers, on the one hand, and Leo Strauss, and his followers, on the other, over how extensive Maimonides thought messianic enlightenment could be. The Cohennian position is much more optimistic than the Straussian. See Steven Schwarzschild, "Moral Radicalism and 'Middlingness' in the Ethics of Maimonides," in *The Pursuit of the Ideal: Jewish Writings of Steven Schwarzschild*, ed. M. Kellner (Albany: SUNY Press, 1990), 137–161 and 302–318 and Michael Kochin, "Morality, Nature and Esotericism in Leo Strauss' *Persecution and the Art of Writing*," *Review of Politics* 64 (2002): 261–83.

58 It is also the position of Martin Luther King, Jr.:

> If we don't have good will toward men in this world, we will destroy ourselves. There have always been those who argued that the end justifies the means, that the means really aren't important. But we will never have peace in the world until men everywhere recognize that ends are not cut off from means, because the means represent the ideal in the making, and the end in process, and ultimately you can't reach good ends through evil means, because the means represent the seed and the end represents the tree.

Cited by Jill Lepore, "Reigns of Terror in America," *The New Yorker*, December 12, 2018.

59 I emphasize that I am about to talk about *aspects* of Maimonides's thought. Maimonides the historical figure was a hard-edged intellectual elitist who anticipated the coming of a messianic king. He was no liberal democrat nor a democratic socialist, despite the best efforts of Hermann Cohen and Steven S. Schwarzschild. See Steven Schwarzschild, "The Democratic Socialism of Hermann Cohen," *HUCA* 27 (1965): 417–38 and Schwarzschild's essays on Jewish eschatology in Kellner, *The Pursuit of the Ideal*, chapters 1, 5, 11, and 13.

60 I have defended this in a series of studies, most recently and most extensively in Kellner and Gillis, *Maimonides the Universalist*, chapter 14.

from Maimonides the understanding that the Torah in question is Abrahamic, not Mosaic; that is, a Torah of ethics, science, and philosophy.[61] Maimonides's messianic naturalism is admitted even by those made uncomfortable by it.[62]

This messianic vision offers us a goal at which to aim, an ideal by which to regulate our behavior. That goal is the realization of the opening chapters of the Bible: *all* human beings are created in the image of God and should be treated, therefore, as Kant would later put it, as ends also, never as means only. Maimonides's naturalism means that this goal can be achieved by human beings, without divine intervention, miraculous or otherwise.

Kant insisted that *ought* implies *can*: if I ought to do something, I must be able to do it. Steven Schwarzschild insisted on a Jewish corollary to that Kantian teaching: if I can achieve some worthwhile goal, then I ought to try to achieve it. Getting ever closer to a messianic world is surely a worthwhile goal. Actually reaching that goal may not be possible, but getting ever closer is.[63] Since we can, we should make every effort to make the world a place in which all human beings are treated as creatures made in the image of God. In effect, Maimonides, Cohen, and Schwarzschild teach us that we ought to devote ourselves to the project of creating a messiah-worthy world.[64]

---

61 For an extended discussion of this admittedly gnomic statement, see ibid., chapter 15.
62 For an elegant and profound exposition of Maimonides's messianic naturalism, see Kenneth Seeskin, *Jewish Messianic Thoughts in an Age of Despair* (Cambridge: Cambridge University Press, 2012).
63 See Schwarzschild, "The Messianic Doctrine in Contemporary Jewish Thought," in *Great Jewish Ideas*, ed. Abraham Millgram (Washington, DC: B'nai B'rith Department of Adult Jewish Education, 1974), 237–259. Many of Schwarzschild's ideas, which influenced my presentation here, are found in his "On Jewish Eschatology," *Pursuit of the Ideal*, chapter 11, 209–228.
64 I found a succinct and to my mind brilliant statement of the position advanced here in an essay by Zev Harvey on views of evil in the philosophic and Kabbalistic traditions:

> The Maimonidean philosophers, unlike the kabbalists and the astrologers, were not primarily concerned about providing comfort as a response to evil. They were more concerned about preventing evil. They were concerned about human responsibility, and the awareness of human responsibility often causes discomfort, not comfort. They insisted that the source of the evils that human beings inflict upon one other is not in some external Satan, but inside the human beings themselves. Since the source of evils is human, we humans can prevent them. We are responsible. One can prevent evils by acting in accordance with reason. One prevents defeat in war not by consulting horoscopes or writing amulets with the names of the proper sefirot on them, but by studying the art of war. Maimonides and his followers sought to understand the psychological and political causes of evil in history in order to determine what actions need to be taken in order to prevent its recurrence. The Kabbalah and Maimonidean

There is something else that Maimonidean messianic universalism and naturalism teaches us: hope. We can hope for (and work towards) a world in which different nations and cultures can value their own contributions to the human mosaic without diminishing the value of others—without wholly *othering* the other. If we can hope, we need not despair: the human condition is not necessarily tragic.[65] That message alone justifies the continued allegiance of the Jewish people to the Torah of Israel and to its destiny.

---

philosophy do represent two opposing approaches to the problem of evil in history. If the former tried to comfort the people with myth, the latter tried to improve their situation with reason.

See Warren Zev Harvey, "Two Jewish Approaches to Evil in History," in *The Impact of the Holocaust on Jewish Thought*, ed. Steven Katz (New York: New York University Press, 2007), 199. For Hermann Cohen himself, see his *Religion of Reason out of the Sources of Judaism*, trans. Simon Kaplan (New York: Frederick Ungar, 1972), 236–261.

65 See Seeskin, *Jewish Messianic Thought*, 42. See also Kenneth Seeskin, "Maimonides and Hermann Cohen on Messianism," *Maimonidean Studies* 5 (2008): 382—"At bottom, commitment to a Messiah amounts to the conviction that the way things are is not the way they have to be."

CHAPTER 4

The Convert as the Most Jewish of Jews

In two separate places, Maimonides goes out of his way to emphasize that seven of the most important of the mishnaic authors (*tannaim*) were descended from King David (himself the great-grandson of Ruth the Moabite). That is not particularly noteworthy. In both places, however, he surprisingly adds that four other key tannaim were proselytes themselves or descended from proselytes. These four are Shemaya and Avtalyon (the teachers of Hillel and Shammai), Rabbi Akiva, and his disciple Rabbi Meir (whose disciple was Judah the Prince, editor of the Mishnah and Maimonides's model in so many ways). The two texts in question are Maimonides's introduction to his commentary on the Mishnah and his introduction to his *Mishneh Torah*.[1]

In the first text (the Mishnah commentary), after listing the seven sages who could claim Davidic descent, Maimonides writes that four other prominent sages came from the community of proselytes (*kehal gerim*): Shemaya, Avtalyon, R.

---

1 Maimonides held that all human beings (Jews and non-Jews alike) are created in the image of God. The issue is analyzed in detail in my *Gam Hem*. This attitude concerning the essential equality of all human beings, together with his emphasis on the theological (as opposed to ethnic) basis of the Jewish religion, led Maimonides to an unusually welcoming attitude towards converts, as will become clear below. Maimonides's attitude towards non-Jews as such should be sharply distinguished from his attitude towards non-Jewish *religions*. For recent studies of the latter subject, see Daniel J. Lasker, "Tradition and Innovation in Maimonides' Attitude toward Other Religions," *Maimonides after 800 Years: Essays on Maimonides and His Influence*, ed. Jay Harris (Cambridge, MA: Harvard University Press, 2007), 167–182 and Lasker, "Rashi and Maimonides on Christianity," in *Between Rashi and Maimonides: Themes in Medieval Jewish Thought, Literature and Exegesis*, ed. Ephraim Kanarfogel and Moshe Sokolow (New York: Yeshiva University Press, 2010), 3–21. On the status of converts in Ashkenaz see Rami Reiner, "Le statut des prosélytes en Allemagne et en France du 11e au 13e siècle," *REJ* 167 (2008): 99–119 and Reiner, "Tough are Gerim: Conversion to Judaism in Medieval Europe," *Hevruta* 1 (Spring 2008): 54–63. On converts in Maimonides's time and place, see the recent dissertation of Moshe Yagur, "'Zehut Datit u-Gevulot Kehilati'im be-Hevrat ha-Genizah (Me'ot 10–13)': Gerim, Avadim, Mumarim" (PhD diss., Tel Aviv University, 2018), 16–71.

Akiva, and Rabbi Meir. In the second text, the introduction to the *Mishneh Torah*, Maimonides provides a detailed list of the forty generations from Moses to Rav Ashi, traditionally taken to be the editor of the Babylonian Talmud. Towards the end of that list, he *chooses* to write: "Shemaya and Avtalyon were proselytes; … Rabbi Akiva ben Joseph was the disciple (*kibbel me* …) of Rabbi Eliezer the Great; Joseph his father was a proselyte. Rabbi Ishmael and Rabbi Meir, son of a proselyte, were the disciples (*kibblu me* …) of Rabbi Akiva."

We learn here that in the eyes of Maimonides the Jewish religion as we know it is largely the product of individuals who were not Jewish by birth, or of those whose fathers were not born Jewish.[2] Why did Maimonides choose to draw attention to this? There is no apparent reason for mentioning that the four tannaim in question were themselves proselytes or descended from proselytes. Furthermore, while there is no doubt that Shemaya and Avtalyon were indeed themselves proselytes[3]—and while in one aggadic passage (Gittin 56a) Rabbi Meir is said to have been descended from Nero (although nowhere is he himself said to have been the son of a proselyte)[4]— there is no explicit statement in any extant Talmudic text that Rabbi Akiva was descended from proselytes, let alone that he was the son of a proselyte.[5]

---

2   Maimonides says nothing about their mothers.
3   See Gittin 57b and the famous story at Yoma 71b concerning their confrontation with an ill-mannered high priest who denigrated them because of their ancestry. On this story, see the discussion of Amram Tropper, *Ke-Homer Be-Yad Ha-Yozer: Ma'asei Hakhamim be-Sifrut Hazal* (Jerusalem: Merkaz Zalman Shazar, 2011), 70–71, 80–81 and the sources cited there.
4   On R. Meir in this context, see Naomi G. Cohen, "Rabbi Meir, a Descendant of Anatolian Proselytes: New Light on His Name and the Historical Kernel of the Nero Legend in Gittin 56a," *Journal of Jewish Studies* 23, no. 1 (1972): 51–59.
5   See Reuven Hammer, *Akiva: Life, Legend, Legacy* (Lincoln: University of Nebraska Press, 2015), 3, 189. Hammer cites BT Ber. 27b ("We can hardly appoint R. Akiba because perhaps Rabban Gamaliel will bring a curse on him because he has no ancestral merit") and comments: "Although some interpreted this to mean that he [R. Akiva] was descended from converts, the meaning is more likely that his ancestry was not from learned or distinguished people." Similarly, see Barry Holtz, *Rabbi Akiva: Sage of the Talmud* (New Haven: Yale University Press, 2017), 15 and 196n29. Aharon Hyman, *Toldot ha-Tannaim ve-ha Amoraim*, 3 vols. (London: n.p., 1910), 3:988, cites Maimonides as the authority for the claim that Joseph father of Akiva was a proselyte! *Sefer Yuhasin* even claims that both he and R. Meir were themselves converts. See Abraham Zacuto, *Sefer Yuhasin ha-Shalem* (Jerusalem: Yerid ha-Sefarim, 2004), 48 for R. Akiva and 56 for R. Meir. A propos citing Maimonides as the source of his own (otherwise unsourced) claim that Joseph father of Akiva was a proselyte, compare Maimonides "Laws of Mourning," iv.4. The last (controversial) phrase there, "one ought not to visit graves," is found in no known source earlier than this text of Maimonides (see Chaim Kanievsky, *Kiryat Melekh* [(Bar Ilan Global Jewish Database]). It appears to be his own addition. In searching for a source, I checked the Bar Ilan University Responsa

It seems evident that Maimonides had something specific in mind in twice drawing attention to this.

What is going on here? Before answering that question let me draw the reader's attention to the views of Judah Halevi, by way of contrast. According to Judah Halevi, the difference between Israel and the nations is so essentialist that even proselytes remain a people apart, not wholly and completely absorbed into Israel. We see this in the following colloquy. In *Kuzari* i. 26 the king asks, "Then your religious Law is a legacy for yourselves only?"[6] In the next paragraph, he receives the following answer:

> The sage said: Yes, [that is so]; but whoever joins us from among the nations especially will share in our good [fortune] (Num. 10:29), although he will not be equal to us. Now, if the requirement of [fulfilling] the religious Law were due to the fact that [God] created us, then [all people,] the white and the black, would indeed be equal in regard to [that obligation] because all of them are His creation, exalted be He. But [the requirement of fulfilling] the religious Law is [in fact] due to His having brought us out of Egypt and His becoming attached to us because we are the choicest (*safwah*) of the descendants of Adam.

It should be recalled that this speech was addressed to a Gentile king who would ultimately convert to Judaism.

Halevi returns to this issue towards the end of the first treatise of the *Kuzari* (i. 115) and in connection with the process of conversion, writes:

> Despite this, the person who enters the religion of Israel [from the outside] is not equal to the native-born Jew, since native-born Jews are specifically qualified for prophecy. The aim of others [should be] to learn from them and to become learned and pious friends of God, [but] not prophets.

What keeps the proselyte from achieving the ultimate religious perfection (prophecy)?[7] According to Halevi that which marks off the Jewish people (and

---

Project CD-ROM and discovered there that the passage in question came from the Higger edition of "*Baraitot le-massekhet soferim*." But Higger, it turns out, cites Maimonides as his source! See Michael Higger, *Massekhet Semahot* (Jerusalem: Makor, 1970), 246.

6   Translations from the *Kuzari* here are those of Barry Kogan, whose kindness in sharing his forthcoming translation (Yale Judaica Series) is much appreciated.

7   It should be recalled that very few Jews by birth reach this status according to Halevi. Thus, his discrimination between native-born Jews and proselytes is largely theoretical. Yisrael

unites them) is their descent from the patriarchs. Thanks to this patrimony, the Jewish people enjoy a unique asset, the *amr al-ilahi* (*inyan elohi* in ibn Tibbon's translation and *davar elohi* in the translations of Kafih and Schwarz).⁸ This special inherited property enables born Jews (and only them) to aspire to fulfill the commandments perfectly, and special individuals among them, to aspire to prophecy. The *amr al-ilahi* is literally hereditary, and shared only by actual descendants of the patriarchs (*Kuzari*, i. 47).⁹

In Halevi's eyes, the distinction between native-born Jew and proselyte is so sharp, that, according to Daniel J. Lasker, it will be maintained even in the messianic era. Lasker shows that Halevi anticipated a messianic era in which there would be two kinds of Jews: those descended from the patriarchs, and those descended from proselytes.¹⁰ Halevi's views may be understood as a perfect contrast to those of Maimonides.

Ben-Simon pointed out to me that, for Halevi, prophecy is not a natural phenomenon (as it is for Maimonides), but is entirely a consequence of God's choosing the prophet—God causes the prophet to prophesy thanks to God's goodness and will. Thus, according to Halevi, it follows that proselytes cannot achieve prophecy not only because they do not have the *inyan ha-elohi*, but because God chooses not to bestow prophecy upon them. It should be noted that in connection with this issue as well R. Aviner moves Halevi into realms he never intended to reach. Halevi's theories are not racist in the modern sense of the term. The *inyan ha-elohi* is a potential that only Jews can actualize, but, in actuality, very few Jews succeed in doing so. A Jew who has not actualized this potential is in no way superior to a non-Jew. For an enlightening discussion of these issues, see Raphael Jospe, "Teaching Judah Halevi: Defining and Shattering Myths in Jewish Philosophy," in *Paradigms in Jewish Philosophy* (NJ: Farleigh Dickinson University Press, 1997), 112–128. Jospe presents Halevi's theory as a rationalist ("scientific" in contemporary terms) attempt to explain historical phenomena—that prophecy is found only among Jews, that miracles were worked for the Jewish people, and that they have survived despite all that has happened to them. My teacher, Steven Schwarzschild, sought to present Halevi's theories in what he called "biologicist" but not racist terms in his posthumous article "Proselytism and Ethnicism in R. Yehudah Halevy," in *Religionsgespraeche im Mittelalter* 4 (1992): 27–41. See also Lippman Bodoff, *The Binding of Isaac, Religious Murder & Kabbalah: Seeds of Jewish Extremism and Alienation?* (Jerusalem: Devorah, 2005), 374–388.

8   On this term, see above, chapter 1, footnote 39.
9   Lasker, "Proselyte Judaism."
10 It should be pointed out that Halevi nowhere diminishes the human character of human beings generally, and certainly not that of proselytes, who can aspire "to become learned and pious friends of God" (Kuzari i. 115). One is tempted to cite George Orwell in *Animal Farm*: "all humans are equal, but some humans are more equal than others." This is the sort of view which seems to underlay R. Herschel Schachter's view that Jews have a greater share of God's image than do non-Jews (see above, chapter 1, footnote 26). It is also fair to note that in practical terms, Halevi is less of an intellectual elitist than is Maimonides, a point emphasized by Hannah Kasher in her review of *Gam Hem*.

Before pressing on with my exposition of Maimonides's views on converts and conversion, I shall discuss a number of other places where Maimonides makes unprecedented claims about proselytes. (It is worth noting that all of the texts I will discuss here are drawn from Maimonides's halakhic works, not from the *Guide of the Perplexed*.)

First, Maimonides subtly rewrites the laws of conversion in his codification of them in "Laws Concerning Forbidden Intercourse," chapters 13 and 14. Clearly basing himself on a *baraita* in Yevamot 47a-b, he writes:

> [13:1]: Israel entered the covenant by way of three rites: circumcision, immersion, and sacrifice. ... [13:4]: Accordingly, the rule for future generations is that when a [male] Gentile (*goy*) wishes to enter into the covenant, to take shelter under the wings of the Shekhinah, and to assume the yoke of the Torah, he requires circumcision, immersion, and the offering of a sacrifice ... as it is said, *as you are, so shall be the convert*[11] (Nu. 15:15), i.e., just as you have entered the covenant by way of circumcision, immersion, and the offering of a sacrifice, so shall the proselyte in the future generations enter by way of circumcision, immersion, and the offering of a sacrifice.

Noteworthy here is Maimonides's implied claim that the Israelites at Sinai were all converts to Judaism.[12] In the following chapter, he gets to the process of conversion itself:

> [14:1–2]: In what manner are righteous proselytes to be received? When one comes forth for the purpose of becoming a proselyte, and upon investigation no ulterior motive is found, the court should say to him: "Why

---

11 Maimonides, like the rest of the tradition, understands the word *ger* here to signify proselyte, not stranger *simpliciter*.

12 For more on this, see Kellner, *Maimonides on Judaism and the Jewish People*, 49–58. Maimonides may be usefully contrasted with Judah Halevi here. For Halevi, the descendants of the patriarchs received the Torah at Sinai because only they could have received it. According to Maimonides, it was the receipt of the Torah that turned ex-slaves into Israel, the chosen people. This point helps us to understand Maimonides's implied rejection of the idea that the patriarchs observed all the mizvot (they themselves were Noachides—at most; their descendants in Egypt—out and out idolaters. On the Israelites in Egypt as idolaters, see Maimonides's "Letter on Resurrection," in *Iggerot ha-Rambam*, ed. Y. Sheilat (Jerusalem: Ma'liyot, 1987), 369. On the patriarchs not observing the commandments of the Torah, see above, chapter 1, footnote 14).

do you come forth to become a proselyte? Do you not know that Israel is at present sorely afflicted, oppressed, despised, confounded, and beset by suffering?" If he answers, "I know, and I am indeed unworthy," he should be accepted immediately. **He should then be made acquainted with the principle of the religion (*ikkar ha-dat*), which is the oneness of God and the prohibition of idolatry. These matters should be discussed at great length**; he should then be told, **though not at great length**, about some of the less weighty and some of the more weighty commandments. Thereupon he should be informed of the transgressions involved in the laws of gleanings, forgotten sheaves, the corner of the field, and the poor man's tithe. Then he should be told of the punishment for violation of the commandments. ... **This, however, should not be carried to excess nor to too great detail, lest it should make him weary and cause him to stray from the good way unto the evil way. A person should be attracted at first only with pleasing and gentle words, as it is said first, *I will draw them with cords of a man, and only then with bonds of love* (Hosea 11:4).**[13]

Despite centuries of attempts, no one has thus far been able to discover a source for Maimonides's additions here.[14] These additions clearly move the focal point of conversion to Judaism from acceptance of the yoke of the commandments to acquiescence to a series of dogmatic statements.[15] They are in themselves surprising (which might explain why they have been ignored by centuries of decisors), but there are more surprises to come.

Maimonides's codification of the laws concerning the so-called "beautiful captive" (*yefat to'ar*) ("Laws of Kings and their Wars," viii. 5) contains another surprise:

---

13 I cite the translation of Louis I. Rabinowitz and Philip Grossman, *The Book of Holiness* (New Haven: Yale University Press, 1965), emended according to the text presented in Yohai Makbili's edition of *Mishneh Torah le-ha-Rambam, Mahadurat Mofet* (Haifa: Or Veshua, 2008). I have placed Maimonides's additions to the Talmudic text in boldface type.

14 For details, see Isadore Twersky, *Introduction to the Code of Maimonides* (New Haven: Yale University Press, 1980), 474–475, Kellner, *Dogma in Medieval Jewish Thought*, 19, and Kellner, *Must a Jew Believe Anything?*, 113.

15 As surprising as this may be in the context of Judaism as it developed before and after Maimonides, it is hardly surprising in the halakhic decisions of the author of the "Thirteen Principles [of Faith]." Note how Maimonides speaks of acceptance of the yoke of *Torah*, not of the yoke of the *commandments*. The significance of this distinction is developed more fully in Kellner and Gillis, *Maimonides the Universalist*.

> What is the law with regard to a captive woman? If after the first coition, while she is still a gentile, she expresses her willingness to accept Judaism [literally: enter under the wings of the Shekhinah] she is immediately immersed for the purpose of conversion. If she is unwilling to accept [the Jewish religion], she remains in his house for thirty days, as it is said, *she shall bewail her father and her mother a full month* (Deut. 21:13). She weeps also for her religion [*datah*] and he does not stop her.[16] She lets her nails grow and shaves her head, in order to become repulsive to him. She remains with him in the house [so that] when he comes in he looks at her, and he will come to loathe her. He behaves patiently with her so that she will accept [Judaism]. If she does, and he desires to marry her, she converts and immerses in the ritual bath as all proselytes do.[17]

What is surprising about this text? In a forthcoming article,[18] I show that Maimonides's statement—"He behaves patiently with her so that she will accept [Judaism]"—has no source in the Talmudic texts on the basis of which he codified the laws concerning the *yefat to'ar*. Furthermore, the "beautiful captive" cannot be forced to accept the tenets of Judaism. Despite that, the master is urged by Maimonides to induce her to do so voluntarily. Why does Maimonides not follow the overall orientation of the rabbinic texts or the attitude of the rest of the halakhot, which he himself decides in accordance with those texts? Why does he not do everything in his power to induce the master to rid himself of this Gentile woman?

In one of his most striking references to proselytes, Maimonides writes the following to Ovadiah, himself a convert. It is a long text, but one worth quoting at length.[19]

---

16 Maimonides may very well have been the first Jewish writer to use the term *dat* to mean "religion" as opposed to "law." See above, in the preface, note 1.

17 I cite the translation of A. M. Hershman, *The Book of Judges* (New Haven: Yale University Press, 1949), 229, with many corrections. While there are some minor textual differences among the various editions of the *Mishneh Torah*, none of them bear on our discussion. My translation here is explained and defended in the article cited in the next note.

18 Menachem Kellner, "The Beautiful Captive and Maimonides's Attitude towards Gentiles," in *Essays for a Jewish Lifetime: The Burton D. Morris Jubilee Volume*, ed. Menachem Butler and Marian E. Frankston (New York: Hakirah Press, forthcoming).

19 For the Hebrew original, see Sheilat, *Iggerot ha-Rambam*, 231–241. Maimonides answered three different questions: on how a proselyte should pray, on free will, and on whether Islam is idolatrous. Here we focus on the first of the three, although the third is relevant as well, as an indication of Maimonides's welcoming attitude towards converts. James Diamond presents a brilliant close reading of this letter in *Converts, Heretics, and Lepers: Maimonides and*

Thus says Moses, the son of Rabbi Maimon, one of the exiles from Jerusalem, who lived in Spain: I received the question of the master Ovadiah, the wise and learned proselyte, may the Lord reward him for his work, may a perfect recompense be bestowed upon him by the Lord of Israel, under whose wings he has sought cover. You ask me if you, too, are allowed to say in the blessings and prayers you offer alone or in the congregation: "*Our* God" and "God of *our* fathers," "You who have sanctified *us* through Your commandments," "You who have separated *us*," "You who have chosen *us*," "You who have inherited *us*," "You who have brought *us* out of the land of Egypt," "You who have worked miracles to our fathers," and more of this kind.

Ovadiah's question makes sense. He is not, after all, part of the congregation of Israel by descent, nor is he descended from those whom God originally chose. Maimonides's answer is unequivocal:

Yes, you may say all this in the prescribed order and not change it in the least. In the same way as every Jew by birth says his blessing and prayer, you, too, shall bless and pray alike, whether you are alone or pray in the congregation. The reason for this is that Abraham our Father taught the people, opened their minds, and revealed to them the true religion [*dat*] and the unity of God; he rejected the idols and abolished their adoration; he brought many children under the wings of the Divine Presence; he gave them counsel and advice, and ordered his sons and the members of his household after him to keep the ways of the Lord forever, as it is written, "For I have known him, to the end that he may command his children and his household after him, that they may keep the way of the Lord, to do righteousness and justice" (Gen. 18:19). Ever since then, whoever adopts Judaism and confesses the unity of the Divine Name, as it is written in the Torah,[20] is counted among the disciples of Abraham our Father, peace be with him. These men are Abraham's household, and he it is who converted them to righteousness.

---

the Outsider (Notre Dame: University of Notre Dame Press, 2007), chapter 1. I cite, with minor emendations, the translation found in Isadore Twersky, *A Maimonides Reader* (West Orange: Behrman House, 1972), 475–476.

20 On the significance of this last clause, see "Laws Concerning Kings and their Wars," viii. 11 and my discussion in *Confrontation*, 241–247.

In the same way as he converted his contemporaries through his words and teaching, he converts future generations through the testament he left to his children and household after him. Thus Abraham our Father, peace be with him, is the father of his pious posterity who keep his ways, and the father of his disciples and of all proselytes who adopt Judaism.[21]

Ovadiah made himself a member of Abraham's household. "Therefore," Maimonides tells him,

> You shall pray, "Our God" and "God of our fathers," because Abraham, peace be with him, is *your* father. And you shall pray, "You who have taken for his own our fathers," for the land has been given to Abraham. ... As to the words, "You who have brought us out of the land of Egypt" or "You who have done miracles to our fathers"—these you may change, if you will, and say, "You who have brought Israel out of the land of Egypt" and "You who have done miracles to Israel." If, however, you do not change them, it is no transgression, because since you have come under the wings of the Divine Presence and confessed the Lord, no difference exists between you and us, and all miracles done to us have been done as it were to us and to you. Thus is it said in the book of Isaiah, "Neither let the son of the stranger, that has joined himself to the Lord, speak, saying, 'The Lord has utterly separated me from His people'" (Is. 56:3). There is no difference whatever between you and us.

Maimonides repeats that, having converted, there is no difference between Ovadiah and Jews by birth. (In this, Maimonides should be contrasted to Judah Halevi.)[22] Because of this equality, he continues:

> You shall certainly say the blessing, "Who has chosen us," "Who has given us," "Who have taken us for Your own," and "Who has separated us," for the Creator, may He be extolled, has indeed chosen you and separated you from the nations and given you the Torah. For the Torah has been given to us and to the proselytes, as it is said, *One ordinance shall be both for you of*

---

21 For a study of the different versions of this paragraph and their significance, see Kellner, "*Farteitcht un Farbessert.*"
22 Having codified them himself, Maimonides was well aware of certain halakhic disabilities pertaining to converts. However, such disabilities are technicalities and in no way diminish the convert's Jewish status. See the chapter on proselytes in Kellner, *Maimonides on Judaism*.

The Convert as the Most Jewish of Jews | 77

the congregation, and also for the stranger that sojourns with you, an ordinance forever in your generations; as you are, so shall the stranger be before the Lord (Num. 15:15). Know that our fathers, when they came out of Egypt, were mostly idolaters;[23] they had mingled with the pagans in Egypt and imitated their way of life, until the Holy One, may He be blessed, sent Moses our teacher, the master of all prophets, who separated us from the nations and brought us under the wings of the Divine Presence, us and all proselytes, and gave to all of us one Law.

Maimonides brings this section of his response to Ovadiah to a dramatic close with the following resounding statement:

Do not consider your origin as inferior. While our descent is from Abraham, Isaac, and Jacob, your descent is from Him through whose word the world was created. As is said by Isaiah: *One shall say, I am the Lord's, and another shall call himself by the name of Jacob* (Is. 44:5).

In this remarkable text, Maimonides turns the proselyte from a second-class Jew (as Judah Halevi would have it)[24] to someone whose Jewish lineage, or *yichus*, is greater than that of born Jews.[25] That is not all. Maimonides continues with a paragraph that deserves special emphasis:

Support for all that we have said to you concerning the fact that you should not alter the accepted text of the blessings is found in Tractate Bikkurim. There we read: a proselyte brings [first fruits] but does not recite,[26]

---

23 Maimonides repeats this claim in a number of places. See explicitly in "Laws Concerning Idolatry," chapter 1 and *Guide*, iii. 32. In this he stands opposed to Judah Halevi (*Kuzari*, I. 97) who maintained that at most only 3,000 out of 600,000 adult male Israelites worshiped the golden calf.
24 See Lasker, "Proselyte Judaism," and the discussion at the beginning of this chapter.
25 See Mordechai Akiva Friedman, *Ha-Rambam, Ha-mashiah be-Teiman ve-Hashemad* [Maimonides, the Yemenite Messiah, and Forced Conversion] (Jerusalem: Makhon Ben-Zvi, 2002), 29n54, 76 for other examples of Maimonides's preference for "spiritual" over biological lineage.
26 The recitation in question (Deut. 16:1–11):

And it shall be, when thou art come in unto the land which the Lord thy God giveth thee for an inheritance, and dost possess it, and dwell therein; that thou shalt take of the first of all the fruit of the ground, which thou shalt bring in from thy land that the Lord thy God giveth thee; and thou shalt put it in a basket and shalt go unto the place since he cannot say "which the Lord promised to our fathers to give to us." When he prays privately he is to say, "Our God and the God of the fathers of Israel;" but when he prays in a synagogue he says "Our God and the God of our fathers," which is an unattributed (*stam*) Mishnah and [thus] reflects the view of R. Meir. This is not the law. Rather, [the law accords with] what was explained in the Jerusalem Talmud: "It is taught in the name of R. Judah: 'A proselyte himself brings and recites.' What is the reason for that? [It is] (Gen. 17:5): *Neither shall thy name any more be called Abram, but thy name shall be Abraham; for the father of a multitude of nations have I made thee.* In the past you [Abraham] were the father of Aram;[27] from now and further you are the father of all humans [*beriyot*]. R. Joshua ben Levi said: 'The law accords with R. Judah.' A case like this came before R. Abbahu and he decided according [the view] of R. Judah." It has thus been made clear to you that you should say "which the Lord promised to our fathers to give to us," and that Abraham is your father and ours, and of all the righteous who follow in his way. The same law holds true for the other blessings and prayers—do not change anything.[28]

---

which the Lord thy God shall choose to cause His name to dwell there. And thou shalt come unto the priest that shall be in those days, and say unto him: "I profess this day unto the Lord thy God, that I am come unto the land which the Lord swore unto our fathers to give us." And the priest shall take the basket out of thy hand, and set it down before the altar of the Lord thy God. And thou shalt speak and say before the Lord thy God: "A wandering Aramean was my father, and he went down into Egypt, and sojourned there, few in number; and he became there a nation, great, mighty, and populous. And the Egyptians dealt ill with us, and afflicted us, and laid upon us hard bondage. And we cried unto the Lord, the God of our fathers, and the Lord heard our voice, and saw our affliction, and our toil, and our oppression. And the Lord brought us forth out of Egypt with a mighty hand, and with an outstretched arm, and with great terribleness, and with signs, and with wonders. And He hath brought us into this place, and hath given us this land, a land flowing with milk and honey. And now, behold, I have brought the first of the fruit of the land, which Thou, O the Lord, hast given me." And thou shalt set it down before the Lord thy God, and worship before the Lord thy God. And thou shalt rejoice in all the good which the Lord thy God hath given unto thee, and unto thy house, thou, and the Levite, and the stranger that is in the midst of thee.

27   The Passover Haggadah (followed by Rashi) glosses this verse as follows: "[A]n Aramean [Laban] tried to destroy our father [Jacob]." Maimonides has no trouble with the literal meaning, that we, the people of Israel, are descended from a wandering Aramean.

28   Twersky did not include this paragraph in his edition of the letter. I therefore translated this part of the letter myself. For an extended discussion of the mishnah from Bikkurim and Maimonides on it, see Shaye J. D. Cohen, *The Beginnings of Jewishness: Boundaries, Varieties, Uncertainties* (Berkeley: University of California Press, 1999), 308–340.

One might (incorrectly) be tempted to conclude that Maimonides's statements here are rhetorical, not halakhic. However, both in his commentary to the Mishnah in Bikkurim[29] and in his *Mishneh Torah*,[30] Maimonides makes it clear that this is not the case. The proselyte's ancestor was not a wandering Aramean who descended to Egypt. However, that is of no importance in this context: the proselyte is descended ideologically, if not biologically, from Abraham. God promised the Land of Israel to Abraham and to the descendants of Abraham, both his biological offspring and his ideological offspring. We thus learn in two separate halakhic texts that Maimonides decides the law in accordance with a view in the Jerusalem Talmud against the view of the Mishnah itself that proselytes must recite the confession of first fruits. His letter to Ovadiah was not mere rhetoric.[31]

Two issues arise here: Maimonides's attitude towards proselytization and his attitude towards the product of proselytization, proselytes. We have seen several expressions of the latter; let us now look at the former. The following passage in positive commandment 3 (concerning love of God) in Maimonides's *Book of Commandments* sets the scene:

> The Sages say that this commandment also includes an obligation to call upon all mankind to serve Him (exalted be He), and to have faith in Him. For just as you praise and extol anybody whom you love, and call upon others also to love him, so, if you love the Lord (to the extent of the conception of His true nature to which you have attained) you will undoubtedly call upon the foolish and ignorant to seek knowledge of the truth which you have already acquired. As the Sifre says, "*And thou shalt love the Lord thy God* (Deut. 6:6]: this means that you should make Him

---

29 In his translation of Maimonides's commentary, R. Kafih notes that this is a later addition, perhaps prompted by his own response to Ovadiah. Moshe Halbertal is more emphatic and opines that Maimonides changed his mind on the issue, after writing to Ovadiah. See his *Maimonides: Life and Thought* (Princeton: Princeton University Press, 2014), 95–96.

30 "Laws Concerning First Fruits," iv.3: "A proselyte must bring first fruits (*bikkurim*) and recite the confession, since Abraham was told, *the father of a multitude of nations have I made thee* (Gen. 17:5), implying that he is the father of everyone who gathers under the wings of Shekhinah; and the Lord's oath was given first to Abraham that his children shall inherit the Land."

31 There is a lively discussion over the charge that some of Maimonides's halakhic writing is meant as rhetoric, not law. For an entry into the discussion, see Yair Lorberbaum and Haim Shapira, "Maimonides's Epistle on Martyrdom in the Light of Legal Philosophy," *Dine Israel* 25 (2008): 123–169.

beloved of man as Abraham your father did, as it is said, *And the souls they had gotten in Haran* (Genesis 12:5)."[32] That is to say, just as Abraham, being a lover of the Lord—as Scripture testifies, *Abraham, who loves Me* (Is. 41:8)—by the power of his conception of God, and out of his great love for Him, summoned mankind to believe, you too must so love Him as to summon mankind unto Him.[33]

This passage puts into perspective a notable ruling of Maimonides. He was asked whether the statement of R. Johanan (Sanhedrin 59a) to the effect that a Gentile who studies Torah incurs the penalty of death was legally binding, and whether one must refrain, therefore, from teaching Gentiles any of the commandments beyond the seven Noachide commandments. Maimonides answers as follows:[34]

> It is the halakhah without a doubt. When the hand of Israel is uppermost over them, we restrain him from studying Torah *until* he converts. But he is not to be killed if he studied Torah, since it says, "incurs the penalty of death" [*hayyav mitah*], but does not say, "is put to death." … It is permissible to teach the commandments to Christians and attract them to our religion, but none of this is permissible to Muslims.[35]

Maimonides goes on to explain that Muslims reject the authenticity of the Torah and thus cannot be convinced by proof texts brought from it. It appears that Maimonides feels that teaching Muslims Torah as a way of attracting them to Judaism is a lost cause and thus not to be undertaken. "But the uncircumcised ones," Maimonides continues—referring to the Christians—"believe that the text of the Torah has not changed." They misinterpret it, but do not reject it. By showing them the correct interpretation, "it is possible that they will turn to the right way."

---

32 Sifre Deut. 6:5.
33 I quote from the translation of Chavel, *The Commandments*, 1:3–4.
34 See J. Blau, ed. and trans., *Teshuvot ha-Rambam*, 4 vols. (Jerusalem: Mekize Nirdamin, 1957–1986), numbers 149 and 284–285).
35 I emphasize the word "until" in this passage (both the Arabic and original have the same Hebrew words: *ad she-yitgayer*), since this seems to show how far Maimonides is from contemporary Orthodox practice which demands relative mastery of halakhah *before* one is allowed to convert. This coheres well with Maimonides's conception of conversion as outlined in "Laws of Forbidden Intercourse," 13 and my discussion in *Maimonides on Judaism*, 85–87 and in *Must a Jew Believe Anything?*, 58–60.

A remarkable feature of this text is the way in which Maimonides states that Jews may actively proselytize.[36] He states that it is permissible to teach Torah to Christians in order to attract them to Judaism. What stares us in the eyes here is evidence for a positive attitude towards proselytization.

We can now examine a text that explains all of the above. After taking the unprecedented step of determining that Judaism has dogmas in his "Thirteen Principles [of Faith]" as they are often called,[37] Maimonides tells us:

> When all these foundations are perfectly understood and believed in by a person, he is within the community of Israel and one is obligated to love and pity him and to act towards him in all the ways in which the Creator has commanded that one should act towards his brother, with love and fraternity. Even were he to commit every possible transgression, because of lust and because of having been overpowered by the evil inclination, he will be punished according to his rebelliousness, but he has a portion [of the world to come]; he is one of the sinners of Israel. However, if a man doubts any of these foundations, he leaves the community [of Israel], denies the fundamental, and is called a sectarian, *epikoros*, and one who "cuts among the plantings." One is required to hate him and destroy him. About such a person it was said, *Do I not hate them, O Lord, who hate thee?* (Psalms 139:21).[38]

I do not plan to repeat here the detailed analysis to which I have subjected this text in a number of places.[39] Suffice to note that in this text Maimonides defines his principles as dogmas in the strict sense of the term: beliefs taught by the highest religious authority (in this case, the Torah itself), acceptance of which is a necessary and a sufficient condition for both being part of the community of Israel and for achieving a share in the World to Come.[40]

---

36 Maimonides encouraged proselytization among Christians, as we just saw, not among Muslims. Doing the latter, of course, would have been very dangerous in Islamic lands.
37 Not everyone agrees that this step was unprecedented. See, for example, David Berger's review of the first edition of my *Must a Jew Believe Anything?* (1999) in *Tradition* 33 (1999): 81–89 (and my response to Berger in the second edition (2006) of the book, 127–147).
38 This paragraph appears at the end of Maimonides's "Thirteen Principles" in his introduction to *Perek Helek* (m. Sanhedrin x). I cite the translation from my *Must a Jew Believe Anything?*, 173–174.
39 In greatest detail in ibid.
40 Rabbi Abraham ben David of Posquieres, known as Rabad (1125–1198), clearly saw—and rejected—the implication that there is no possibility of *shegagah*, inadvertence, playing an

What Maimonides does here is nothing short of astonishing. He uses his dogmas to define *what* a Jew is, not *who*. He ignores questions of descent altogether, and takes his dogmatic definition of Judaism as defining the community of Jews whose members one is obligated to love.⁴¹ In his *Mishneh Torah* he repeats almost all of his principles (scattered throughout the first volume *Sefer ha-Madda*), and in a variety of ways uses them to explain other halakhot.⁴² It must be understood that what we have here, for the very first time, is Judaism as a *religion*, defined by its beliefs in the first instance, by its practices secondarily,⁴³ and by descent as a distant third, which Maimonides largely ignores.⁴⁴

We are coming to the end of our inquiry and fast approaching the point where we can draw the discussion together and explain the upshot of the texts we have seen here. What is the essential element in Jewish identity? What is it that makes one a Jew? The post-biblical tradition seems to offer two choices. One can hold that there is something inherent in one's very nature which makes one a Jew. On such a view, which I have called an "essentialist" position,⁴⁵ there is some metaphysical or mystical essence that inheres in every Jew, by virtue of which he or she is a Jew. This view explains why it is that one cannot, as it were, "resign" from Judaism. On the alternative view, being Jewish is primarily a matter of commitment. There is no essential, immanent, metaphysical, or mystical difference between Jew and Gentile. Jews in the fullest sense of the term are those who have made a particular intellectual commitment. Gentiles are

---

    exculpatory role here. See his gloss to Maimonides, "Laws of Repentance," III.6–7, discussed below (chapter 6) and in my *Dogma*, 89.

41 Note should be made of "Laws of Character Traits (*De'ot*)," vi. 4 in which Maimonides parallels the obligation of love towards proselytes to the obligation to love God (Deut. 6:5).

42 Discussion: Kellner, *Dogma in Medieval Jewish Thought*, 21–24.

43 The commandments of Judaism are tools; as such, they could, in principle, be different (if, for example, historical circumstances had been different when they were given); they are, in other words, institutions that affect social status, but do not affect ontological status. For details see chapter 1 in Kellner, *Confrontation*, "The Institutional Character of Halakhah."

44 This formulation relies upon a distinction between individuals recognized as Jewish by halakhah and who are obligated to fulfill the commandments, on the one hand, and those who, for lack of a better term, are, in addition to being born Jews, are also true *Yisrael* (Israelites, as in "All Israelites have a share in the world to come"—Mishnah Sanhedrin x.1). For a defense of this distinction see Kellner, "Steven Schwarzschild, Moses Maimonides, and 'Jewish Non-Jews,'" in *Moses Maimonides (1138–1204): His Religious, Scientific, and Philosophical Wirkungsgeschichte in Different Cultural Contexts*, ed. Goerg K. Hasselhoff and Oftried Fraise (Wuerzburg: Ergon, 2004), 587–606) and *Confrontation*, 238–241.

45 In *Maimonides on Judaism*, where the points sketched in this paragraph are presented in detail. I revisit the issue in even greater detail in *Confrontation* and in *Gam Hem*. See also above, chapter 2.

those who have not (yet) done so. For Maimonides, that commitment involves intellectual acquiescence to certain doctrines. Since the nature of being Jewish in this sense is understood in terms of the acceptance of certain views, and since he expected that in the Messianic era all human beings would see the truth of these views and accept them,[46] Maimonides could not but view conversion in a positive light. Why? Because, as we saw above, Maimonides the decisor determined that in order to convert, one must accept as true certain basic theological/philosophical teachings.

Maimonides teaches that the essence of being and becoming a Jew, and of earning a place in the world to come, involves the intellectual acceptance or rejection of certain views. While one can be coerced into behaving in a particular fashion, one cannot be coerced into accepting the truth of certain doctrines. Maimonides turns Judaism, *ideally if not practically,* into a "synagogue of true believers."[47]

While there are conflicting views within the tradition about proselytes, some very positive, some very negative,[48] the rabbinic tradition never encouraged proselytization.[49] For Halevi, converts could only become the equals of native Jews after many generations of intermarriage between them. For certain strands of the Midrash and for the *Zohar,* conversion as such was not really possible. Converts were actually persons of Gentile parentage into whom intrinsically Jewish souls happened to find their way. Conversion then was not really the issue, so much as returning an errant soul to its proper place. Gentiles, not having such souls, could never truly convert to Judaism.[50] Maimonides rejected these views altogether, welcomed sincere proselytes wholeheartedly, allowed for proselytization, and adopted a warmly positive attitude towards the whole issue of conversion. Given that we are fundamentally all the same, and

---

46 On Maimonides on the messianic era, see chapter 14 in Kellner and Gilles *Maimonides the Universalist.*

47 I emphasize these words since nothing I write here is meant to imply that I hold that Maimonides sought to reject received halakhah about being born to a Jewish mother as defining who is a Jew. Nor should it be taken to imply that Maimonides was not proud of the Jewish people and his being part of it. For a discussion of Maimonidean locutions which could mistakenly be understood as if he taught that Jews are in some essential way different from and superior to non-Jews, see Kellner, *Confrontation,* 250–264, and in greater detail, *Gam Hem,* chapter 8.

48 A dated, but still useful discussion: Bernard Bamberger, *Proselytism in the Talmudic Period* (Cincinnati: Hebrew Union College Press, 1939).

49 Contrary to Sand, *The Invention of the Jewish People,* 173–178.

50 On the views of the Kabbalah concerning Gentiles and converts, see above, chapter 1, footnote 28.

given that one day all humans would accept the Torah,[51] Maimonides had no reason to have reservations about sincere proselytes, and may even have seen in the welcoming of proselytes an anticipation of the messianic era. This attitude finds expression in his discussion of the laws of the "beautiful captive," in which the master is exhorted to bring about her conversion to Judaism.

Pulling all of the issues discussed here together, it turns out that, for Maimonides, one cannot really be born Jewish in the fullest sense of the term. Ideally, Judaism is not something that can be inherited passively, it must be achieved. The pattern was set by Abraham and then again by his descendants and those who joined them at Sinai. The most Jewish Jews, then, are not those whose biological *yichus* is impeccable, but those who choose to be Jews, converts. Thus, David, king of Israel, the progenitor of the future messiah, is the great-grandson of a proselyte, Ruth (the Moabite); among the central creators of that Judaism, as described in Maimonides's *Mishneh Torah* were two proselytes and the sons of two proselytes. Jews celebrate the giving of the Torah on Shavuot. That Torah was, is, and will be, given to *all* human beings (*kol ba'ei olam*)[52]—nothing symbolizes this fact more than the status of proselytes.

All human beings are potential proselytes; upon conversion, they are halakhic Jews in the fullest sense of the term. The question of the status of Gentiles in the messianic era, and the question of the status of Maimonidean Gentiles today, will be taken up in chapters 5 and 6 below.

---

51 See Kellner, *Science in the Bet Midrash: Studies in Maimonides*, 291–320 and Kellner and Gillis, *Maimonides the Universalist*, chapter 14.

52 See Hirshman, *Torah lekhol Ba'ei Olam*.

CHAPTER 5

Aher[1]—Then, Now, and in the Future: Othering the Other in Judaism

1. WHY BOTHER?

If one is asked to characterize Jewish attitudes towards the other in any but a straightforwardly historical context, an important question arises. Why bother? Why preserve Judaism and/or Jewish identity? The answer to be presented here is that one stream of Judaism offers a unique ethical perspective in its thinking about the non-Jewish other. But, once that ideal has been articulated, do we still need the Jews? Jewish messianism as taught by Maimonides provides an answer. Maimonidean naturalist and universalist messianism is both a challenge to create a world in which the messiah could come, and a promise that the human condition is not ultimately tragic. Until that message is universally adopted and acted upon, Judaism still has a task.

In this chapter, I will attempt to describe traditional Jewish attitudes towards non-Jews[2] and also stake out a position of my own, privileging one set of those attitudes over others. I set myself the challenge of preserving the category of the other without overly othering the other and without becoming an out and out relativist. The latter is important to me, since I believe that truth matters and that epistemological and moral relativism are self-contradictory and dangerous.[3] My ultimate mission here will be to show that one can use traditional Jewish sources to lessen the traditional tendency of othering the other

---

1   (Rabbi) Elisha ben Abuyah, the notorious first-century apostate tanna, was called Aher, the "Other One." On Elisha, see chapter 3 in Diamond, *Converts, Heretics, and Lepers* and Yehudah Liebes, *Het'o shel Elisha* (Jerusalem: Akademon, 1990).
2   See: Laurence J. Silberstein and Robert L. Cohn, eds., *The Other in Jewish Thought and History: Constructions of Jewish Culture and Identity* (New York: New York University Press, 1994).
3   See Ophelia Benson and Jeremy Stangroom, *Why Truth Matters* (London: Continuum, 2006) and Jerome Gellman, *God's Kindness Has Overwhelmed Us*, 33.

without diluting those sources beyond recognition. The Jewish tradition has both universalist and particularist elements. The former emphasize the commonality of all human beings as created in the image of God; the latter emphasize the (alleged) special nature of Jews and, it is usually thought to follow, the special nature of the Jews' relationship with God. At the end of this chapter, I will also sketch out a messianic justification for emphasizing Jewish universalism and for maintaining certain Jewish teachings.

2. MUST THERE BE OTHERS?

In order to "worry" about the status of the other in Judaism (ignoring the issue of what it means to speak of "Judaism"), one must start from the assumption that there is some positive good in remaining Jewish, that is, remaining as the other from the perspective of non-Jews. Unless one is willing to affirm that there is some good reason to remain Jewish and pass on elements of Judaism to subsequent generations, is there any reason not to simply assimilate and disappear, as the novelist Michael Chabon appears to suggest?[4] The issue takes on special urgency in light of the chilling point made by the philosopher and theologian Emil Fackenheim, mentioned above in chapter 2. Fackenheim pointed out that Jews were murdered in the Holocaust because their great-grandparents refused to assimilate; had their great-grandparents converted to Christianity, their progeny would have been spared. To remain Jewish, Fackenheim challenged his listeners, was to make a choice fraught with moral implications and, possibly life or death for one's descendants.[5]

---

4   See: Michael Chabon, "Those People, Over There," *Tablet*, May 30, 2018 https://www.tabletmag.com/jewish-arts-and-culture/262965/michael-chabon-commencement.   Chabon, of course, is not the first to raise this challenge. Emmanuel Levinas stated in 1975: "We must answer a youth that sees in the particularism of Judaism, in the world of the commandments and of true Jewish distinctiveness, only support for an anachronism, for a world that is passing away." See Levinas, "Ideology and Idealism," in *Modern Jewish Ethics: Theory and Practice*, ed. Marvin Fox (Columbus: Ohio State University Press, 1975), 122. Levinas, of course, seeks to provide an answer to that youth. For a valuable analysis of the many contemporaries who go under the rubric of "new diasporists," see Allan Arkush, "From Diaspora Nationalism to Radical Diasporism," *Modern Judaism* 29 (2009): 326–350.

5   Fackenheim clearly thought that Jews should remain Jewish. He is well known for introducing the "614th commandment": Thou shalt not give Hitler posthumous victories (by assimilating). The emotional weight of that cry has gotten weaker with each passing year, but, beyond that, one would hope that there are positive reasons for remaining Jewish. See Emil Fackenheim, *To Mend the World: Foundations of Future Jewish Thought* (New York: Schocken, 1982), 213.

Remaining self-consciously Jewish without affirming at least some element of important truth in Judaism may thus be immoral, or, at the very least, irresponsible. In a world in which not only the hoi polloi, but also the academic elites, shamelessly repeat antisemitic tropes only two generations after the Holocaust, remaining a Jew is a *choice* fraught with moral implications.[6]

Assuming all this to be the case, would it not be immoral of me to remain Jewish, raise my children as Jews, and hope that they will raise theirs to be Jewish? Moreover, much of my career has been devoted to showing that a humane and universally oriented Judaism can be appropriately grounded in Jewish texts and teachings. Much of that writing was motivated by the desire for tenure and promotion (and thus sought to adhere to appropriate canons of academic objectivity), but there was often a subtext also. That subtext was to show that one could responsibly present a picture of Judaism attractive enough to enable Jews to remain within the fold despite being aware of the many less than edifying aspects of Jewish traditions and of parts of the Jewish community. If I have enabled even one person to remain within the Jewish community for no objectively good reason, have I endangered, God forbid, the lives of her or his descendants?

I do not believe in the existence of nonhyphenated human beings. To be human is to born into a culture that supports and is supported by a community.[7] One can dream of a world in which this is not the case, one can *imagine*,

---

6   I grew up in an environment such that when members of the previous generation talked about antisemitism, I thought they were trapped in an old world that happily no longer existed. From 1946 when I was born, to 2000, when the second intifada broke out, I can only recall two small events in my entire life that might have been caused by antisemitism. Until I moved to Israel, no one ever tried to harm me because I was Jewish. Now, people throw rocks, rockets, and bullets at me because I am a Jew. The rise of antisemitism in this millennium shook my entire being. I thought that the Holocaust had made it impossible to be an antisemite, but I was wrong. (I am not one of those people who thinks that every criticism of Israel is antisemitic, but I think a lot of it is.)

7   This is one way of reading Michael J. Sandel, *Liberalism and the Limits of Justice*, 2nd ed. (Cambridge: Cambridge University Press, 1998). Sandel is followed by Rabbi Jonathan Sacks. See his *The Politics of Hope* (London: Jonathan Cape, 1997). I recently came across a summary of Isaiah Berlin's views on the subject which resonate with mine:

> Not all needs, desires and values are shared by everyone, but many are common to the great majority of human beings, whatever time, place or society they belong to. If it were not so, we could not understand, assess and communicate with others. One of our shared needs is to belong to a community whose language and form of life we can effortlessly negotiate, recognizing them as a central part of our identity. This is the basis of cultural nationalism, a peaceable cousin of political nationalism, and one we

with John Lennon, "one world" without borders and without nationalities,[8] but that is to live in a fantasy world, not that in which we actually find ourselves.[9] In the aftermath of WWII many wonderful people shared that dream (in my youth, I was enthused by it); but, if nothing else, recent events have shown it to be a pipedream.[10]

Even those who see in this dream the ultimate fulfillment of Judaic messianism must admit that perhaps Hermann Cohen was right: messianic fulfillment is an ideal towards which humanity should aim, but (absent divine intervention, which Cohen did not expect) can never really reach.[11] We should of course aim for the ideal, but while we do so we have to keep ourselves grounded in actual realities.

Admitting that human beings need specific communities, why ought one of them be *Jewish*? Why not assimilate, as so many Jews in the West are doing with great success? At the very least, wholesale assimilation would solve the "Jewish problem" and rid the world of antisemitism. It is not enough to say that in so doing the human mosaic would be diminished. Of course, that is true, but the human mosaic is diminished every day as languages, cultures, communities, and nations disappear. This process has been happening for centuries. How many of the ancient nations, cultures, languages, and so forth mentioned by Herodotus have left any trace? Does anyone miss them today? Would it be so horrible if an ancient historian centuries hence were to devote a career (and earn tenure and promotion in the process) to unearthing the crumbling remains of a culture called "Judaism"? Does anyone today lose sleep over the disappearance of the Phrygians, their language and culture?[12]

None of these questions arises for a person who believes fully that God chose the Jews to be a "special treasure" (Exod. 19:5, etc.) and revealed the

---

should not aspire to eliminate in favour of cosmopolitanism, which Berlin called "the shedding of all that makes one most human".

See Henry Hardy, "Isaiah Berlin: Against Dogma," *TLS*, https://www.the-tls.co.uk/articles/isaiah-berlin-against-dogma/.

8   See https://www.google.com/search?client=firefox-b-d&q=john+lennon+imagine.
9   For a very amusing, if very serious, critique of Lennon's imaginary dream, see Ze'ev Maghen, *John Lennon and the Jews: A Philosophical Rampage*, 2nd ed. (Jerusalem: Toby Press, 2015).
10 As we saw above in chapter 3, Isaac Deutscher thought that nationalism was passé; Israel returned to the international stage too late.
11 On Hermann Cohen's messianism, see Seeskin, "Maimonides and Hermann Cohen on Messianism."
12 For a dramatic exposition of something along these lines, see the opening volumes of Isaac Asimov's *Foundation* series.

Torah at Sinai specifically to them. One need not follow Halevi, Kabbalah, Hasidut, Rav Kook, and so forth in believing that God was forced in effect to make the choice by the special nature of the Jews.[13] One can follow God and Maimonides and affirm that the Torah was serious when it taught that all human beings are fully and equally made in His image, and also follow Maimonides in affirming that (for reasons to be addressed below) the Jews are in some nontrivial sense God's chosen people. One can also follow those rabbinic figures (with whom Maimonides likely agreed) who held that the Torah was ultimately meant for all humankind.[14]

When the Israelites were surrounded by brutal idolaters, preserving their communities and teachings certainly made sense. If we assert that monotheism marks an intellectual and moral advance over polytheism, then (to the extent that Jews were truly monotheists)[15] preserving Jewish communities and teachings certainly made sense in a polytheistic world.[16] But today, when the vast majority of human beings are decent, moral individuals (whatever their religious beliefs) and where very many Jews who take their Judaism seriously are only marginally monotheist (at least according to Maimonides)[17] and very often do not live up to their own ideals, is the preservation of Judaism really that important?

My religious beliefs aside, I know that I am a Jew simply because I was born and raised as one. Nevertheless, whether it makes sense or no, I am the sort of Jew who takes pride in his heritage. For reasons of sentiment at the very least, and perhaps out pure stubbornness, I want to see that heritage continue.

---

13 On Halevi on how and why God chose the Jews, see his *Kuzari*, i. 27, 96, 115 and ii. 36, 44, 56. See also Novak, *The Election of Israel*, 200–225. On the other varieties of Jewish particularism mentioned here, see above, chapter 1. In the meantime, let it be noted that thinkers like Judah Halevi, the authors of the *Zohar*, Maharal of Prague (c. 1525–1609), Shneur Zalman of Lyady, founder of Habad (1745–1813), and R. Abraham Isaac Kook, were all convinced that Jews are distinguished from Gentiles by some essential characteristic which made Jews ontologically distinct from and superior to Gentiles. As pointed out above in chapter 3, this view has no source in the Hebrew Bible at all and very few clear-cut sources in rabbinic literature, but it came to dominate medieval and post-medieval Judaism. (This is hardly surprising, given the way in which the Gentile world threatened the Jews for much of this period.)

14 For the doctrine itself, see Hirshman, *Torah Lekhol Ba'ei Olam*. Maimonides's messianic universalism will be discussed below.

15 See Kenneth Seeskin, "When Did the Bible Become Monotheist?," The Torah.com, 2019, https://www.thetorah.com/article/when-did-the-bible-become-monotheistic.

16 See, Lenn Evan Goodman, *God of Abraham* (New York: Oxford University Press, 1996).

17 See below, chapter 7.

But I also want to see it continue in a way attractive enough to enable Jews to take continued pride in it despite being aware of the many far from attractive (at least to me) aspects of our traditions and community.

Let me rephrase the point in terms of the title of an essay I contributed to a festschrift in honor of Rabbi Lord Jonathan Sacks: "We are Not Alone."[18] I want to address those fellow Jews who believe that Judaism has something unique and valuable to contribute to the world, while cheerfully admitting that other nations and cultures also have something unique and valuable to contribute to the world—we are not alone. Can we find traditional sources that teach (or, at the very least, imply) that the Torah is true and still the other/"foreigner" is no less cherished by God than are the Jews?

3. PARTICULARISM/UNIVERSALISM

We have seen that Judah Halevi and the many who follow him in the Jewish tradition[19] largely deny that God cherishes all humanity equally—Jews truly are alone. In addition, they also maintain that there is something uniquely special about *Jews* as such. For them, the question, "why remain Jewish?," has an obvious answer. Maimonides, by contrast, rejects the claim that Jews as such are in any way different from non-Jews as such.[20] In that case, why remain Jewish? His answer is simple: there is something uniquely special about *Judaism* as such.[21] This unique teaching will ultimately be accepted by all of humanity.[22]

Let us assume that we wish to retain enough Jewish uniqueness to justify remaining Jewish despite Fackenheim's challenge, without so othering the other as to fall into the camp of Halevian and Kabbalistic particularlists. These latter, it must be admitted, represent the overwhelming majority of contemporary Jewish Orthodoxy. To do so, it seems that we must adopt a modified

---

18 See above chapter 2.
19 For one expression of Halevi's impact on later (Kabbalistically inflected) thinkers, recall Isadore Twersky's concise comment: "In many respects, R. Judah Halevi, Nahmanides, and the Maharal constitute a special strand of Jewish thought—threefold, yet unified." See above, chapter 3, note 23 and the other sources cited there.
20 See Kellner, *Confrontation* throughout and chapter 7 in particular and Kellner, *Gam Hem*. However, see chapter 3, note 25.
21 As already noted, this uniqueness is expressed popularly in Maimonides's "Thirteen Principles," on which, see Kellner, *Must a Jew Believe Anything?*; halakhically in "Laws of the Foundations of the Torah," i–iv; and philosophically in the *Guide of the Perplexed*.
22 For Maimonides's messianic texts, see Kellner and Gillis, *Maimonides the Universalist*, chapter 14.

Maimonideanism, that is, the claim that there is something about Judaism itself that is worth preserving.[23] I will return to this issue at the end of this chapter.

4. JEWISH OTHERS—THE BIBLE, HALEVI, MAIMONIDES

Let us now return to a brief biblical account of Jews and their others (surveyed above in chapters 2 and 3). Abraham, the progenitor of those whom we now call Jews, first appears at the end of the eleventh chapter of Genesis, twenty generations having passed since creation. For Halevi and those who follow him, Abraham was specifically chosen by God: as we have seen, Halevi maintained that in the ten generations from Adam to Noah, and in the ten generations from Noah to Abraham, a line of descent developed (or, perhaps more accurately, was caused to develop by God) of individuals capable of achieving prophecy. This special subset of humanity continued to develop through Abraham (but not through his brother Haran, his nephew Lot, or the children of his second wife Keturah),[24] through Isaac (but not through his brother Ishmael), and through Jacob (but not through his brother Esau) and finally to all of Jacob's descendants, the children of Israel/Jacob.

---

23 It has to be a modified Maimonideanism, since his own views are saturated with his Aristotelian understanding of the universe and his hard-edged intellectualist elitism. It also has to be a modified Maimonideanism, since Maimonides himself had no problem with "the tyranny of the majority"—when that majority reflects an accurate understanding of truth. See Jonathan Sacks, "The Dignity of Difference: Exorcizing Plato's Ghost," in *The Dignity of Difference: How to Avoid the Clash of Civilizations*, 2nd ed. (New York and London: Continuum, 2003), 45–66. Lest it be thought that I personally want to live in such a world, let me make clear that I understand that Maimonides might be one of the enemies of the open society criticized by Karl Popper and that his vision of liberty is not the one that Isaiah Berlin and I prefer. Maimonides, after all, was a universalist, not a pluralist, and he was convinced that truth is one, objective, and unchanging—no relativist he. If virtue is knowledge, then ignorance of the truth is immoral and also a form of mental illness. However, on the other hand, because of his universalism, Maimonides adopted a kind of pluralism: there can be salvation outside of the synagogue, so long as one accepts the philosophic truth ultimately taught by the synagogue. Thus, *contra* Isaac Deutscher's "non-Jewish Jews," Maimonides, through Steven Schwarzschild channeling, as it were, Hermann Cohen, could speak of Jewish non-Jews. See Kellner, "Steven Schwarzschild, Moses Maimonides, and 'Jewish Non-Jews,'" and *Confrontation*, 229–234. In a review of my book, *Maimonides on Judaism and the Jewish People*, David Novak points out (*Shofar* 11 [1992], 150–152) that by rejecting Halevi's emphasis on innate Jewish uniqueness, Maimonides runs the danger of turning Jews into a heresy-hunting communion of true believers. I sought to reply to that important challenge in *Must a Jew Believe Anything?*

24 See above, chapter 1, footnote 10.

It is important to recall that the doctrine of the chosen people, while certainly central to Jewish self-understanding, is not unique to the Jews.[25] The Jews, however, may be the first people to ground their chosenness in a covenant with God. Why did God enter into the covenant with the patriarchs Abraham, Isaac, and Jacob, and their descendants?[26] There is surprisingly little discussion of this point in the Bible itself. There are many iterations of the idea that God chose the Jews out of love for their ancestors, but why did God love their ancestors?[27] As noted, Judah Halevi and Maimonides essayed answers to this question, answers that reflect very different understandings of what Judaism is. For Halevi, God in effect had no choice in the matter: the choice of the patriarchs and their descendants after them was determined by their special qualities. For Maimonides, God did not choose the Jews; rather, the Jews (or, more precisely, their progenitor, Abraham) chose God. The covenant with Abraham's descendants was both a fulfillment of a divine promise made to Abraham and a reward to him for discovering God.[28] The Torah itself seems to support the view of Maimonides rather than that of Halevi. The clearest expression of this might be Deuteronomy 7:6–9:

> For thou art a holy people unto the Lord thy God: the Lord thy God hath chosen thee to be His own treasure, out of all the peoples that are upon the face of the earth. The Lord did not set His love upon you, nor choose you, because ye were more in number than any people—for ye were the fewest of all peoples—but because the Lord loved you, *and because He would keep the oath which He swore unto your fathers*, hath the Lord brought you out with a might hand, and redeemed you out of the house of bondage, from the hand of Pharaoh king of Egypt."[29]

---

25 For a study of the surprising number of nations which have seen themselves as "chosen" see above, chapter 2, note 1. For a recent statement of the Jewish doctrine of election in a nonparticularist vein, see: Gellman, *God's Kindness Has Overwhelmed Us*. For another nonparticularist approach, see Eugene Korn, "One God, Many Faiths: A Jewish Theology of Covenantal Pluralism," in Korn and Pawlikowsky, *Two Faiths, One Covenant?*

26 I ignore God's previous covenant with all humanity after the Flood. See Gen. 7:21–22. The Talmudic rabbis extrapolated from this the seven Noachide commandments, on which see Novak, *The Image of the Non-Jew in Judaism*.

27 See above, chapter 3 on election.

28 While writing this sentence it struck me that one might use the reward for Abraham mentioned here as support for the claim (which I do not accept) that Maimonides denied the possibility of actual reward after death, since the promised reward is this-worldly. The issue is not relevant here and hinges on the debated question of what metaphysical truths Maimonides thought we could actually acquire.

29 Emphasis, of course, added. See also Gen. 17:1–4, Deut. 4:31–40, and Deut. 10:14–15.

God's choice of Israel reflected no special quality of Israel's, but, rather, a promise made to their ancestors. This and similar verses can be read differently, but this seems to be the simple sense, and it is certainly the way that Maimonides (but not Jewish particularists) have read them.

As noted above, Maimonides and Halevi and their respective followers all agree that the nation which came to be called Jews was chosen by God. For Halevi, this is a function of the special nature of the Jewish people, established at the moment of creation. For Maimonides this choice was a function of an event that did not have to occur—it did not have to have been the ancestor of the Jews who rediscovered God.

Joel Kaminsky has argued conclusively that the Bible itself distinguishes among the elect, the anti-elect (such as Amalek and the Seven Canaanite nations, condemned to destruction)[30], and the vast run of humanity, whom Kaminsky styles the "non-elect."[31] By and large, when not crossing the orbit of Israel, the Bible shows little interest in the non-elect, that is, in the other who does not directly challenge the hegemony of Torah in the Land of Israel.[32]

The Bible is, of course, a complex document, but until the book of Ezra there appear to be no texts which clearly support Halevi over Maimonides, that is, which support the claim that the Jewish people are in some ontological fashion innately superior to non-Jews, to the other.[33] Indeed, as already cited above, Christine Hayes,[34] maintained that

> The rabbis seem eager to disassociate themselves from Ezran holy seed rhetoric and related Second Temple traditions that denounced even casual interethnic unions as capital crimes, subject to the vengeance of zealots. They rule that those who read a universal prohibition of intermarriage into the Bible are to be severely suppressed (M. Megillah 4:9). The rabbis' failure to take up Ezra's ban on foreign wives and their children—indeed,

---

30 For biblical texts, medieval responses, and modern studies, see Kellner, "And Yet, the Texts Remain."
31 See above, chapter 3, footnote 7.
32 See Altmann, *Tolerance and the Jewish Tradition*, 6. Compare further, Christine Hayes, "The 'Other' in Rabbinic Literature," in *The Cambridge Companion to the Talmud and Rabbinic Literature*, ed. C. Fonrobert and M. Jaffee (Cambridge: Cambridge University Press, 2007), 243–269.
33 A propos Halevi, it is important to note that his own views on the special nature of the Jewish people bear all the hallmarks of Shi'ite influence. See again Krinis, *God's Chosen People* and above, chapter 1, footnote 8.
34 Hayes, "The 'Other' in Rabbinic Literature," 246–247.

their very reversal of this program by allowing conversion—is all the more remarkable in light of the rabbis' general perception and presentation of themselves as Ezra's (indirect) successors.

Assuming that Hayes is correct, we have here an example of a rabbinic attempt to resist the conversion of biblical universalism to a hard-edged particularism. We will see below examples of the opposite tendency.

There is also a strain of eschatological universalism in the Bible (such as Isaiah 40–66).[35] This strain found dramatic exposition in Maimonides's refusal to see non-Jews as any less human than Jews (and hence as any less loved by God)[36] and certainly in his accounts of the messianic era.[37] Eschatological universalism may be seen as undercutting the genocidal passages found in the Hexateuch.[38] There is also much evidence that these passages made Talmudic rabbis and medieval authorities uncomfortable.[39]

5. TWO FURTHER RABBINIC ATTEMPTS TO KEEP THE OTHER OTHER

Despite this apparent discomfort, and Judah Halevi and his followers to the contrary, the Bible seems in many ways to be much more universalist than were some of the Talmudic rabbis. This is clearly seen in the rabbinic treatment of two important biblical terms, *ger* (stranger, alien, sojourner) and *re'a* (fellow, often mistranslated as neighbor).[40]

---

35 For a sophisticated analysis of these twenty-two chapters, see Joel Kaminsky and Anne Stewart, "God of All the World: Universalism and Developing Monotheism in Isaiah 40–66," *Harvard Theological Review* 99 (2006): 139–163.
36 See Kellner, *Gam Hem*.
37 On these accounts, see below in this chapter.
38 See Kellner, "And Yet, the Texts Remain." From my point of view, there are all too many who see no problem with these genocidal commands.
39 For the Talmudic rabbis, see James A. Diamond, "King David of the Sages: Rabbinic Rehabilitation or Ironic Parody?" *Prooftexts* 27 (2007): 373–426. For medieval thinkers, see the article by Kellner cited in the previous note.
40 For more on the move which I detect from biblical universalism to later particularism, see Leon Roth, "Moralization and Demoralization in Jewish Ethics," in *Is There a Jewish Philosophy?* (London: Littman Library of Jewish Civilization, 1999), 128–143. See also Hirshman, "Rabbinic Universalism in the Second and Third Centuries": 113: "Jewish universalism was not born in the first centuries of this era. At best, one should speak of a renaissance or recrudescence, depending on one's perspective, of the explicit universalism in the Bible. Even in the Bible one can distinguish between a messianic and eschatological universalism, and the historically grounded universalism of Isaiah 40–66." For a further dramatic example of a move from universalism to particularism, compare biblical teachings about Esau/Edom

The Bible teaches, "Love the ger, because you were *gerim* [pl. of *ger*] in the Land of Egypt" (Deut. 10: 19). That seems clear enough: the Israelites in Egypt were strangers, aliens, sojourners there. Thus, Jews, of all people, should be sensitive to the needs of strangers, and the like, in their midst. However, the rabbinic tradition is overwhelmingly consistent in reading this verse as if it refers to the *ger tsedek*, or proselyte, one who converted to Judaism and is thus a Jew, not a stranger, alien, or sojourner.[41] The proselyte is, of course, the locus of many discussions of Judaic tolerance, pluralism, universalism, and so forth.[42]

It is worthwhile to emphasize this point. In his famous halakhic responsum to Ovadiah the proselyte, discussed above in chapter 4, Maimonides insists that proselytes are Jews, period. In Maimonidean eyes, they are the best of Jews, since their Judaism is the result of conviction and choice, not simply birth.

Returning to our discussion, just as Jewish tradition narrows the focus of love of the *ger* from love of the stranger, sojourner, and so forth, to love of the proselyte, so does the tradition largely frame the focus of the famous verse "Love thy neighbor (*re'a*) as thyself" (Lev. 19: 18) so that it refers only to Jews.

(Gen. 25) with the way in which he is described by some of the Talmudic rabbis and certainly by Rashi (See Rashi on Gen. 25:22–23 and Gen. 27:22, 27, and 34). See further Gerson Cohen, "Esau as Symbol in Early Medieval Thought," in *Jewish Medieval and Renaissance Studies*, ed. Alexander Altmann (Cambridge, MA: Harvard University Press, 1967), 19–48 and Asaf Turgeman, "Typological Exegesis Concerning the Image of Esau in Rabbinic Midrash and in Medieval Exegesis," *Sha'anan* 18 (2009): 53–66 (Hebrew). On Rashi on Esau see also Eric Lawee, *Rashi's Commentary on the Torah: Canonization and Resistance in the Reception of a Jewish Classic* (Oxford: Oxford University Press, 2019), 31 and 209–211 and Avraham Grossman, *Rashi* (Oxford: Littman Library of Jewish Civilization, 2012), 101–104 and in the index under "Esau."

41 Deut. 10:19 teaches that one is obligated to love the *ger*, since we were *gerim* in the land of Egypt. Exod. 22:20 teaches that one may not defraud the ger. In both instances, references to these verses in rabbinic literature assume that ger in these contexts mean proselyte. See, for example the Talmud (bB. Mets. 59b), following the Mishnah (mB. Mets. iv. 10), and, for one example out of several in midrashic literature, *Midrash Tehilim (Shoḥar Tov)*, 146. Maimonides summarizes this tradition in his *Book of Commandments*, positive command-ment 207 and negative commandments 252 and 253. See also his "Laws of Character Traits," vi. 3. Warren Zev Harvey has written a sophisticated but as yet unpublished study focusing on the issue of the *ger*.

42 For an entry into the discussion, see Kellner, *Maimonides on Judaism and the Jewish People*, chapter 6. An extremely important study on Maimonides on proselytes is Diamond, *Converts, Heretics, and Lepers*, chapter 1. See also chapter 4 above. Of course, the Talmud also preserves passages unfriendly to proselytes. See Bamberger, *Proselytism in the Talmudic Period*, esp. 163–165.

Who is the neighbor whom one must love? It is not, it turns out, the person living next door, whatever their religion or ethnicity. At the very least, it is the fellow Jew and, in some even more particularist readings, only Jews who keep all the commandments.[43]

---

43 Ernst Simon, "The Neighbor (Re'a) Whom We Shall Love," in Fox, *Modern Jewish Ethics*, 29–56. Of course, the immediate context of the verse itself suggests the narrower reading. Despite that, prominent twentieth-century (Orthodox) rabbinic figures have included non-Jews in the obligation of neighborly love. See, for example, Baruch Halevi Epstein (1860–1941) in his commentary *Baruch She-Amar* on Avot iii. 14 (Tel Aviv: Am Olam, n.d.), 121–123. Epstein cites many examples of the use of the term *re'a* as applying to all human beings and cites R. Akiva in support of his interpretation. This very moving text was brought to my attention by Eric Lawee. R. Epstein was preceded by Rabbenu Bahya ben Asher (1255–1340) in his commentary on Exod. 20:13 ("You shall not murder"), who understands the term *re'a* to refer explicitly to non-Jews. See further David Ellenson, "Rabbi Hayim David Halevi on Christians and Christianity: An Analysis of Selected Legal Writings of an Israeli Authority," in *Transforming Relations: Essays on Jews and Christians throughout History in Honor of Michael A. Signer*, ed. Franklin Harkin (Notre Dame: Notre Dame University Press, 2010), 340–361. Rabbi Hayyim David Halevi (1924–1998) was Chief Rabbi of Tel Aviv. Ellenson cites his *Aseh Lekha Rav*, vol. 9 (Tel Aviv, 1989), 64–65. On p. 65, Rabbi Halevy explicitly distinguishes Christians from Christianity, and applies the commandment of neighborly love to Christians as humans made in the image of God, citing Avot iii. 14 in the process. That text reads (in the translation of Sefaria.org, https://www.sefaria.org.il/new-home):

> He [R. Akiva] used to say: Beloved is man for he was created in the image [of God]. Especially beloved is he for it was made known to him that he had been created in the image [of God], as it is said: "for in the image of God He made man" (Genesis 9:6). Beloved are Israel in that they were called children to the All-Present. Especially beloved are they for it was made known to them that they are called children of the All-Present, as it is said: "you are children to the Lord your God" (Deuteronomy 14:1). Beloved are Israel in that a precious vessel was given to them. Especially beloved are they for it was made known to them that the desirable instrument, with which the world had been created, was given to them, as it is said: "for I give you good instruction; forsake not my teaching" (Proverbs 4:2).

For another example, see David Shapiro, *Yesodei ha-Dat ha-Universalit Al Pi Mekorot ha-Yahduat* (New York: Bloch, 1936), 36–37. The Israeli chief rabbi Ben-Zion Meir Hai Uziel (1880–1953) also insisted that the commandment of neighborly love encompassed non-Jews. See Zvi Zohar, "Rabbi Uziel—Individual, Nation, Humanity," in *Ha-Rav Uziel: Hagut, Halakhah, ve-Historiah*, ed. Zvi Zohar et al. (Ramat-Gan: Bar-Ilan University Press, 2020), 75–102, esp. 80–82 (Hebrew). Further on Rabbi Uziel, see Marc Angel, *Loving Truth and Peace: The Grand Religious Worldview of Rabbi Benzion Uziel* (Northvale: Jason Aronson, 1999). For a good example of a scholarly study which simply ignores the narrow reading, assuming that the expression refers to all human beings, see Chaim Reines, "The Self and Other in Rabbinic Ethics," in *Contemporary Jewish Ethics*, ed. Menachem Kellner (New York: Sanhedrin Press, 1978), 162–174. For an extensive survey of sources, see Reinhard Neudecker, "'And You Shall Love Your Neighbor as Yourself—I Am the Lord' (Lev 19:18) in Jewish Interpretation," *Biblica* 73 (1992): 496–517.

Presenting these two terms in this fashion reflects what I admit to be a prejudice of mine: that the Jewish tradition, from the Bible onward, is fundamentally universalist, becoming ever more particularist as Jewish history became ever more difficult.[44] Over the generations, it became more and more difficult to see the non-Jew as a fellow creature made equally in the image of God. Thus, we find a kind of ethnic particularism developing and growing especially from the Middle Ages onward.[45]

6. WHO IS FULLY CREATED IN THE IMAGE OF GOD—AND IS THUS NOT TRULY OTHER?

One might expect that belief in one God who created all human beings in the divine image should lead to a universalist ethic, according to which all human beings are equal in the eyes of God and equally beloved by God. A well-known mishnaic text (M. Sanhedrin iv.5), one that was the basis for a Koranic sura (v.35),[46] makes the point emphatically and explicitly:[47]

> How were the witnesses inspired with awe? Witnesses in capital charges were brought in and intimidated [thus]: perhaps what you say is based only on conjecture, or hearsay, or is evidence from the mouth of another witness, or even from the mouth of a trustworthy person: perhaps you are unaware that ultimately we shall scrutinize your evidence by cross-examination and inquiry? Know then that capital cases are not like monetary cases. In civil suits, one can make monetary restitution and thereby effect his atonement; but in capital cases he is held responsible for his blood and the blood of his [potential] descendants until the end of time, for thus we

---

44 By "universalist" here I mean the view that all human beings are fully created in the image of God and all are objects of God's concern. It will be objected that my prejudice ignores the biblical doctrine of election—a popular accusation among individuals seeking to contrast Judaic narrowness with, say, Christian universalism. For accurate accounts of what biblical election actually entails, see the writings of Levenson and Kaminsky, cited above in chapter 3, footnote 7.

45 Ethnic particularism, often expressed in terms of ontological superiority, became dominant in the Jewish middle ages, but it was hardly the only view. For a detailed analysis of Maimonides's rejection of this view, and his affirmation that all human beings are indeed created in the image of God, see Kellner, *Gam Hem*.

46 See Menachem Kellner, "A New and Unanticipated Textual Witness to the Reading, 'All Who Kills a Single Person—It Is as if He Destroyed an Entire World,'" *Tarbiz* 57 (2007): 565–566 (Hebrew).

47 Further on rabbinic attitudes towards non-Jews, see Hayes, "The 'Other' in Rabbinic Literature."

find in the case of Cain, who killed his brother, that it is written: *the bloods of thy brother cry unto me*: not the blood of thy brother, but the bloods of thy brother, is said—i.e., his blood and the blood of his [potential] descendants. Alternatively, *the bloods of thy brother*, teaches that his blood was splashed over trees and stones.

For this reason was man created alone, to teach you that whosoever destroys a single soul, Scripture imputes [guilt] to him as though he had destroyed a complete world; and whosoever preserves a single soul, Scripture ascribes [merit] to him as though he had preserved a complete world. Furthermore, [he was created alone] for the sake of peace among men, that one might not say to his fellow, "My father was greater than yours."

And that the sectarians might not say: "There are many ruling powers in heaven."

Again, to proclaim the greatness of the Holy One, blessed be He: for if a man strikes many coins from one mold, they all resemble one another, but the Supreme King of Kings, The Holy One, blessed be He, fashioned every man in the stamp of the first man, and yet not one of them resembles his fellow.

Therefore, every single person is obliged to say: the world was created for my sake.

This text would seem to teach the following lessons (among others):

- Each person is a world unto himself or herself and should, therefore, be treated as such.
- Every human being is, in terms of his or her humanity, equal to all other human beings—none is more noble than the other, more precious than the other, more worthy than the other.
- Unlike coins, each person is unique (and can never be replicated or replaced—the loss of any single human being is thus tragic).
- If each person is obliged to say that the world was created for his or her sake, then, in the words of Immanuel Kant, humans must be treated as ends also, and never as means only—after all, if I am the object of creation, so is every other human being.[48]

---

48 To my mind, Nazism is the clearest antithesis to this approach: stripping human beings of their identity, tattooing numbers on their arms (numbers are simply placeholders—there is nothing unique about each of them), killing them outright, or working them to death, all these are expressions of the idea that these people are means only, and not ends at all.

It would seem also to follow from the above that each person is in some sense responsible for the whole world—each and every human should be a guarantor for all the others.[49]

However, being the God of the Western monotheist religions must be a frustrating experience. Many Western monotheists have managed to avoid the universalist consequences of the notion that all human beings are created in the divine image, by arguing that if there is only one God, then there can be only one "approved" way of approaching that God, and all other approaches are illegitimate. Further, if one's share in the world to come depends upon one's (correct) relationship to that one God, then theological mistakes can be eternally deadly.[50] In other words, if that one God vouchsafed to humanity a message expressing crucially important truths, competing messages are not only mistaken, but also culpably false; in the eyes of many Christians and Muslims over the generations, failure to accept the true message yields an eternity of suffering in hell.[51]

Seeking to make certain that God is wholly frustrated, the Jewish tradition preserves another version of our mishnaic text. In almost all versions of the Mishnah published since the invention of printing, we find the following instead of the text cited above: "For this reason was man created alone, to teach you that whosoever destroys a single *Jewish* soul, Scripture imputes [guilt] to him as though he had destroyed a complete world; and whosoever preserves a

---

49 The Talmud gives expression to this idea (with respect to Jews, at least): "All Israelites are guarantors/responsible for each other" (Shev. 39a). (Note that in context, the assumption being discussed is whether the whole world is responsible for violations of the Torah.)

50 Historically this has been more of problem for premodern Christianity and many versions of contemporary Islam. However, if historically Christianity and Islam have had more opportunities than Judaism to put religious particularism into actual practice, this may have only been because Jews have not had the opportunity to do so, as Judah Halevi *seems* to admit to the King of the Khazars. See Judah Halevi, *Kuzari* i. 114–115.

51 On Christianity, see Eugene Korn, "Extra Synagogam Sallus Est? Judaism and the Religious Other," in Religious Perspectives on Religious Diversity, ed. Robert McKim (Leiden: Brill, 2016): 37–62. Concerning Islam, I asked a colleague, an expert on Islam, about eternal damnation for Jews and Christians. He answered, "Very difficult question to answer. On the one hand, Qur'an 2:62 states that 'the believers and the Jews and the Christians and the Sabeans—all those who believe in God and the Last Day and do good works—their reward is prepared for them by their Lord, neither shall they ever grieve.' On the other hand there are those [Islamic] exegetes who believe that this verse has been 'abrogated' by another, which is far less ecumenical, and in a well-known hadith Muhammad says, 'I swear by Him in whose hand is my life, that no member of this people, Jew or Christian, who hears me but does not believe in what Allah sent me with, will be other than a denizen of the fire'. Two Muslims, three answers." This quip is another indication of Islam's dependence upon Judaism.

single *Jewish* soul, Scripture ascribes [merit] to him as though he had preserved a complete world."[52] It is easy to prove that the text cited above, and not the particularized contemporary version, was the original version in the Mishnah.[53] A universalist text has been stripped of its original meaning and made to serve a particularist agenda. God can only try …

Judaism has until recently been dominated by particularist tendencies, tendencies which distanced and disadvantaged the foreigner/other. I cannot prove but wish to assert that this can be understood as a response to historical realities: the revolutionary rise of Judaic monotheism in a polytheistic world and the vicissitudes of Jewish history. I maintain, in other words, that while Jews have historically tended towards particularist tendencies, Judaism itself (to the extent that there is such a thing) has always managed to preserve the universalist message of humanity—all of it—being created in the image of God.[54] Of course, this may simply be an expression of my own prejudices, as mentioned above.

7. OTHERS OTHERED—THEN AND NOW

Continuing with our discussion, it is only fair to conduct a brief survey of the ways in which this divine agenda has been thwarted.

Who is the biblical other? Skipping the first twenty generations of biblical history, and restricting our view to Abraham's family, it would appear that the first others are Abraham's nephew Lot and Ishmael, Abraham's firstborn son, but not his heir (Gen. 18). From the text itself, we get no hint that Ishmael's rejection was connected to a defect in him or to any special desert of Isaac's.

---

52 For a particularly odious example of this usage, see the comment of Maharsha (R. Shlomo Edels, 1555–1631) to Sanhedrin 37a on our text (Sanhedrin iv. 5).

53 Ephraim E. Urbach, "'Whoever Saves One Soul … [mSan 4:5]': The History of a Recension," In *Me-Olamam Shel Hakhamim: Kovets Mehkarim* (Jerusalem: Magnes, 1988), 561–577 (Hebrew). Further on our text here, see Roth, "Moralization and Demoralization," 128–129.

54 This remains a live issue today. In a *New York Times* book review, Hillel Halkin made fun of someone for holding views similar to those I defend here: "Weiss fails to realize that herself is an example of the wishful thinking about Judaism that is ubiquitous among American Jewish liberals. One might call this the Judaism of the Sunday school, a religion of love, tolerance, respect for the other, democratic values and all the other virtues to which American Jews pay homage. This is a wondrous Judaism indeed—and one that has little to do with anything that Jewish thought or observance has historically stood for." See Hillel Halkin, review of *How to Fight Antisemitism*, by Bari Weiss, *New York Times*, September 10, 2019, https://www.nytimes.com/2019/09/10/books/review/how-to-fight-anti-semitism-bari-weiss.html.

Esau has a legitimate claim upon his brother Jacob and in the text itself he is treated in a fairly sympathetic manner. Jacob and his dysfunctional family take up a large portion of the book of Genesis. As progenitors of the "Children of Israel [Jacob]" they are the opposite of "others." Other descendants of Abraham are largely ignored, but not the descendants of his nephew Lot, the Moabites and Amonites (Deut. 23: 4–8). Among the other others we find enemies (Amalek and the seven Canaanite nations—Kaminsky's "anti-elect"), idolaters in the Land of Israel and the "mixed multitude."[55] With the exception of the Moabites and Amonites, all the other others are othered by virtue of their ideology and/or behavior, not by virtue of their descent (at least according to Maimonides).[56]

Who is the rabbinic other? Candidates include women (there is a whole order of the Mishnah devoted to women, but not one devoted to men), *amei ha-aretz* (often understood as ignoramuses), gentiles,[57] various sectarians, the evil son of the Haggadah, and so forth. Converts occupy an anomalous position: fully Jewish (despite certain disabilities) on the one hand, but treated by some of the rabbis with reservations.[58]

Who is the medieval other? Karaites and, a new category, heretics.[59] The most othered of medieval others is the non-Jew, at least in the Kabbalistic

---

55 Rashi identifies the mixed multitude with converts (Exod. 12:38); given the negative attitude towards the mixed multitude in many rabbinic texts, this might be taken to indicate a negative attitude towards converts on Rashi's part. See, however, his commentary on Exod. 18:27. The issue demands further study.

56 The rabbis found a way around the biblical prohibition of allowing Moabites and Amonites in the community of Israel (Deut. 23:4). See M. Yadayim iv. 4. For Maimonides, see Kellner, "And Yet, the Texts Remain."

57 See Adi Ophir and Ishay Rosen-Zvi, *Goy: Israel's Multiple Others and the Birth of the Gentile* (Oxford: Oxford University Press, 2018). This book must be used with caution. See Christine Hayes, "The Complicated Goy in Classic Rabbinic Sources," in *Perceiving the Other in Ancient Judaism and Early Christianity* ed. Michal Bar-Asher Siegal et al. (Tuebingen: Mohr Siebeck, forthcoming).

58 Bamberger, *Proselytism*. See above chapter 4 and the chapter on proselytes in Kellner, *Maimonides on Judaism*.

59 For support for the claim that theological heretics are a new form of other, see Kellner, *Must A Jew Believe Anything?* In the second edition of that book I reply to David Berger's critique of this claim. On Karaites see Ya'akov Blidstein, "Maimonides's Attitude Towards Karaites," *Tehumin* 8 (1988): 501–510 (Hebrew), and Blidstein, "The 'Other' in Maimonidean Law," *Jewish History* 18 (2004): 173–95. See also Daniel J. Lasker, "Maimonides and the Karaites: From Critic to Cultural Hero," in *Maimonides Y Su Eoca*, ed. Carlos del Valle et al. (Madrid: Sociedad Estatal de Conmemoraciones Culturales, 2007), 311–325. In most cases, Karaites and heretics were condemned as heterodox, without being excluded from the nation of Israel.

tradition. Influenced by Halevi and, perhaps, by Ezra, we have seen that many Kabbalists developed a notion of Jewish ontological superiority over non-Jews.[60]

Who is the modern other? Judaism and the Jewish people are so deeply fractured in the world today that a very large percentage of Jewish others are other Jews. The intra-Jewish situation is remarkably fluid after several generations of relative rigidity.[61] In Israel the divide between Haredim of various stripes and non-Haredim is exacerbated by issues of army service, education, and sharing the burden. In its early days, the Reform movement was demonized by some contemporary Orthodox rabbis.[62] Fifty years ago, when my lovely wife and I were married by her late father in the sanctuary of his Conservative synagogue, two very close (and beloved) relatives stayed outside, on the grounds that it is forbidden to enter a non-Orthodox synagogue. Many Orthodox spokespersons in Israel today still condemn Reform and Conservative Judaism as heretical.[63] Today, outside of Israel, there appears to be less tension between the groups.

As to non-Jewish others, there appears to be a sharp divide between Haredi Jews of various stripes, and all others. The Haredi position is, on the face of it, clear-cut: Gentiles are ontologically distinct from Jews and inferior to them. This is even the case with respect to Habad which, of all Haredi groups, would appear to be most open to interactions with the outside world and, one would expect, willing to consider Gentiles as full human beings. With respect to non-Haredim, it is fair to say that the closer one is to Haredi attitudes, the more one tends to emphasize the inherent superiority of Jews over Gentiles.

---

60 Nevertheless, see the surprising number of Kabbalists who also looked forward to a redemption characterized by wholesale conversion to Judaism cited by Reuven Kimelman in his study of *Lekha Dodi*: *"Lekha Dodi" ve-Ḳabalat Shabat. Ha-Mashma'ut ha-Mistit* (Jerusalem: Magnes, 2003), chapter 4.

61 For details, see: Adam Ferziger, "From Demonic Deviant to Drowning Brother: Reform Judaism in the Eyes of American Orthodoxy," *Jewish Social Studies: History, Culture, Society* 15 (2009): 56–88 and Ferziger, "The Role of Reform in Israeli Orthodoxy," in *Between Jewish Tradition and Modernity*, ed. Michael Meyer and David Myers (Detroit: Wayne State University Press, 2014), 51–66.

62 See David Ellenson, "Traditional Reactions to Modern Jewish Reform: The Paradigm of German Orthodoxy," in *History of Jewish Philosophy* ed. Daniel H. Frank and Oliver Leaman (London: Routledge, 1996), 651–673.

63 For details, see Kellner, *Must A Jew Believe Anything?*

8. OTHERS TOMORROW—A MODIFIED MAIMONIDEANISM

My discussion here basically repeats the last section of chapter 3, just as the title of this section reflects that section as well. As we saw there, Maimonides bids Jews to anticipate the coming of the messiah. In the messianic era foreseen by Maimonides, human beings would be free to devote themselves to the Torah *and its wisdom*. Such devotion will make those wise enough to engage in it "worthy of life in the world to come." The point of the messiah's coming is thus to help human beings bring about a peaceful society enjoying the just allocation of resources and devoted to the cultivation of the intellect.

As we saw above, Maimonides brings his most extensive discussion of the messiah to a dramatic summation in "Laws of Kings," xii: 4. With that text, he ends the entire *Mishneh Torah*, anticipating a messianic era characterized by enlightenment and (therefore) peace. Messianic Torah, Maimonides insists, has something important and valuable to teach the whole world. Given that people will be enlightened and peaceful, and those who can will devote themselves to science (*ma'aseh bereshit*) and philosophy (*ma'aseh merkavah*), Maimonides had no reason to expect that those descended from Abraham, Isaac, and Jacob, and those not so descended, would worship God in different ways. His vision of the messianic era is truly universalist.

What can we learn from this? As I insisted above (at the end of chapter 3), this gives us much reason for hope. In Maimonides's view, the point of the messianic era is to bring the Torah *lekhol ba'ei olam*, to all human beings. This messianic vision offers us a goal at which to aim, an ideal by which to guide our behavior. That goal is the realization of the opening chapters of the Bible: *all human beings are created in the image of God* and should be treated, therefore, as ends also, never as means only.

Maimonides's naturalism means that this goal can be achieved by human beings, without divine intervention, miraculous or otherwise. Kant insisted that *ought* implies *can*: if I ought to do something, I must be able to do it. As noted above, Steven Schwarzschild insisted on a Jewish corollary to that Kantian teaching: if I can achieve some worthwhile goal, then I am obligated to try to achieve it. Getting ever closer to a messianic world is surely a worthwhile goal. Actually reaching that goal may not be possible, but getting ever closer is.[64] Since we can do it, we should make every effort to make the world a place in which all human beings are treated as creatures made in the image of God.

---

64 See Schwarzschild, "The Messianic Doctrine in Contemporary Jewish Thought."

In effect, Maimonides, Cohen, and Schwarzschild teach us we ought to devote ourselves to the project of creating a messiah-worthy world.

To repeat myself: there is something else that Maimonidean messianic universalism and naturalism teaches us: hope. We can hope for (and work towards) a world in which different nations and cultures can value their own contributions to the human mosaic without diminishing the value of others—without wholly othering the other. If we can hope, we need not despair: the human condition is not necessarily tragic.

CHAPTER 6

Tolerance

1. INTRODUCTION—THE PROBLEM

In this chapter, I will develop *a* concept of religious tolerance out of the sources of Judaism. Like the other chapters in this book, this chapter is a work of constructive Jewish theology. It is also a polemic, arguing for a version of tolerance that rejects both the "Scylla of relativism and the Charybdis of absolutism."[1]

My intention here is to develop a strong version of religious tolerance, without shading over into some form of pluralism and without sacrificing the idea that truth and falsity are important distinctions. My version of tolerance will not involve pity or condescension towards those who do not share my religious positions, and will involve more than simply "putting up with" religions other than my own. I will explain these terms through the course of what I write here.[2] I also seek an approach to religious tolerance that could be adopted by traditionalist followers of other religions, should they so choose, as well as by Jews in their relations with each other.

Rather than defining what I mean by a strong version of tolerance, let me cite an example of it, from what struck me originally as a surprising source: the (Orthodox) Rabbinical Council of America (RCA) issued a policy statement on inter-religious dialogue (1964).[3] After affirming that "each religious community is endowed with intrinsic dignity and metaphysical worth," the RCA statement went on to maintain: "Only full appreciation on the part of all of the singular role, inherent worth and basic prerogatives of each religious community will

---

1 Reuven Kimelman, "Judaism and Pluralism," *Modern Judaism* 7, no. 2 (1987): 137.
2 On these various approaches, see Alan Brill, *Judaism and Other Religions: Models of Understanding* (New York: Palgrave Macmillan, 2010), 9, 16–17; and Gellman, *God's Kindness Has Overwhelmed Us*, 31–42.
3 An organization that, I suspect, would be less happy today with the statement than it was in 1964. For background to this assessment, see Samuel C. Heilman, *Sliding to the Right: The Contest for the Future of American Jewish Orthodoxy* (Berkeley: University of California Press, 2006).

help promote the spirit of cooperation among faiths."[4] Given the way in which it was promulgated—published as an appendix to a programmatic article on the subject of inter-religious dialogue by the leading rabbinic figure in the RCA's world (Rabbi Joseph B. Soloveitchik)[5]—this statement carried great weight.

---

4   Appended to: Joseph Ber Soloveitchik, "Confrontation," *Tradition* 6, no. 2 (1964): 5–29. See further: Reuven Kimelman, "Rabbis Joseph B. Soloveitchik and Abraham Joshua Heschel on Jewish-Christian Relations," *Me'orot* 4 (2004): 1–21; Eugene Korn, "The Man of Faith and Religious Dialogue: Revisiting 'Confrontation,'" *Modern Judaism* 25, no. 3 (2005): 290–315. Here is the text of the full statement:

> STATEMENT ADOPTED BY THE RABBINICAL COUNCIL OF AMERICA AT THE MID-WINTER CONFERENCE, FEBRUARY 3–5, 1964
>
> We are pleased to note that in recent years there has evolved in our country as well as throughout the world a desire to seek better understanding and a mutual respect among the world's major faiths. The current threat of secularism and materialism and the modem atheistic negation of religion and religious values makes even more imperative a harmonious relationship among the faiths. This relationship, however, can only be of value if it will not be in conflict with the uniqueness of each religious community, since each religious community is an individual entity which cannot be merged or equated with a community which is committed to a different faith. Each religious community is endowed with intrinsic dignity and metaphysical worth. Its historical experience, its present dynamics, its hopes and aspirations for the future can only be interpreted in terms of full spiritual independence of and freedom from any relatedness to another faith community. Any suggestion that the historical and meta-historical worth of a faith community be viewed against the backdrop of another faith, and the mere hint that a revision of basic historic attitudes is anticipated, are incongruous with the fundamentals of religious liberty and freedom of conscience and can only breed discord and suspicion. Such an approach is unacceptable to any self-respecting faith community that is proud of its past, vibrant and active in the present and determined to live on in the future and to continue serving God in its own individual *way*. Only full appreciation on the part of all of the singular role, inherent worth and basic prerogatives of each religious community will help promote the spirit of cooperation among faiths.
>
> It is the prayerful hope of the Rabbinical Council of America that all inter-religious discussion and activity will be confined to these dimensions and will be guided by the prophet (Mic. 4:5). *Let all the people walk, each one in the name of his god, and we shall walk in the name of our Lord, our God, forever and ever.*

    This statement was made in the context of Vatican II and the many Jewish discussions of how to respond to that initiative. Rabbi Soloveitchik's article laid down the parameters of permissible dialogue with (primarily in his case) the Catholic Church.

5   Much has been written by and about Rabbi Soloveitchik (1903–1993), the undisputed leader of what was once called Modern Orthodoxy. See Eli Turkel, "Partial Bibliography of works by and about Rabbi Joseph B. Soloveitchik Zt"l": http://www.cs.tau.ac.il/~turkel/. Two valuable studies: Daniel Rynhold and Michael J. Harris, *Nietzsche, Soloveitchik, and*

I personally found this a surprising statement. It speaks of religious *communities* and religious *faiths*; it thus ignores the ethnic component of Judaism (on which, more below) and adopts the view of Judaism as a religion, like Protestantism and Catholicism (in 1964 very few American Jews had ever seen let alone met a Muslim).[6] More importantly, it also acknowledges that Christianity has a singular role[7] and inherent worth, not to mention being "endowed with intrinsic dignity and metaphysical worth."[8]

This is the strong form of tolerance that I seek: acknowledging that other religions (not just Christianity and Islam) have a singular role in their respective cultures and *inherent religious* worth.[9] Once I acknowledge that with respect to other faiths, I am on strong grounds to insist that followers of other religions acknowledge the singular role and inherent worth of Judaism.

Having said that, I am faced with a serious problem. Is it possible to arrive at the strong form of tolerance without adopting a pluralist stance towards truth? Jews, Christians, and Muslims have traditionally seen the teachings of their respective religions to be exclusively true. Indeed, this is a consequence of their monotheism. The issue of religious tolerance arises urgently in the context of Western monotheisms.

Much of this chapter will involve the elucidation of ideas drawn from the writings of the greatest Jewish legist and thinker, Moses Maimonides. It is important to emphasize at the outset that I seek to build on Maimonidean ideas

---

Contemporary Jewish Philosophy (Cambridge: Cambridge University Press, 2018); and Schwartz, *Religion or Halakha*.

6 For a prominent expression of this perspective, see Will Herberg, *Protestant—Catholic—Jew: An Essay in Religious Sociology* (Chicago: University of Chicago Press, 1955).

7 Of course, this could be taken as a form of *praeparatio evangelica*, which, as we will see below, is precisely Maimonides's move.

8 One could water down the admission that Christianity has inherent worth by adopting Alan Brill's locution concerning certain patronizing medieval Jewish attempts to make space for what we might call tolerance of Christianity. Brill points out that certain medieval authorities maintained that Christianity is "monotheistic enough for Gentiles." See Brill, *Judaism and Other Religions*, 179. This can hardly be said of Islam as Maimonides sees it. For Maimonides Islam is every bit as monotheist as Judaism. For two of many studies, see Lasker, "Tradition and Innovation" and Eliezer Schlossberg, "Maimonides's Attitude towards Islam," *Pe'amim* 42 (1990): 38–60 (Hebrew). Ya'akov (Gerald) Blidstein refutes the (idiosyncratic) claim of R. Yisrael Ariel (b. 1939) that Maimonides held Muslims to be idolaters. See Blidstein, "The Status of Islam in Maimonidean Halakhah," in *Rav-Tarbutiut Be-Medinah Demokratit U-Yehudit*, ed. Avi Sagi, Menachem Mautner, and Ronen Shamir (Tel Aviv: Ramot, 1998), 465–476 (Hebrew).

9 I realize that in putting the matter this way, I am denying the claim of these other religions to universal (exclusive) validity. So be it. Judaism never made that claim about itself.

to arrive at a form of theological tolerance. I do not claim for one moment that Maimonides himself would be happy with what I have done with and to his writings. He was a twelfth-century figure whose life had been turned upside down more than once by Muslim persecution. Like many medieval universalists, he would probably be baffled by our interest in developing a doctrine of theological tolerance. For Maimonides, Judaism (at least as he presented it) is true; Christianity and Islam are at best pale imitations.[10]

Why write about tolerance at all? I have a problem: I would like my views to be tolerated, even respected. Does consistency demand that I tolerate and even respect views with which I strongly disagree? How should I behave if those views with which I strongly disagree result in actions which I abhor?[11] This is one way of putting what has been called the "paradox of toleration."[12] I have a second, related problem: I would like to think that truth matters[13] and that the distinction between truth and falsity remains valid, despite the attacks of postmodern thinkers. However, if truth really matters, how can I tolerate falsity? I have a third problem: should I tolerate the intolerant?

For reasons that will become clear below, issues such as these have been less of a problem for Judaism than they have been for classical Christianity and Islam. However, I am not only a Jew, I am also (perhaps primarily)[14] a citizen in a democratic polity. As such, the "paradox of toleration" obtains in matters not directly connected to Jewish views of other religions. Let us take examples torn from today's headlines in the West:

---

10 On Christianity and Islam as imitations of Judaism, see Maimonides's *Epistle to Yemen*, in Halkin and Hartman, *Crisis and Leadership*, 93–131. Despite this view, Maimonides envisioned a role for Christianity and Islam in the messianic process. See his *Mishneh Torah*, "Laws of Kings and their Wars," xi. 4 (uncensored version). For details, see Kellner and Gillis, *Maimonides the Universalist*, chapter 14.

11 Putting the matter this way frees me from the obligation of considering whether tolerance is a virtue, and, if so, deciding if it is intimately bound up with liberalism. On this question, see Susan Mendus, *Toleration and the Limits of Liberalism* (Atlantic Highlands: Humanities Press International, 1989) and Will Kymlicka, "Two Models of Pluralism and Tolerance," in *Toleration: An Elusive Virtue*, ed. David Heyd (Princeton: Princeton University Press, 1996), 81–105.

12 On the paradox of toleration, see Bernard Williams, "Toleration. An Impossible Virtue?," in Heyd, *Toleration*, 18–27.

13 See Benson and Stangroom, *Why Truth Matters*. Since truth matters, normative theological pluralism is no option, based as it is on the idea that there can be many competing "truths." I will take this up below and in my conclusion to this chapter.

14 This is why my views will be of no interest to Jewish particularists, of whom there are (too) many.

- I support the rights of women to control their own bodies, including the right to have an abortion (at least up to the point of fetal viability).[15] Many of those who oppose abortion maintain that there is a conflict of rights in this case: the right of the mother to her own body versus the right of the fetus to live. Since I do not believe that zygotes and fetuses have rights, ought I tolerate such "pro-life" forces?[16]
- I support the rights of homosexuals to live their lives unmolested and with all the rights of heterosexuals, including marriage. However, like Islam and apparently classical Christianity, my religious tradition treats male homosexuality as an abomination, worthy of capital punishment. How ought I to behave?
- To my mind, individuals who seek to impose boycotts, divestment, and sanctions (BDS) on the State of Israel in general and upon Israeli academe in particular are either culpably misinformed or simply evil.[17] A few years ago, I was confronted by a problem in this regard. Sitting on an academic committee approving grants made by the State of Israel I was confronted by an application from an Israeli academic prominent in the boycott Israeli academia campaign. Should one boycott the boycotters?

Must I tolerate those who oppose abortion and those who seek to deny equal civil rights to homosexuals and those who support "conversion therapy"? Must I tolerate (and fund) individuals who seek to undermine the very academic world in which they (and I) function?

---

15 Personally, I do not think that abortion ought to be used casually, or as a form of birth control, but I still do not think that I have the right to tell women what to do with their bodies.

16 In strictly halakhic terms, the issue is certainly complex. I would like to draw attention, however, to the fact that *Tradition*, the journal of the (Orthodox) Rabbinical Council of America, published an article by Dr. Fred Rosner, called "The Jewish Attitude toward Abortion," *Tradition* 10 (1968): 48–71, reprinted in Kellner, *Contemporary Jewish Ethics*, 257–269. Rosner is a physician, not a rabbi, and is careful to cite Orthodox rabbinic opinions. He shows that there is a wide variety of (Orthodox) rabbinic opinions on when abortion may be permitted. In the fifty years since Rosner published his article it appears that there has been a hardening of (Orthodox) rabbinic opinion on the subject, with rabbis sounding occasionally like Catholic priests or evangelical ministers. A discussion of why that has taken place belongs to the sociology of contemporary Orthodox Judaism, which I am happy to leave in the competent hands of sociologists.

17 This, of course, is hardly the place to go into the issue. For details, see Cary Nelson, *Israel Denial: Anti-Zionism, Anti-Semitism, & the Faculty Campaign Against the Jewish State* (Bloomington: Indiana University Press, 2019).

The three examples cited here raise the "paradox of toleration" very clearly. I myself may have clear opinions on how to respond to the paradox in these cases, but my opinion on these matters is of no relevance to the issue before us, namely, how tolerant can a traditionally oriented Jew be of Christians and Muslims (or, for that matter, of believers in nonmonotheistic faiths)? To rephrase: What can I say to a Jew who accepts the idea that the Torah is in some real sense the record of God's revelation? How can I urge that person to acknowledge the inherent worth and metaphysical dignity of religions that deny the truth of the Torah, either because it has been superseded, or because it is a counterfeit?

It is obvious that this last question has not really confronted Jews—at the very least—since the destruction of the Second Temple in Jerusalem in 70 CE. To be troubled by the question of tolerance, one must be in a position to tolerate. A weak and persecuted community does not have to worry about tolerating others; it is too busy, as it were, trying to be tolerated by those others. Now that the State of Israel exists, the question of theological tolerance of other religions by Jews has become a live and pressing matter.

The issue in Israel is often phrased in terms of idolatry (*avodah zarah*, alien or foreign worship), one of the three "cardinal sins" in Judaism.[18] The general question, what constitutes idolatry, is of great contemporary relevance in Israel: growing ties with Hindu India raise questions about the relevance of classic views of idolatry; the constantly growing contributions of evangelical Christian organizations to Israeli Jewish institutions raise questions about whether or not Christianity should be treated as idolatry.[19] In chapter 7 below I address the question of whether Christianity (in all or some of its many, many forms) is to be considered idolatry. It should be emphasized that this is not a light matter in Jewish eyes: *avodah zarah*, as noted, is one of the three so-called "cardinal sins" of Judaism; it is settled law that one must submit to martyrdom rather than engage in *avodah zarah*, murder, or commit certain forms of sexual immorality. Whether or not Christianity is considered *avodah zarah* is also not a light matter considering the vast numbers of Jews who over the generations chose martyrdom over forced conversion to Christianity. Are we to say that their sacrifice was mistaken, in vain, since God would not have been disappointed, as it were, had they submitted to baptism since Christianity is not *avodah zarah*?[20]

---

18 The other two are murder and sexual immorality. On the three "cardinal sins" see: Maimonides, *Mishneh Torah*, "Laws of the Foundations of the Torah," v. 2, and below in chapter 7.
19 I treat the question of whether or not Christianity is *avodah zarah* in chapter 7 below.
20 Maimonides maintained that one must die rather than submit to forced conversion to Christianity. He maintained as a religious decisor of the first rank that one ought not die rather

It is of, course, not only in the State of Israel that the issue arises. Jewish communities around the world must ask themselves how best to cooperate with non-Jews in a world in which all religion seems to be constantly under siege by the forces of secularism.

When I wrote the first draft of this chapter, I argued that the issue of theological tolerance arises most emphatically in the context of the three Western monotheisms. Recent events in India have shown how narrow my focus was. However, unlike Indian religions, all three Western traditions present themselves as based upon divinely revealed texts. Each of these texts, especially as received by their respective traditions, claims to teach truth in some important and significant manner. While there are many areas of agreement among these texts, there are even greater areas in which they do not agree. Not all three can be equally true. Jews, Christians, and Muslims have historically claimed that their respective traditions are true and that the other two are partially or even wholly false. The issue of tolerance arises in this context.

2. TOLERANCE AMONG JEWS AND TOWARDS OTHER FAITHS

Most contemporary discussions of tolerance in Jewish contexts relate to intra-Jewish tolerance: Can one group of Jews accept other groups as in some sense Jewishly legitimate?[21] As the old saw has it, "two Jews, three views"— there has never been a lack of debates among Jews over what Judaism is, or even

---

than submit to forced conversion to Islam. Christianity in his eyes is *avodah zarah*, Islam is not. See above, note 8, on Christianity and Islam. On submitting to forced conversion to Islam, see Maimonides, "Epistle on Martyrdom," in Halkin and Hartman, *Crisis and Leadership*, 30.

21 There is occasionally respectful tolerance *within* the (Orthodox) halakhic community. The challenge, of course, is to find ways of promoting tolerance towards Jews whose Judaism is significantly different than one's own. For studies, see Martin Goodman et al., eds., *Toleration within Judaism* (London: The Littman Library of Jewish Civilization, 2013); Aviezer Ravitzky, "The Question of Tolerance in the Jewish Religious Tradition," in *Hazon Nahum: Studies in Jewish Law, Thought, and History Presented to Dr. Norman Lamm on the Occasion of His Seventieth Birthday*, ed. Yaakov Elman and Jeffrey S. Gurock (New York: Yeshiva University Press, 1997), 359–391; and Aviezer Ravitzky, "The Question of Tolerance: Between Pluralism and Paternalism," in *Ḥarut Al ha-Luḥot* (Tel Aviv: Am Oved, 1999), 114–138 (Hebrew). Further valuable statements and studies include Altmann, *Tolerance and the Jewish Tradition*, Kimelman, "Judaism and Pluralism," and Suzanne Stone, "Tolerance Versus Pluralism in Judaism," *Journal of Human Rights* 2 (2003): 105–17. I present an argument in support of intra-Jewish tolerance in Kellner, *Must a Jew*.

whether it might be.²² As is often the case with intragroup polemics, it may be hard for outsiders even to see the differences between the groups. Ask a contemporary Reform Jew, for example, to explain the difference between "modern Orthdoxy" and "open Orthodoxy" and you are likely to meet with a total lack of comprehension.²³ Similarly, if you ask a contemporary American Orthodox Jew to explain why there are so many political parties in Israel, each of them claiming to represent "true Jewish Orthodoxy" you will probably find the same lack of comprehension. Freud's "narcissism of small differences" indeed. Luckily for us, however, these questions may be set aside, since our challenge is to mount an argument in favor of tolerance on the part of Jews vis-à-vis other religions and not towards each other.

We thus seek a Jewishly serious basis for a position of tolerance towards non-Jewish religions. Is that possible?

The first stirrings of an attempt to ground a Jewish vision of tolerance may be found in the writings of Moses Mendelssohn (1729–1786), strongly influenced as he was by the European Enlightenment. In his book *Jerusalem* (1783), Mendelssohn presents a defense of religious tolerance and pluralism. His views are ably summarized by Raphael Jospe:

> Mendelssohn argues that Judaism adds no dogmas, no eternal truths necessary for salvation, to the basic rational truths of natural religion, namely the existence of God, providential reward and punishment, and the immortality of the human soul, on the grounds that these truths must be rationally accessible to all humans in all times and all places, and cannot be revealed. … Mendelssohn's theory establishes the basis for two modern corollaries that are basic pillars of the Enlightenment ideology of religious toleration. First, since all positive religions, with their diverse theoretical doctrines and ritual practices, share a common, universal rational basis and morality, the state can and must tolerate diversity and be neutral in religious areas. Second, since the truths essential for human happiness are rationally accessible to all, there is no basis for claiming exclusivity of salvation. A different and more positive relationship among religions is

---

22 See above, preface, note 1, on my use of the term "Judaism."
23 For an entry into the lively discussion around "open Orthodoxy," see Zev Farber, "Torah Min ha-Shamayim: A Guide to the Four Questions," TheTorah.com, 2013, http://thetorah.com/torah-four-questions/. Two recent books by Jerome Yehudah Gellman are exemplary of the new openness: *God's Kindness Has Overwhelmed Us* and *This Was from God: A Contemporary Theology of Torah and History* (Boston: Academic Studies Press, 2016).

therefore not only practically possible, in terms of political toleration, but also theoretically desirable, in terms of pluralism.[24]

Without specific reference to Mendelssohn, Eugene Korn cites Jacob Katz to the effect that it was the budding Christian tolerance during this period that significantly influenced the development of a positive halakhic (Jewish legal) attitude toward Christians held by traditionalist Orthodox rabbis who came after Mendelssohn.[25]

With the rise of reform movements in nineteenth-century European Judaism, the reaction of that stream which came to be called "Orthodox" was harsh and uncompromising. Reform was once viewed as a form of apostasy,[26] as "demonic deviance." Over the last two centuries, the attitudes of almost all exponents of Jewish orthodoxy outside of Israel have moderated dramatically.[27] There are, of course, many reasons for this change of attitude, but it certainly

---

24 Raphael Jospe, "Moses Mendelssohn: A Medieval Modernist," in *Sepharad in Ashkenaz: Medieval Knowledge and Eighteenth-Century Enlightened Jewish Discourse*, ed. Andrea Schatz, Irene Zwiep and Resianne Fontaine (Amsterdam: Royal Netherlands Academy of Arts and Sciences, 2007), 107–40, esp. 123–124. Further on Mendelssohn see Alexander Altmann, *Moses Mendelssohn: A Biographical Study* (Tuscaloosa: University of Alabama Press, 1973).
25 Eugene Korn, "The People Israel, Christianity, and the Covenantal Responsibility to History," in *Covenant and Hope*, ed. Robert W. Jenson and Eugene Korn (Grand Rapids: Eerdmans, 2012), 145–172. Korn cites Jacob Katz, *Exclusivism and Tolerance* (New York: Schocken, 1962). On our issue directly, see Steven Schwarzschild, "Do Noachites Have to Believe in Revelation? (A Passage in Dispute between Maimonides, Spinoza, Mendelssohn, and Herman Cohen): A Contribution to a Jewish View of Natural Law," in Kellner, *The Pursuit of the Ideal*, 29–59.
26 David Ellenson, himself longtime head of the main Reform seminary Hebrew Union College has examined the issue objectively and in detail. See, for example, his "Traditional Reactions to Modern Jewish Reform: The Paradigm of German Orthodoxy," in *History of Jewish Philosophy*, ed. Daniel Frank and Oliver Leaman (London: Routledge, 1997), 651–673 and "The Orthodox Rabbinate and Apostasy in Nineteenth-Century Germany and Hungary," in *Tradition in Transition: Orthodoxy, Halakhah and the Boundaries of Modern Jewish Identity* (Lanham: University Press of America, 1989), 161–184. On the use of these motifs in contemporary Israeli orthodoxy, see Adam Ferziger, "The Role of Reform in Israeli Orthodoxy," in *Between Jewish Tradition and Modernity*, ed. Michael Meyer and David Myers (Detroit: Wayne State University Press, 2014), 51–66.
27 See Adam Ferziger, "From Demonic Deviant to Drowning Brother: Reform Judaism in the Eyes of American Orthodoxy," *Jewish Social Studies: History, Culture, Society* 15 (2009): 56–88. Ferziger is the author of several studies on this phenomenon. See, among others, his "Religion for the Secular: The New Israeli Rabbinate," *Journal of Modern Jewish Studies* 7 (2008): 67–90 and *Beyond Sectarianism: The Realignment of American Orthodox Judaism* (Detroit: Wayne State University Press, 2015).

has taken place.[28] Thus, there is growing intra-Jewish tolerance on the part of many Orthodox figures, but, it must be admitted, not the strong tolerance of respect which I seek to ground this chapter.

3. POSSIBLE SOLUTIONS FOR LIVING TOGETHER BEYOND TOLERANCE

Tolerance is only one way of looking for ways to live with other faiths in mutual respect. I want to examine and reject a number of other options.

3a. Pluralism

We can solve our problem by affirming theological pluralism, the assertion that other religions are no less true than one's own. If one can assume that other religions are also true, there is no need for tolerance towards those other religions.[29] There are a number of problems with this approach (aside from the fact that it makes writing this chapter otiose). Most importantly, theological pluralism is based upon a notion of epistemological relativism—truth is relative, and, hence, truth does not *really* matter.[30] As stated above, in this chapter I want to avoid the challenge put so well by Reuven Kimelman of adopting neither the "Scylla of relativism [nor] the Charybdis of absolutism." I want to arrive at a position of tolerance without being forced to abandon the claim that truth matters (on which more below).

I define epistemological relativism as the claim that truth is not one, absolute, and knowable, but variable, depending upon historical circumstance,

---

28 Among the reasons advanced for this change: Orthodox triumphalism ("the Jewish future is ours, we therefore can and ought to be magnanimous"), the rise of worldwide antisemitism, financial need, but most of all a growing sense of Orthodox responsibility for the Jewish people as a whole. This latter was spearheaded by the Habad movement, but now finds spirited acceptance in Orthodox outreach (*kiruv*) institutions. For details, see Ferziger, "From Demonic Deviant".

29 For important contemporary expositions of pluralist views, see Eugene Korn, "One God, Many Faiths: A Jewish Theology of Covenantal Pluralism," in *Two Faiths, One Covenant?*; Korn, "Extra Synagogam Sallus Est?"; and Reuven Kimelman, "Irving Greenberg, For the Sake of Heaven and Earth: The New Encounter Between Judaism and Christianity," *Modern Judaism* 27 (2007): 103–125. On Greenberg's version of pluralism, see also Eugene Korn, "Idolatry and the Covenantal Pluralism of Irving Greenberg," in *A Torah Giant: The Intellectual Legacy of Rabbi Dr. Irving (Yitz) Greenberg*, ed. Shmuly Yanklowitz (Jerusalem: Urim Publications, 2018), 59–70.

30 Raphael Jospe does not agree with this assertion. For his important (if ultimately unsuccessful) attempt to ground theological pluralism without being forced into epistemological relativism, see his "Affirming Chosenness and Pluralism: Ritual Exclusivity vs. Spiritual Inclusivity," forthcoming.

point of view, and so forth: "true for you, but not for me." An epistemological relativist should have no problem agreeing with Judah Halevi's philosopher who deduced from the conflicting truth claims of Judaism, Christianity, and Islam that they were all equally false.[31]

3b. Noahides

One way Jews have sought to avoid intolerance is by granting (some) non-Jews the status of Noahides. Jewish tradition teaches that the "sons of Noah" (i.e., all human beings after the Flood and before Sinai) were given seven divine commandments).[32] Of these seven, six involve forbidden behaviors (worshiping idols, murder, sexual immorality, theft, blaspheming God, eating flesh torn from a living animal) and one positive commandment: to establish courts of law. These seven commandments are often construed as a kind of universal morality, making demands of Jews and non-Jews alike. Non-Jews who satisfy these seven are considered righteous.

I sense a heavy dose of condescending paternalism in this approach.[33] In the words of Alan Brill, Christianity (which I cite here as a possible contemporary example of Noahism) is "monotheistic enough for Gentiles," but not, of course, truly and fully monotheistic. (I hasten to emphasize that this patronizing position is not Brill's own) Indeed, Maimonides, the greatest Jewish legal and philosophical authority of the last millennium (at least), insisted that in order to count as a Noahide one must explicitly accept and obey the Noahide commandments, not because they are reasonable, but because they are taught

---

31 Halevi, *Kuzari*, i: 1 (end).
32 A vast amount has been written on the Noahide commandments. David Novak is the author of a comprehensive study of the subject: *The Image of the Non-Jew in Judaism: An Historical and Constructive Study of the Noahide Laws* (New York: E. Mellen Press, 1983). See also his "Maimonides and Aquinas on Natural Law," in David Novak, *Talking with Christians: Musings of a Jewish Theologian* (Grand Rapids: Eerdmans, 2005), 67–88. Further on Maimonides and Noahism, see Schwarzschild, "Do Noachites Have to Believe in Revelation?"; Howard Kreisel, "Maimonides on Divine Religion," in *Maimonides After 800 Years: Essays on Maimonides and His Influence* Jay Harris (Cambridge, MA: Harvard University Press, 2007), 151–166; and Dov Frimer, "Israel, the Noahide Laws and Maimonides: Jewish-Gentile Legal Relations in Maimonidean Thought," in *The Legacy of Maimonides: Religion, Reason, and Community*, ed. Yamin Levy and Shalom Carmy (New York: Yashar Books, 2006), 96–110.
33 Elijah Benamozegh (1822–1900) would have rejected this assessment. See Elijah Benamozegh, *Israel and Humanity*, trans. Maxwell Luria, (Mahwah: Paulist Press, 1995). See also Luria on Benamozegh: "Rabbi Eliyahu Benamozegh: Israel and Humanity," Jewish Ideas.com, 2017, https://www.jewishideas.org/article/rabbi-eliyahu-benamozegh-israel-and-humanity-0.

in the Torah of Moses.[34] On this view, to be a Noahide is to be a self-consciously watered down Jew. On this view also, the vast majority of humanity that has never heard of Torah would be left out in the cold.

Further, as Eugene Korn has shown, the vast majority of medieval and early modern decisors in Christian Europe found a middle path, originally charted by the medieval Talmudic commentators known as Tosafists, between pluralism and viewing Christianity as rank idolatry: Christianity is forbidden idolatry (*avodah zarah*) when practiced by Jews, but not when practiced by Gentiles.[35] As noted, on this approach "Christianity is monotheistic enough for Gentiles," but certainly not for Jews. Tolerant, perhaps, but hardly respectful.

3c. (Messianic) Universalism[36]

Another way of avoiding intolerance is by adopting some form of messianic universalism. A common way of presenting this view is to say that, in effect, Christianity is correct: when the messiah (actually) comes, Judaism will cease to be an ethnically based religion, but the universal religion of all humankind. Christianity's basic mistake was in thinking that the messiah has already come.[37]

---

34 Maimonides, *Mishneh Torah*, "Laws of Kings and their Wars," viii. 11. Maimonides is often misconstrued as maintaining there that only such Noahide non-Jews have a share in the world to come. For Maimonides a non-Jew who orders her/his life on the basis of rational acceptance of the equivalence of Noahide commandments is still a full-fledged Noahide in good standing in God's eyes and will have a share in the world to come. See Kellner, *Confrontation*, 241–249.

35 Eugene Korn, "Rethinking Christianity: Rabbinic Positions and Possibilities," in *Jewish Theology and World Religions*, ed. Alon Goshen-Gottstein and Eugene Korn (London: Littman Library of Jewish Civilization, 2012), 196–197.

36 Much, but not all the writing on Judaic universalism is apologetic in tone. On a wholly nonapologetic plane, for the Bible see the book and articles by Kaminsky and the articles by Levenson cited above, chapter 3, footnote 7; for rabbinic Judaism, see Gerald Blidstein, "A Note on Rabbinic Missionizing," *Journal of Theological Studies* 47 (1996): 528–31. Menachem (Marc) Hirshman has isolated a strain of universalism in rabbinic thought. See his "Rabbinic Universalism in the Second and Third Centuries." Hirshman continues his examination of this strain of rabbinic thought in his "Election and Rejection in the Midrash," *Jewish Studies Quarterly* 16 (2009): 71–82. For Maimonides's views, see Kellner, *Confrontation*; and Kellner, *Science in the Bet Midrash: Studies in Maimonides*, chapters 16–20. For Maimonides's geonic background, see David Sklare, "Are the Gentiles Obligated to Observe the Torah? The Discussion Concerning the Universality of the Torah in the East in the Tenth and Eleventh Centuries," in *Be'erot Yitzhak: Studies in Memory of Isadore Twersky*, ed. Jay Harris (Cambridge, MA: Harvard University Press, 2005), 311–346.

37 I ignore other mistakes of Christianity, such as original sin and the divine nature of the messiah, among others.

This universalism is one way of construing the position of Maimonides. He included the following passage in his major exposition of messianism:[38]

> Even of Jesus of Nazareth, who imagined that he was the messiah, and was put to death by the court, Daniel had prophesied, as it is written, *And the children of the violent among thy people shall lift themselves up to establish the vision; but they shall stumble* [Dan. 11: 14]. For has there ever been a greater stumbling-block than this? All the prophets affirmed that the messiah would redeem Israel, save them, gather their dispersed, and strengthen [observance of] the commandments. But he [Jesus] caused Israel to be destroyed by the sword, their remnant to be dispersed and humiliated. He was instrumental in changing the Torah and causing the world to err and serve another beside God. But it is beyond the human mind to fathom the designs of the Creator; for our ways are not His ways, neither are our thoughts His thoughts. All these matters relating to Jesus of Nazareth, and the Ishmaelite [Mohammed] who came after him, only serve to clear the way for King messiah, to prepare [*letaken*] the whole world to worship God with one accord, as it is written, *For then will I turn to the peoples a pure language, that they all call upon the name of the Lord to serve Him with one consent* [Zeph. 3: 9]. How so? The messianic hope, the Torah, and the commandments have become familiar topics—topics of conversation [among the inhabitants] of the far isles and many people, uncircumcised of heart and flesh. They are discussing these matters and the commandments of the Torah. Some say, "Those commandments were true, but have lost their validity and are no longer binding"; others declare that they had an esoteric meaning and were not to be taken literally; that the messiah has already come and revealed their occult significance. But when the true King messiah will appear and succeed, be exalted and lifted up, they will forthwith recant and realize that they have inherited nothing but lies from their fathers, that their prophets and forebears led them astray.[39]

---

38 Maimonides, *Mishneh Torah*, "Laws of Kings and their Wars," xi. 4. For detailed commentary on the texts cited in this section, see Kellner and Gillis, *Maimonides the Universalist*, chapter 14.

39 Seth Avi Kadish (personal communication) pointed out to me that Maimonides here rejects the two basic ways that classical Christianity dealt with the Hebrew Bible: supercessionism and spiritualization.

Maimonides affirms that Christianity and Islam have crucial roles in the messianic advent. Since the task of the messiah is "to prepare the *whole* world to worship God with *one accord*," and since, as Maimonides often stresses, no miracles are to be involved, for the messiah to come the world must be monotheized, as it were. That is the role assigned by God to Christianity and Islam.[40]

Having discussed Christianity and Islam, Maimonides turns, in the final, climactic chapter of the *Mishneh Torah* to the main contours of the messianic era. In the first paragraph of the last chapter of the *Mishneh Torah* ("Laws Concerning Kings and Their Wars," 12:1), Maimonides writes:

> Let it not enter your mind that in the days of the messiah any aspect of the regular order of nature will be abolished or some innovation will be introduced into the world of nature; rather, the world follows its accustomed course. The verse in Isaiah [11:6], *the wolf shall dwell with the lamb, the leopard lie down with the kid* is an allegory and metaphor. Its meaning is that Israel will dwell in security with [those who were] the wicked nations of the earth, which are allegorically represented as wolves and leopards, as it says [Jer. 5:6]: *the wolf of the desert ravages them. A leopard lies in wait by their towns.* Those nations will all adopt the true religion [*dat ha'emet*]. [In consequence,] they will neither rob not destroy; rather, they will eat permitted foods in peace and quiet as Israelites, as it says, *the lion, like the ox, shall eat straw.*[41] All similar things written about the messiah are allegories, and in the days of the messianic king everyone will understand which matters were allegories, and also the meaning hinted at by them.

What does the expression *dat ha'emet* mean in this context? In a number of places, I have argued that Maimonides means that in the messianic era (or, more accurately, by the time it reaches fruition since it is, after all, a process and not an event) all human beings will worship God from a position of absolute

---

40 It is of interest to note how the verse from Zephaniah contrasts with the story of the Tower of Babel, anticipating as it does a time when peace reigns because all people speak one language (presumably Hebrew, not Esperanto). It should also be noted that this passage was censored from premodern editions of the *Mishneh Torah*. By whom? That is hard to say. See Kellner, "Farteitcht un Farbessert."

41 Note that according to this proof-text, the lion and the ox eat the *same* food. For an alternative reading of this paragraph, according to which messianic Gentiles fulfill the seven Noachide commandments but remain Gentiles, see Chaim Rappoport's critique of Kellner in *Meorot* 7, no. 1 (next note).

spiritual equality.⁴² Whether that means that all non-Jews will convert formally to Judaism,⁴³ that they will be absorbed into Israel in some other fashion, or that the distinction will become in some way significantly less important than it is now, is open to question. What is clear is that the relevant distinctions between Jew and non-Jew will disappear by the time that the messianic process has reached completion. In making this claim, I stand opposed to those who interpret Maimonides in a more particularist fashion, according to which even at the end of days for Maimonides the Jews will remain God's chosen people, especially beloved, and distinct from the mass of humanity. I also stand opposed to those who might want to read Maimonides in a pluralist fashion, as if he holds that in the messianic era many different paths will lead equally to God. Rather, I read him as a messianic universalist.

Maimonides makes our point in the resounding last paragraph of the *Mishneh torah*, as we have seen above.⁴⁴

> The Sages and Prophets did not long for the days of the messiah that they might exercise dominion over the world, or rule over the nations, or be exalted by the peoples, and not in order to eat and drink and rejoice, but so that they be free to devote themselves to the Torah and *its wisdom*, with no one to oppress or disturb them, and thus be worthy of life in the world to come, as we explained in "Laws of Repentance" (ix. 2). Then there will be neither famine nor war, neither jealousy nor strife. Good things will be

---

42 See Menachem Kellner, "Maimonides's *True Religion*—for Jews, or All Humanity?" *Me'orot* 7, no. 1 (2008): 1–24; and Kellner and Gillis, *Maimonides the Universalist*, chapter 14.

43 As I argue in *Maimonides on Judaism and the Jewish People*, 39–58. Maimonides was not alone in this view. See the surprising number of Kabbalists who also looked forward to a redemption characterized by wholesale conversion to Judaism cited by Reuven Kimelman in his study of the hymn "Lekhah Dodi": *"Lekhah Dodi" ve-Kabbalat Shabbat*, chapter 4. Maimonides's son Abraham likely understood his father in much the way as we present him here: "And the meaning of 'a kingdom of priests' [Exod. 19: 6] is that the priest of a congregation is its leader, for he is its most honored member and serves as its model, inasmuch as the members of the congregation will walk in his footsteps and through him will find the straight path. Thus, God said, 'You, by observing My commandments, will become the leaders of the world. Your relationship to them [the nations of the world] will be like the relationship of the priest to his congregation. All the world will follow in your wake, they will imitate your actions, and walk in your path.' This is the understanding that I received as the explanation of this verse from my father and master, of blessed memory." Abraham ben Maimonides, *Commentary on Genesis and Exodus*, ed. S. D. Sasoon and E. Weisenberg, 303 (Arabic original) and 302 (Hebrew translation); note that this book is available for download at https://hebrewbooks.org/https://hebrewbooks.org/.

44 See above, in chapters 3 and 5.

abundant, and delicacies as common as dust. The one preoccupation of the whole world will be only to know [*lada'at*] the Lord. Hence [they][45] will be very wise, knowing [*yod'im*] things now unknown and will apprehend knowledge [*da'at*] of their Creator to the utmost capacity of the human mind, as it is written: *For the land shall be full [ki mal'ah ha'arets] of the knowledge [de'ah] of the Lord, as the waters cover the sea* [Isa. 11:9].

The peak of messianism for Maimonides is to bring all human beings to the point where they abandon idolatry (and all that idolatry stands for, namely, brutality and stupidity) and embrace monotheism. Remember, the messiah will "prepare the whole world to worship God with one accord, as it is written, *For then will I turn to the peoples a pure language, that they all call upon the name of the Lord to serve Him with one consent* [Zeph. 3:9]." This will come about without miraculous intervention.[46] If the messiah is meant to "to prepare the whole world to worship God with one accord," then the world must be made ready to accept belief in one God in order to make the messiah's mission possible. Converting the entire world from paganism to refined monotheism in one fell swoop would be a miracle of gargantuan proportions. Such a change can only come about miraculously since, as Maimonides teaches in the *Guide* (iii. 32; Pines, 526), "a sudden transition from one opposite to another is impossible. And therefore man, according to his nature, is not capable of abandoning suddenly all to which he was accustomed." Thus, in order for Judaic messianism to reach fruition, the world needs Christianity and Islam to pave the way for the messiah's advent. Maimonides is perhaps the most universalist of premodern Jewish thinkers, but, as a messianic exclusivist, he had no room for non-Jewish religions in his messianic world.[47]

---

45 On this term, see above, chapter 1, note 53.
46 The claim that the messianic advent comes about without interruptions in the order of nature is, as it were, a leitmotif of Maimonides's discussions of messianism. Here, too, see Kellner and Gillis, *Maimonides the Universalist*, chapter 14.
47 Messianic particularists, of course, such as the Habad movement, have even less room for non-Jewish religions in their messianic world. There will be Non-Jews, but they will be Noahides, subservient to the Jews. For a typical statement of Habad attitudes on non-Jews in the messianic era, see Menachem Krengel, *Sha'arei Geulah* (New York: Kehat, 1992), 188–205 and Alon Dehan, *Go'el Aharon: Mishnato ha-Meshiḥit shel Rabbi Menachem Mendel Schneerson* (Tel Aviv: De Smerik, 2004), 535–577. Not only Habad affirms messianic particularism. Daniel J. Lasker is the author of an important and widely cited study showing that according to Judah Halevi, in the messianic era all humanity will accept Judaism, but the "new Jews" will constitute a separate community. See Lasker, "Proselyte Judaism."

We have surveyed pluralism, Noahism, and messianic universalism. None of them provides a basis for the strong sort of tolerance that I seek.

3d. Particularism

Of course, historically, the most prevalent option has been to reject tolerance altogether and affirm some sort of Judaic particularism. Particularism comes in many varieties and flavors. We can hardly survey them all here.[48] Perhaps a useful way of entering our subject is by very briefly reminding ourselves of the history of two words, *ger* (stranger, alien, sojourner) and *re'a* (fellow, often translated neighbor). They were, as we saw above, largely framed in particularist, not universalist, terms. By way of contrast, we saw there and in chapter 4 above, how Maimonides casts proselytes and proselytism in very positive terms.

I admitted above (chapter 5) that presenting these two terms in this fashion reflects a prejudice of mine: that the Jewish tradition, from the Bible onward, is fundamentally universalist, becoming ever more particularist as Jewish history became ever more difficult.[49] Over the generations, it became more and more difficult to see the non-Jew as a fellow creature made equally in the image of God. Thus, we find a kind of ethnic particularism developing and growing especially from the Middle Ages onward.[50] Going into this matter would take us far afield, since our interest in this chapter is in finding a Jewishly serious form of theological tolerance. Explaining why that is hard to find in Jewish sources is hardly what we are about here.

3e. Judaic Religious Tolerance—finally

Tolerance comes in many flavors. There is a weak version, typical of Judaism over the generations, of not being interested in other religions, so long as the Jews were left alone. This is the view expressed by the rabbi in the musical *Fiddler on the Roof*:

---

48 For studies of Judaic particularism, see above, chapter 3, note 28.
49 For the meaning of the term "universalist" here, see above, chapter 5, footnote 44.
50 As noted above, ethnic particularism, often expressed as some form of ontological superiority, became dominant in the Jewish middle ages, but it was hardly the only view. For a detailed analysis of Maimonides's rejection of this view, and his affirmation that all human beings are indeed created in the image of God, see Kellner, *Gam Hem Keruyim Adam*.

the rabbi's son asks if there is "a proper blessing for the czar." The rabbi responds, "A blessing for the czar?" He ponders awhile, then pronounces: "Of course: May God bless and keep the czar—far away from us. Amen."

This is meant to be amusing, but it actually expresses an important point. All the rabbi wanted from the czar was to be left alone. As long as the czar was not persecuting the Jews, what he did was his business. Let God bless the czar and keep him (as in the priestly blessing, *May the Lord bless you and keep you* [(Nu. 6:23]), and let the czar leave the rabbi and his flock to their own devices. The rabbi has no interest in the czar, certainly not in his theology, and has no objection to God showering blessings upon the him.

Why has the rabbi no such interest? The reason behind this lack of interest is simple to state, but rarely understood by non-Jews, and has recently become the focus of debate among scholars of Judaism, some of whom have barely hidden political agendas.[51] What is that reason? Judaism, unlike Christianity and Islam, makes no pretensions of being a universal religion; indeed, it is hard to see it as "only" a religion in the sense that Christianity and Islam are religions (however one defines the term). Judaism is the religion *of* the Jewish people,[52] or the religion *that constitutes* the Jewish people.[53] Jews, defined as members of the Jewish people, have held many religious views (on which, more below) and generally have been uninterested in the religious views of other peoples. Jewish history and texts do not call for crusades and jihad against unbelievers.[54]

So far, the weak version of tolerance means lack of interest. Another version of weak tolerance can be "putting up with" or pitying.[55] This is hardly the sort of tolerance sought here. I do not seek for non-Jews to put up with me, condescend towards me or, worse, pity me. I shall thus not seek a version of tolerance towards non-Jews that involves my "putting up" with them, condescending towards them, or pitying them.

---

51 For example, Shlomo Sand perverts scholarship for political ends. He is, sadly, very much not alone. See his *The Invention of the Jewish People*.
52 Solomon Schechter (1847–1915) is often quoted as having stated that "Judaism is the religion of the Jewish people."
53 Sa'adia Gaon (882–942) stated, "Our people is only a people by virtue of its Torahs [i.e., written and oral]." See Sa'adia Gaon, *Book of Belief and Opinions*, trans. Samuel Rosenblatt (New Haven: Yale University Press, 1948), iii. 7, 158 (emended).
54 See Altmann, *Tolerance and the Jewish Tradition*, above, chapter 3, note 8.
55 Abraham Joshua Heschel calls for reverence of the other, not tolerance in the sense of condescension or pity. See Heschel, "No Religion is an Island," *Union Seminary Quarterly Review* 21 (1966): 123.

Before moving on, allow me to present one personal story illustrating the tolerance of pity. Many years ago, before making *aliyah* (moving) to Israel, my family and I were close to two other religious families in the community in which we then lived: the family of the local Orthodox rabbi and a family of evangelical Christians, with whom we shared many social and cultural attitudes. All three families once got together for a barbecue in the rabbi's back yard. Mary, the teenage daughter of our evangelical friends was playing with the rabbi's son, then a toddler. Suddenly Mary burst into bitter tears. When asked why, she explained: "Ploni [the rabbi's son] is such a wonderful, sweet little boy, and is still destined to burn in hell!" Well-meaning, I suppose, but certainly condescending and pitying.

There is a second reason for the *Fiddler* rabbi's lack of what we might call theological interest in the thinking and doing of non-Jews: Judaism, whatever it is, makes no claims of exclusivism. Jewish texts and teachers have never called upon all non-Jews to become Jewish so as to be "saved" (whatever that might be)[56]. It has long been settled Jewish doctrine that outside of the synagogue there *can* be salvation.[57]

As noted already at the beginning of this chapter, I seek a strong version of tolerance, one grounded in Jewish texts and teachings, and one that a person committed to the truth of Torah could accept. Having said that, I am faced with a serious problem. Is it possible to arrive at the strong form of tolerance without

---

56 Jewish texts express the idea captured by the word "salvation" by talking of having a share in the world to come. Aside from an endless stream of jokes, the Jewish tradition has never arrived at a clear understanding of what that means. Minimally, it is expected that in some fashion or other the righteous will be rewarded after death and the wicked punished. For an introduction to the discussion, see Steven Schwarzschild, "On Jewish Eschatology," in Kellner, *The Pursuit of the Ideal*, 209–228.

57 If there is anything in Jewish theology which may be considered settled doctrine it is that righteous non-Jews (*hasidei umot ha-'olam*) enjoy a share in the world to come. For studies, see: Eugene Korn, "Gentiles, the World to Come, and Judaism: The Odyssey of a Rabbinic Text," *Modern Judaism* 14 (1994): 265–87; Korn, "Extra Synagogam Sallus Est?"; Hannah Kasher, "Three Punishments Which are One, According to Maimonides," *Sidra* 14 (1988): 39–58 (Hebrew); Jacob Katz, "The Vicissitudes of Three Apologetic Statements," *Zion* 23–24 (1958–59): 174–93 (Hebrew); Ronen Lubitch, "The Righteous among the Nations of the Earth in the Thought of R. Hayyim David Halevi: Kabbalah and Natural Justice in the Question of the Attitude Towards Gentiles," in *Yahadut Shel Hayyim: Iyyunim be-Yetsirato ha-Hagutit-Hilkhatit Shel ha-Rav Hayyim David Halevi*, ed. Zvi Zohar and Avi Sagi (Jerusalem: Keter, 2007), 215–234 (Hebrew); Michael Zvi Nehorai, "'Righteous Gentiles Have a Share in the World to Come,'" *Tarbiz* 61 (1992): 465–87 (Hebrew); Nehorai, "A Portion in the World to Come for the Righteous/Sages of the Nations," *Da'at* 50–52 (2003): 97–105 (Hebrew).

adopting a pluralist stance towards truth? Jews, Christians, and Muslims have traditionally seen the teachings of their respective religions to be exclusively true. Indeed, this is a consequence of their monotheism. The issue of religious tolerance arises urgently in the context of Western monotheisms.

3f. Monotheism and Intolerance

In chapter 5 above we discussed the attempt to minimize the universalist message of Mishnah Sanhedrin iv. 5. That attempt involved replacing the implication of the belief in one God who created all human beings in the divine image with a reading that emphasized the special privileged status of the people of Israel. However, as noted above, being the God of the Western monotheist religions must be a frustrating experience. Not only Jews tinkering with a mishnaic text, but many Western monotheists have managed to avoid the universalist consequences of the notion that all human beings are created in the divine image. They do this by arguing that if there is only one God, then there can be only one "approved" way of approaching that God, and all other approaches are, as it were, not kosher. In other words, if that one God vouchsafed to humanity a message expressing crucially important truths, competing messages are not only mistaken, but also culpably false; in the eyes of many Christians and Muslims over the generations, the failure to accept the true message yields an eternity of suffering in hell. As with the terms *ger* and *re'a* (sojourner, neighbor), here in this passage from the Mishnah a universalist text has been stripped of its original meaning and made to serve a particularist agenda.

For Halevi this special subset of humanity is related to the rest of the human race as the heart is related to the rest of the body: the most important organ, without which the other organs cannot survive and which itself, if we take the analogy further, cannot survive without them. Maimonides, on the other hand, taught that it was Abraham who chose God, not the other way round, and in consequence of that choice, God entered into a covenant with Abraham, his son and grandson, and ultimately with their descendants at Sinai.[58] As we have seen, Maimonides and Halevi both agree that the nation which came to be called Israel was chosen by God. For Halevi, this is a consequence of the special nature of the Jewish people. According to Maimonides this is ultimately a function of an historically contingent event—it did not have to be the ancestor of the Jews who rediscovered God.

---

58 Maimonides, "Laws of Idolatry," chapter 1. For discussion, see above, chapter 1.

Monotheism is thus part of our problem (and, one hopes, part of the solution). However, so is truth.

3g. Truth

Maimonides is well known for having insisted, "accept the truth whatever its source."[59] Hidden behind this injunction is the view that truth is one, objective, unchanging, and largely knowable. This is hardly a surprising claim to find in the writings of a medieval monotheist, but it must be admitted that it has a hard edge. On the one hand, this statement leads to universalism: all human beings who acknowledge the truth are "in the club," as it were. Nevertheless, allied with this universalism, we find a sharp elitism:[60] those who fail to acknowledge the truth are at best mistaken and probably evil.[61] To the extent that acknowledging truth is the key to God's favor, failure to arrive at the truth is a serious matter indeed.

Can someone who accepts that her or his religion is true in some serious sense truly tolerate someone who rejects or even questions that truth? The simplest solution to this problem is to abandon the Maimonidean understanding of truth as one, objective, unchanging, and knowable. This is the epistemological relativism of various postmodernists.[62] I have yet to find a version of postmodernism which is not self-refuting, but that is not the tack to be taken here.[63] Once I am willing to accept the relative nature of truth, the need to justify tolerance disappears and this chapter can end at this point. Religious pluralism, as a normative stance, simply obviates the need for tolerance.

---

59 Maimonides, "Introduction to the Commentary on the Tractate Avot," in *Ethical Writings of Maimonides*, trans. Raymond Weiss and Charles Butterworth (New York: Dover, 1983), 60.

60 On Maimonidean elitism, see Kellner, *Confrontation*, 16 and index under "elitism"; Remi Brague, "Athens, Jerusalem, Mecca: Leo Strauss's 'Muslim' Understanding of Greek Philosophy," *Poetics Today* 19 (1998): 235–259; Gad Freudenthal, "The Biological Foundations of Intellectual Elitism: Maimonides vs. Al-Farabi," *Maimonidean Studies* 5 (2008): 293–324; and Rynhold and Harris, *Nietzsche Soloveitchik, and Contemporary Jewish Philosophy*, 268–277. See above, chapter 2, footnote 20 on Hannah Kasher's critique of Maimonides in this regard.

61 Rabbi Elhanan Wasserman, martyred by the Nazis in 1941, was a strict antimodernist (and anti-Zionist). He held that God's existence and providence were so evident that only a hedonist, seduced by the pleasures of this world, could possibly be an atheist. See the chapter on Wasserman in Diamond and Kellner, *Reinventing Maimonides*, 107–148.

62 For as good a defense of this impossible approach as can be found, see Miriam Feldmann-Kaye, *Jewish Theology for a Postmodern Age* (London: Littman Library of Jewish Civilization, 2019).

63 For a brief but telling exposition of this position, with citations of relevant studies, see Gellman, *God's Kindness Has Overwhelmed Us*, 33.

So why not give up on the notion of objective truth and become religious pluralists? Aside from the fact that truth *does* matter (without agreeing on some standards of truth and falsity, I do not see how any real communication can take place), for Jews the issue take on special urgency. As noted above (in chapter 2), I once heard Emil Fackenheim assert that people were killed by the Nazis because at least one of their great-grandparents was Jewish; had that ancestor converted to Christianity, their descendents would have been spared. To remain Jewish, Fackenheim challenged his listeners, was to make a choice fraught with moral implications and, possibly life or death for one's descendents.

Remaining theologically Jewish without affirming at least some element of important truth in Judaism is thus actually immoral, or, at the very least, irresponsible.[64] What can I do? I want to claim that Judaism (whatever that might be) is true but I do not want to claim that other religions are false.

3h. Proposed Solution

I would like to propose a way out of our impasse. I will phrase it in terms of Jewish texts and teaching, but it could be adopted by followers of other religious traditions as well. Put simply, to say that Torah teaches truth is not to say that Jews actually understand that truth fully. One might even want to follow thinkers like Tamar Ross and Jerome Gellman (both influenced by Rabbi Kook) who maintain that our approximation of Torah truth grows ever greater and deeper, not the further we get from Sinai, but the closer we get to the messianic era.[65] However, one need not go that far to find a traditional Jewish warrant for the assertion that our understanding of Torah is far from deep and full.

Examining the figure of Moses will elucidate the point. Maimonides was the first authoritative Jewish teacher to affirm that Judaism had dogmas in the strict sense of the term (doctrines taught by the Torah, correct acceptance of which was both a necessary and sufficient condition for being part of the Jewish collective and for achieving a share in the world to come).[66] Judaism, he taught, consists of thirteen core beliefs. Of them,

> [t]he seventh foundation is the prophecy of Moses, our Teacher; to wit, it should be known that: Moses was the father of all the prophets—of those

---

64 See above, chapter 5, notes 5 and 6 for an expansion on this point.
65 For Ross, see her *Expanding the Palace of Tora: Orthodoxy and Feminism* (Waltham, MA: Brandeis University Press, 2004); for Gellman, see the works cited above in note 23.
66 See Kellner, *Dogma in Medieval Jewish Thought*.

who came before him and of those who came after him; all were beneath him in rank and that he was the chosen of God from among the entire species of humanity and that he comprehended more of God, may He be exalted, than any man who existed or will exist, ever comprehended or will comprehend, and that he, peace upon him, reached a state of exaltedness beyond humanity and became included in the level of angels. There remained no veil which he did not pierce, no material hindrance burdened him, and no defect, whether small or great, mingled with him. The imaginative and sensible faculties in his perception were stripped from him, his desiderative faculty was still and he remained pure intellect only. For this reason, they remarked of him that he discoursed with God without the intermediary of an angel.[67]

Despite the facts that Moses was the greatest of all prophets who ever lived or ever will live;[68] that he comprehended more of God than any other human who ever lived or will live; that he became, in effect, an angel; and that there "remained no veil which he did not pierce," so much so that God spoke to him, as it were, face to face (Nu. 12:8); despite everything, there was much about God that Moses did not comprehend.[69]

This we learn from Maimonides's statement in *Guide of the Perplexed* i. 54 that despite all his greatness, Moses remained a human being, and as such was limited in what he could know of God:

> Moses our Teacher, the master of those who know, made two behests, both answered: first, that God acquaint him with His true Reality, and second (although he asked this first) to make Himself known through His attributes. God answered by promising Moses knowledge of all His attributes, revealing that His attributes are His acts, and teaching him that one cannot know Him as He really is but awakened him to an intellectual plane

---

67 I cite the translation of David Blumenthal as found in Kellner, *Must a Jew Believe Anything?*, 168–169
68 Including even the messiah; see Maimonides, *Mishneh Torah*, "Laws of Repentance," ix. 2.
69 For surveys of the places in his writings where Maimonides deals with the exalted nature of Moses and his prophecy, see Alfred Ivry, "The Image of Moses in Maimonides's 'Thought,'" in *Rambam. Shamranut, Mekoriut, Mahapkhanut*, ed. Aviezer Ravitzky (Jerusalem: Merkaz Zalman Shazar, 2008), 481–499 (Hebrew); and Hannah Kasher, "Maimonides' Interpretation of the Story of the Divine Revelation in the Cleft of the Rock," *Da'at* 35 (1995): 29–66 (Hebrew).

from which he could reach the summit of human awareness. What Moses knew then has been grasped by no one else before or since.[70]

Moses made two requests of God in Exodus 33: to know God's ways, and to behold God's presence. Maimonides interprets this latter request as a desire to know God's true reality, that is, to know God as God truly is. God's ways, Maimonides teaches here, are what we would call the laws of nature, God's acts. However, to know God as God truly is cannot be achieved by any human being, even one as supreme as Moses.

If divine truth in and of itself was hidden from Moses, how much more so it is hidden from us.[71] Ought we not extend that modesty to our claims to understand the truths taught by Torah?

God's ultimate unknowability is one of the fundamental teachings of Maimonides's entire philosophy. It also underlies his widely cited interpretation of the Talmudic dictum that the Torah speaks in human language.[72] Why must the Torah speak in human language as opposed to expressing the truths of God in, as it were, God's language?[73] The Torah is addressed to human beings, not to angels,[74] and human beings are, by their very creaturely nature, incapable of actually knowing God as God is. This should certainly undermine any claims to theological certainty.

---

70 Pines, 123.
71 Kellner, "Maimonides on the Science of the *Mishneh Torah*." See pages 170 and 192 on the infinite tasks that are astronomy and metaphysics (which explains why we, and even Moses, can never achieve full knowledge of God) and 176ff on the fallibility of the Rabbinic sages. If the authors of Mishnah and Talmud could make mistakes on theological issues, how much more can we be mistaken on such issues. Further on this latter point, see Menachem Kellner, *Maimonides on the "Decline of the Generations" and the Nature of Rabbinic Authority* (Albany: SUNY Press, 1996).
72 Maimonides took the rabbinic statement that the Torah speaks in human language to mean that much of the Torah ought to be understood metaphorically. For entry into the discussion, see Amos Funkenstein, "'Scripture Speaks the Language of Man': The Uses and Abuses of the Medieval Principle of Accommodation," *Philosophes Medievaux* 26 (1986): 92–101; Joshua L. Goldin, "On the Limits of Non-Literal Interpretation of Scripture from an Orthodox Perspective," *Torah u-Madda Journal* 10 (2001): 37–59; Sara Klein-Baslavy, "The Philosophical exegesis," in *Hebrew Bible / Old Testament: The History of its Interpretation* ed. Magne Saebo (Goettingen: Vandenhoeck and Ruprecht, 2000), 302–320.
73 Mystics, of course, are not restrained in this matter to the same degree as philosophers, who, by and large, aim for an understanding of God, as opposed to an experience of God.
74 Ber. 25b and parallels; see Christine Hayes, "The Torah was not given to Ministering Angels: Rabbinic Aspirationalism," in *Talmudic Transgressions: Engaging the Work of Daniel Boyarin*, ed. Charlotte Fonrobert et al., Supplements to the Journal for the Study of Judaism 181 (Leiden: Brill, 2017), 123–160.

This point is importantly buttressed, as Eugene Korn pointed out to me (personal communication), by a variety of Talmudic and later texts, which fault Abraham for having misunderstood God's command concerning the sacrifice of Isaac. Abraham was not meant to sacrifice Isaac, but to offer a sacrifice to God *with* Isaac. Given the central importance that later Jewish texts attached to the *aḳedah*, the binding of Isaac, and its place in the liturgy, this is a striking claim, but it is found in a number of sources (known to Maimonides).[75] If Abraham could misinterpret God's message, and if Moses was unable to plumb the depths of knowledge of God, how much more should we adopt a stance of epistemological modesty when it comes to affirming the truths of Torah.[76]

There is another lesson we should learn from Moses. Not only did he reach the summit of human awareness but he was also the most modest of all human beings (Nu. 12:3). The mishnaic tractate Avot teaches (iv. 4) that one must be excessively humble. In his extensive commentary on this passage, Maimonides cites Moses as the exemplar of human humility.[77] Why was Moses so humble? Knowing better than any other human being how little he actually knew of God, Moses was more aware than most of his human frailty.[78] If Moses, the greatest of all human beings, was excessively modest, should we not be too?[79]

---

75 Korn notes: "This is the interpretation offered *in Ta'anit* 4a; *Genesis Rabbah* 55:5 and 56:8; *Pesikta Zutra* 44." Korn also points to Rashi on Gen 22:2 and R. Abraham Isaac Kook (*Letters* II: 379)—neither of whom were known to Maimonides—about the first there is no proof on way or the other, but about the second, there obviously can be no question.

76 See Eugene Korn, "Religious Violence, Sacred Texts and Theological Values," in *Plowshares into Swords? Reflections on Religion and Violence*, ed. Robert W. Jensen and Eugene Korn (Jerusalem: Center for Jewish Christian Understanding and Cooperation, 2014), Kindle ed.

77 It is of great interest, but not actually relevant to our point, that in his commentary on this text Maimonides cites a Sufi story about humility. See Herbert Davidson, *Moses Maimonides: The Man and His Works* (Oxford: Oxford University Press, 2005), 94n104. See also Raymond L. Weiss, *Maimonides's Ethics: The Encounter of Philosophic and Religious Morality* (Chicago: University of Chicago Press, 1991), 40.

78 Further on Moses's humility, see James Diamond, "Exegetical Idealization: Hermann Cohen's Religion of Reason out of the Sources of Maimonides," *Journal of Jewish Thought and Philosophy* 18 (2010): 56.

79 As Daniel J. Lasker pointed out to me (personal communication), a Christian might say that Jews did not fully understand God's revelations despite all the obvious hints to their real meaning, namely Christianity. I imagine that very few Christians would want to say that Moses himself did not fully understand God's revelation.

3i. Maimonidean Mistakes[80]

We have now shown that according to Maimonides, Moses's theological apprehensions were limited by his humanity. We can also show that there is hardly a Jew alive today who, if pressed, would not admit that Maimonides himself erred on crucial theological issues. In the *Mishneh Torah*'s "Laws Concerning Repentance," iii. 6, Maimonides writes that "The following have no portion in the world to come, but are cut off and perish, and for their great wickedness and sinfulness are condemned forever and ever." In paragraph 7 he specifies one of the groups of people there mentioned:

> Five classes are termed sectarians [*minim*]: he who says that there is no God and that the world has no ruler; he who says that there is a ruling power but that it is vested in two or more persons; he who says that there is one Ruler, but that He has a body and has form; he who denies that He alone is the First Cause and Rock of the universe; likewise he who renders worship to anyone beside Him, to serve as a mediator between the human being and the Lord of the universe. Whoever belongs to any of these five classes is termed a sectarian.[81]

On this text, Maimonides's acerbic critic, R. Abraham ben David (Rabad), writes:

> Why has he called such a person [he who says that there is one Ruler, but that He has a body and has form is] a sectarian? There are many people greater than, and superior to him, who adhere to such a belief on the basis of what they have seen in verses of Scripture, and even more in the words of the aggadot [Talmudic stories] which corrupt right opinion about religious matters.[82]

---

80 As noted above, Maimonides was an extreme intellectual elitist. Hearing me talk about his elitist views once so annoyed my wife that I posted a list of Maimonides's mistakes on our refrigerator so she would be angry with him, not me. His intellectual elitism led the list.

81 I cite the translation of Moses Hyamson (New York: Feldheim, 1974), 84b. Hannah Kasher subjects the terms in this paragraph to detailed analysis in *Al ha-Minim, ha-Kofrim, ve-ha-Epikorsim be-Mishnat ha-Rambam* (Tel Aviv: Ha-Kibbutz ha-Meuhad, 2011). Zev Harvey points out that our paragraph parallels the first five of Maimonides's thirteen principles. See Zev Harvey, "The Question of God's Incorporeality in Maimonides, Rabad, Crescas, and Spinoza," in *Minhah le-Sarah*, ed. in S. Rosenberg et al. (Jerusalem: Magnes, 1994), 63–78 (Hebrew).

82 I cite the text as translated by Isadore Twersky in *Rabad of Posquieres: A Twelfth-Century Talmudist* (Philadelphia: Jewish Publication Society, 1980), 282. A more moderate version of Rabad's gloss has been preserved. See Kellner, *Dogma in Medieval Jewish Thought*, 89.

I do not believe that Rabad was affirming the corporeality of God (after all, those who do believe in divine corporeality are *misled* by Torah verses and aggadot "which corrupt right opinion about religious matters"); rather he was affirming that one is allowed to be mistaken about that issue. However, for Maimonides God's corporeality is an issue about which no one is permitted to remain mistaken, not even "little children, women, and the dull and deficient" (*Guide* i. 35; Pines, 81).[83] The important point for our purposes here is that Rabad recognizes that Maimonides does not allow for inadvertence (*shegagah*) with respect to theological matters. A sincere mistake about God is still a mistake and constitutes heresy. It follows that worship of a god about which one is objectively mistaken is *avodah zarah*.[84]

I would be surprised if many contemporary Jews would accept Maimonides's views on this matter and not those of Rabad. Few would be willing *say* that Maimonides was simply wrong on the fact of God's absolute incorporeality—rather they act on that view. Proof of my claim here is that David Berger is clearly correct: on strict Maimonidean terms, contemporary Habad Hasidism is heretical, and, when pressed, many would be willing to admit that this is correct.[85] Do any other contemporary rabbinic figures in Orthodoxy follow up on that admission and impose upon followers of Ḥabad the considerable restrictions that Maimonides and others would have us impose upon heretics? Hardly.

---

83 Let it be noted that Maimonides, unlike almost all other medieval figures (Jewish, Christian, or Muslim), held women to be fully human, fully created in the image of God. See Menachem Kellner, "Misogyny: Gersonides vs. Maimonides," in *Torah in the Observatory: Gersonides, Maimonides, Song of Songs*, ed. Menachem Kellner (Boston: Academic Studies Press, 2010), 283–304. Maimonides's misogyny is halakhic, not philosophical. Hannah Kasher has recently addressed this issue (with apparently less sympathy for Maimonides) in "Maimonides on the Intellects of Women and Gentiles," in *Interpreting Maimonides*, ed. Charles Manekin and Daniel Davies (Cambridge: Cambridge University Press, 2018), 46–64.

84 In his statement at the end of his "Thirteen Principles" Maimonides defines his principles as dogmas in the strict sense of the term: beliefs taught by the highest religious authority (in this case, the Torah itself), acceptance of which is both a necessary and sufficient condition for both being part of the community of Israel and for achieving a share in the world to come. Rabad clearly understood Maimonides to be insisting that in these matters *shegagah*, inadvertence, cannot play an exculpatory role. Rabad strongly rejects this view of Maimonides's.

85 See David Berger, *The Rebbe, the Messiah, and the Scandal of Orthodox Indifference* (London: Littman Library of Jewish Civilization, 2001); Berger, review of *Must a Jew Believe Anything?*, by Menachem Kellner, *Tradition* 33 (1999): 81–89, and my response in Kellner, *Must a Jew Believe Anything?*, 2nd ed., 127–148.

Lip service is paid to Maimonides's strict criteria of theological orthodoxy, but it is only lip service.[86]

It would be easy to show (and in fact, I have shown[87]) that very few contemporary Orthodox Jews pass Maimonides's own tests for theological orthodoxy. Maimonides erred on important matters, and so can we.

3j. Pluralism, Again

Why can I not simply say that Judaism is true for Jews, Christianity for Christians, and Islam for Muslims? This ignores the ethnic component of Judaism. Just as Maimonides is "also" a rabbi,[88] Judaism is not only a religion, since it is also an ethnicity, whereas Christianity and Islam are indeed "only" religions, that is, faith communities transcending ethnic/national lines. The ethnic component of Judaism is a central part of its religious self-understanding. Jews are both members of a religion and members of a nation. To put the matter simply, Judaism teaches not only that the Torah is God's revelation, but that also that the Jews are God's chosen people. The question of what that latter claim means is no less debated than the meaning of the former, but neither claim is denied by professing Jews.[89]

No less importantly, to say that Judaism is true for Jews, Christianity is true for Christians, and Islam is true for Muslims makes a mockery of the sort of truth we have been seeking here and simply sneaks religious pluralism in through the back door.

Further, I know that I am Jewish only thanks to accidents of birth and upbringing. Several years ago I read Jonathan Haidt's book *The Righteous Mind:*

---

86 On this lip service, see Kellner, *Dogma in Medieval Jewish Thought*, 207–217. Further on this, see Marc Shapiro, *The Limits of Orthodox Theology: Maimonides's Thirteen Principles Reappraised* (London: Littman Library of Jewish Civilization, 2004).

87 See below in chapter 7.

88 Jolene S. Kellner, my lovely wife of fifty years, likes to remind me to tell my students that as much as Maimonides was a philosopher, he was *also* a rabbi.

89 This not the place to go into the matter, but to say that Jews have understood the notion of the chosen people in dramatically different ways is an understatement. See above, chapter 3 and Kellner, *Confrontation*, chapter 7. Since the chosen people doctrine is often used by antisemites, allow me to remind the reader that many nations have made the same claim about themselves. See above chapter 2, note 1. In the context of this chapter, see also the interesting reflections of Paul Mendes-Flohr, "Israel: In Pursuit of Normalcy—Zionism's Ambivalence towards Israel's Election," in *Many Are Chosen: Divine Election and Western Nationalism*, ed. William R. Hutchison and Hatrmut Lehman (Minneapolis: Fortress Press, 1994), 201–224. Mendes-Flohr points to the recent invention of the term "chosen people" and its reliance on Christian self-understanding.

Why Good People are Divided by Politics and Religion, which resonated with me deeply. Haidt shows that our deepest convictions are rarely (if ever) the result of rational argument. Rationality, he maintains, is primarily used to justify our antecedently held positions—positions that are the result of many factors, rational argument often the least of them. Haidt helped me to understand why it is that people whom I respect (and often love) hold views that to me are clearly and evidently wrong. In their eyes, my views are equally wrong (about which, "of course," *they* are wrong). My Judaism may only be an accident of birth and upbringing, and has not remained static over the years, but I have never been tempted to give it up.

Despite knowing all this, I cannot free myself from the strong feeling that Christianity and Islam make demands upon my credulity that Judaism does not. I rarely rely upon Judah Halevi in my Jewish thinking, but here I do: The Khazar king rejects Islam on the grounds that he has no way of judging if the language of the Koran is really as miraculous as the Muslim spokesperson insists (to which I add that so much of the Koran is clearly drawn from earlier Jewish sources). He rejects Christianity on the grounds of its blatant irrationality. Both the king and I, not having been brought up on these beliefs, have no reason to accept them.[90] I am not asserting that Judaism is free of nonsense (would that it were so!), but there seems to be much less of it than in other faiths, when examined from an "objective" (i.e., my) perspective.

3k. Pluralism, yet Again—and Rejected Again

I would like to take one final stab at pluralism since, by personal predilection it is the position with which I am most comfortable. My late mentor and friend, Steven S. Schwarzschild (1924–1989), used to assert (with tongue only partially in cheek) that many people whom he admired (such as Immanuel Kant and the later Sartre) were Jewish non-Jews.[91] Playing on Isaac Deutscher's discussion of non-Jewish Jews (such as Spinoza and Freud)[92] Schwarzschild maintained that ethnicity, religious identification, and practice (or lack thereof)

---

90 For two of many relevant studies by Daniel J. Lasker, see: "Popular Polemics and Philosophical Truth in the Medieval Jewish Critique of Christianity," *Journal of Jewish Thought and Philosophy* 8 (1999): 243–59 and *Jewish Philosophical Polemics against Christianity in the Middle Ages*, 2nd ed. (Oxford: Littman Library of Jewish Civilization, 2007).
91 Kellner, "Steven Schwarzschild, Moses Maimonides, and 'Jewish Non-Jews'" and *Confrontation*, 229–234.
92 On Deutscher see above, chapter 3.

aside, some non-Jewish philosophers were, in effect, philosophically Jewish. By this, he meant that they preached and practiced a form of ethical monotheism.[93]

Let us seek to recast Schwarzschild's point in terms drawn from Maimonides. As noted above, Maimonides innovated the claim that in order to be counted as a member of the Jewish community and in order to earn a share in the world to come, one had to accept thirteen fundamental teachings. I have argued that in order to be consistent, Maimonides would have to admit that only the first five of his "Thirteen Principles" are actually necessary for full membership in the Jewish community.[94] These five are: God' existence, unity, incorporeality, transcendence,[95] and that God alone may be worshiped. A Jew can say, building on and out of Maimonides, that an immoral person (Martin Heidegger comes to mind) cannot really be a philosopher. Thus, to be a Maimonidean Jewish non-Jew is, once again, to be an ethical monotheist. However, if this is enough, why be Jewish? Why not be, in effect, a Noachide, a watered-down Jew?

I fear that I am stuck without pluralism, messianic or otherwise, and will have to make do with tolerance.

31. Final Thoughts

A respected friend who read this chapter for me said that it appears that I am trying to square the circle. That may be a polite way of saying that I am trying to eat my cake and have it, too. Other friends have pointed out that in my day-to-day life I behave like a theological pluralist: trying to live while letting others live (up to a point, of course: I strongly believe that brutality and intolerance must be resisted). I want therefore to restate what I am trying to accomplish in this chapter.

As I said above, if I want to be tolerated as a Jew by individuals many of whose beliefs contrast sharply with core beliefs of historical Judaism, then how can I not tolerate them as well? Why do I want to both tolerate and be tolerated

---

93 Schwarzschild was originally an ordained Reform rabbi, but of a very traditionalist bent—as evidenced by his ultimate membership in the (Conservative) Rabbinical Assembly, and his close relations with two major Orthodox rabbinic figures, Rabbis Joseph Soloveitchik and Issac Hutner (for details, see my introduction to Schwarzschild's *The Pursuit of the Ideal*, 1–14). I do not think that his basic criterion of who a non-Jewish Jew is (emphasis on ethics and philosophical monotheism) is a function of his Reform background. It is, rather, a function of his appreciation of Hermann Cohen.
94 Kellner, *Confrontation*, 233–238.
95 More literally, "ontic precedence."

(in the strong sense of the term used in this chapter)? Above, I defined the strong sense of tolerance as acknowledging that other religions (not just Christianity and Islam) have a singular role in their respective cultures and *inherent religious* worth. Were I willing to withdraw behind the walls of a cultural ghetto, imposed by others or self-imposed, it would then be enough for me to leave others alone in the hope and expectation that they would leave me alone. Were that the case, there would be no problem. But that is not enough. Historically, it was all that could be hoped for.[96] We, however, are challenged to do more.

I want to affirm the truth of Torah, but not be so sure of myself that I can condemn every other view (within and without Judaism) as false. Why affirm the truth of Torah? I recently came across an interesting sentence in Gibbon's *Decline and Fall*: "The various modes of worship, which prevailed in the Roman world, were all considered by the people, as equally true; by the philosopher, as equally false; and by the magistrate, as equally useful."[97] If that is all we sought, this would have been a very short chapter: each of us could undertake to "put up with" the others and be done with it. We seek more.

Thankfully, I will, of course, find truly tolerant (i.e., respectful) partners among many Christians and Muslims, and among followers of other religions. However, they will not be any more representative of their communities than I am of mine. I have had this experience often: engaging in trialogues (Jews, Christians, and Muslims), I find much in common with my fellow participants (despite all the differences between us). We all admit, ruefully, that when we return to our synagogue, church, or mosque it will be hard to find many of our fellow worshipers interested in sharing our respectful openness towards the religious other.

For religious tolerance to be serious, each side must not be expected to relinquish the truth claims of their respective religions. To do so would be to give up devotion to the God of Abraham, Isaac, and Jacob and replace it with intellectual acquiescence to the existence of the God of the philosophers. Instead of speaking to God, we would speak about God. Instead of being believers, we would become metaphysicians. Instead of believing *in* God, we would

---

96 Paul Mendes-Flohr quotes Franz Rosenzweig to the effect that the Christian ignored the Jew in order to be able to tolerate him, and the Jew ignored the Christian in order to allow himself to be tolerated. See Mendes-Flohr, *Jewish Philosophy: An Obituary* (Yarnton: Oxford Centre for Hebrew and Jewish Studies, 1999), 20n24, https://www.ochjs.ac.uk/wp-content/uploads/2011/09/4th-Frank-Green-Lecture-Jewish-Philosophy-An-Obituary.pdf.

97 Edward Gibbon, *The History of the Decline and Fall of the Roman Empire*, abr. ed. (London: Penguin Books, 2000), 35.

believe *that* God exists. Judaism, Christianity, Islam would cease to be sources of knowledge and become only cultural artifacts.⁹⁸

The solution offered here (epistemological modesty about religious beliefs) may satisfy few (it will not satisfy many of the people with whom I pray to God, not about God, in my synagogue), but it allows me (and people like me) to relate to our religions seriously while being truly respectful of others, within Judaism, and without.

I occasionally quote Oliver Cromwell. He (allegedly) exhorted his troops: "Put your trust in God, but keep your powder dry." To me, that sounds like an excellent characterization of Judaism in general and of religious Zionism in particular (*ein somkhin al ha-nes*—trust not in miracles). I shall close here with another Cromwell quote, addressed to all those so confident of their faith that they are dismissive of other faiths (or other understandings of their own faiths): "I beseech you, in the bowels of Christ, think it possible you may be mistaken."⁹⁹

---

98 This paragraph owes much to Alexander Altmann, "The God of Religion, the God of Metaphysics, and Wittgenstein's 'Language Games,'" *Zeitschrift für Religions- und Geistesgeschichte* 39 (1987): 289–306. Buber's distinction between belief *in* and belief *that* is developed in Kellner, *Must a Jew Believe Anything?*, chapter 1.

99 For both Cromwell quotes, see https://en.wikiquote.org/wiki/Oliver_Cromwell.

CHAPTER 7

Christianity

1. THESIS

My thesis is simple: without exception, rabbinic authorities who convict Christianity of *avodah zarah* (idolatry; literally, alien/foreign worship) rely on Maimonides to do so. Logical consistency and intellectual honesty would then demand that they must also convict Nahmanides, Kabbalists, Hasidim, R. Haim of Volozhin (1749–1821), and much of the so-called Lithuanian yeshiva world and many others of *avodah zarah*.[1] Put another way, my argument here is that Maimonides's views on the nature of *avodah zarah* are problematic for anyone who subscribes to those aspects of contemporary Judaism that are infused with Kabbalah. Most aspects of contemporary Judaism (not just Orthodoxy) are infused with Kabbalah. The question arises: Why condemn Christianity as *avodah zarah* on Maimonidean grounds while giving a pass to Kabbalah-inflected Judaisms?

Not giving such Judaisms a pass is a heavy price to pay for the "pleasure" of condemning Christians as idolaters. I will show that if we follow Maimonides in convicting Christians of idolatry, we cannot avoid convicting all those listed above. I personally have no interest in condemning Christians or Kabbalists of idolatry. It is not that I am in particular an admirer of Christianity as such, or that I think that it is true and Judaism false (heaven forfend!), or that I am some sort of religious pluralist;[2] rather, for a number of reasons I see no point in calling Christianity idolatry. We will see below that the Talmudic sages themselves realized that idolatry as understood in the Bible was no longer a live option or a real threat. If that was true then, it is all the more so true today. Idols of wood and stone are not the challenge we face today, nor is worship of heavenly bodies.

---

1 I will briefly treat of Nahmanides and other Kabbalists below. For R. Haim, see his *Nefesh ha Hayyim* (Bnai Brak, 2009), gate 1, chapter 3 (p. 4); chapter 9 (p. 33); chapter 22 (p. 75); and gate 2, chapter 6 (p. 105), among many, many examples.
2 See chapter 6 above, and Menachem Kellner and Jolene Kellner, "Respectful Disagreement: A Response to Raphael Jospe," in Goshen-Gottstein and Korn, *Jewish Theology and World Religions*, 123–133.

However, worship of false ideals certainly is.³ Our struggle with idolatry should focus on that, not on followers of Jesus of Nazareth, however mistaken we find them to be.

Beyond that, I will show here, almost no one actually follows Maimonides in his thinking about the nature of God and of faith in God.⁴ Such thinking led him to denounce Christianity as idolatry—but it would also lead him to denounce almost all those living Jews who take their Judaism seriously as idolaters. If you do not want to follow Maimonides there, how in good conscience can you follow him in seeing Christianity as idolatry?

The general question, What constitutes idolatry?, is of great contemporary relevance in Israel: growing ties with Hindu India raise questions about the relevance of classic views of idolatry; the constantly growing contributions of evangelical Christian organizations to Israeli Jewish institutions raise questions about whether or not Christianity should be treated as idolatry.⁵ I know

---

3   See Kenneth Seeskin, *No Other Gods: The Modern Struggle Against Idolatry* (New York: Behrman House, 1995).

4   Aside from paying lip service to his views, how many Jews really follow the consequences of Maimonides's understanding on the nature of Jewish faith? The clearest proof that few do is that while David Berger's attack on Habad is clearly on the mark in Maimonidean terms, no other rabbi has publicly supported him. For details see the previous chapter, footnote 85.

5   The question of whether or not Christianity is *avodah zarah* usually arises in the following contexts: May one enter a church? For one detailed discussion—published under the auspices of the Orthodox Union's Israel Center—see the sources found under the title "Entering Churches and Mosques" at https://www.rabbimanning.com/wp-content/uploads/2016/04/Online-Web-Resources-2016.pdf. May one participate in a Christian ceremony (see the previous source)? May one accept financial support from Christians and Christian institutions? This latter issue comes up often in Israel today. Prominent opponents include R. Shomo Aviner (see forty-two separate pages on his extreme opposition to Christianity at http://shlomo-aviner.net/index.php/%D7%A7%D7%98%D7%92%D7%95%D7%A8%D7%99%D7%94:%D7%A0%D7%A6%D7%A8%D7%95%D7%AA_(%D7%9E%D7%90%D7%9E%D7%A8%D7%99%D7%9D) and R. Eliyahu Zini who devoted a whole book to denouncing the practice—*Hesed le-Umim Hatat* (Haifa: Yeshivat Or Vishua, 2018). Rabbi Eliezer Melamed (an Israeli Orthodox rabbi and the rosh yeshiva of Yeshivat Har Bracha, rabbi of the community Har Bracha, and author of the book series Peninei Halakhah) published three article in the (settler) newspaper *Ba-Sheva* (see: https://www.inn.co.il/News/News.aspx/277905) in which he uses quotations from Rav Kook to support a basically universalist approach to non-Jews. His main concern is to argue that philo-Jewish evangelicals are sincere and that Jews may accept financial support from them. Catholics, he maintains (correctly), do not treat statues in their churches as idols, and do not pray to them. He goes so far as to surmise that even Maimonides would be lenient with respect to Protestants. His articles were subjected to detailed, even ferocious, criticism by Rabbi Yehonatan Simhah Blass, "Contributions of Evangelicals and the Law Forbidding Expressions of Gratitude to Priests," *Tehumin* 34 (Sivan 5774/June 2014): 214–224 (Hebrew). Strictly

nothing about Hinduism and will leave that discussion to experts who know what they are talking about. Here I wish to deal with the claim that Christianity (in all or some of its many, many forms)[6] is to be considered *avodah zarah*. It should be emphasized that this is not a light matter in Jewish eyes: *avodah zarah* is one of the three so-called "cardinal sins" of Judaism: it is settled law that one must submit to martyrdom rather than engage in *avodah zarah*, murder, or commit certain forms of gross sexual immorality.[7] Whether or not Christianity is considered *avodah zarah* is also a significant matter considering the vast numbers of Jews who over the generations who were murdered by Christians (as Christians) or who chose martyrdom over forced conversion to Christianity.[8]

Let me begin by making two "meta-halakhic" assertions. First, despite what many Orthodox rabbis will tell you, halakhah has a history. Second, as such it is not a mathematical science, but halakhic decisions reflect the ideological commitments of those making them. This last point is reflected in Blu Greenberg's famous (if perhaps exaggerated) comment that "Where *there's a rabbinic will, there's a halakhic way.*"

---

speaking, if Christianity is *avodah zarah*, then no business may be conducted with Christians in Israel on Sundays, or three days before Sunday (Mishnah AZ, chapter 1). I know of no rabbi who actually decides halakhah in this fashion. Many of the most strident opponents of accepting financial or other assistance from Christians (because Christianity is idolatry) claim to be followers of Rav Kook the elder. For an analysis of his actual views see Karma Ben-Johanan, "Wreaking Judgment on Mt. Esau: Christianity in R. Kook's Thought," *Jewish Quarterly Review* 106 (2016): 76–100 and the sources cited there. The views of his son, Rabbi Z. Y. Kook, are presented in *Yahadut ve-Nazrut* (Judaism and Christianity), ed. Shlomo Aviner (Jerusalem: Sifriyat Hannah, 2001).

6   I will ignore the fact that there is no such thing as "Christianity" *simpliciter*—in this I follow most of the many rabbis to whose writings I will allude here. It is equally true that there is no such thing as Judaism *simpliciter*, of course.

7   On the three "cardinal sins" see: Maimonides, "Laws of the Foundations of the Torah," v. 2 and above, chapter 6.

8   It ought to be noted that a minority of Orthodox rabbis (some of them quite prominent) argue that Christianity is not *avodah zarah*. See, for example, Chief Rabbi Isaac Herzog, "The Rights of Minorities According to Halakhah," *Tehumin* 2 (1981): 169–199 (Hebrew); and Marc Shapiro, "Is It Permissible to Enter a Church? First Publication of a Responsum by Ha-Ga'on R. Eliezer Berkovitz on the Matter," *Milin Havivin* 4 (2011): 43–50. Note further the views of Nachum Rabinovitch (*Melumedei Milhamah* [Ma'aleh Adumim: Ma'aliyot, 1992], 145) and David Shapiro, *Studies in Jewish Thought*, vol. 2 (New York: Yeshiva University Press, 1981), 272–275. It may not be a coincidence that all four of these figures reached rabbinic maturity outside of Israel. See further the "Orthodox Rabbinic Statement on Christianity," CJCUC.org, December 3, 2015, http://cjcuc.org/2015/12/03/orthodox-rabbinic-statement-on-christianity/. The five dozen Orthodox rabbis who signed this statement, some of them prominent, do not reject Christianity as *avodah zarah*.

2. CHRISTIANITY/IDOLATRY?

Such being the case, questions concerning the claim that Christianity is idolatry immediately arise: first, our contemporaries *could* choose to follow the widely accepted dictum that the ancient rabbis destroyed the evil inclination for idolatry.[9] This being the case, there is no real idolatry anymore—rather, contemporary "idolaters" are simply aping, as it were, their forbears, not actually worshiping idols or other false gods. Second, one *could* choose to follow the views of Menahem ha-Me'iri (1249–1310) who made something like the following argument: true idolatry always involves morally corrupt behavior; our Christian neighbors are not morally corrupt; therefore, Christianity is not true idolatry.[10] In effect, Me'ri anticipated Martin Luther King, Jr.: individuals should be judged by the content of their characters, not by the church that they attend. Mei'iri moves the discussion from idolatry to idolaters, from a class to individuals. Individuals whose religion makes them brutal, or allows them to be brutal, are idolaters and their religion is therefore idolatry. People whose religion does not make them brutal, or allow them to be brutal, are not idolaters, and their religion is not idolatry.[11] This contrasts with the view of Maimonides, who, in many of his writings, focuses on the theology of idolatry, and less on the practice of idolatry. Maimonides changes the focus of idolatry from forbidden behavior to philosophical error.[12] This is, of course, consistent

---

9 AZ 17a-b; Sanh. 64a; Yoma 69b. Compare Sanh. 102b, which implies that the evil inclination for idolatry was strong during the period of the First Temple, but no longer since its destruction. See further Yitzhak Melamed, "Idolatry and Its Premature Rabbinic Obituary," in *Jewish Philosophy Past and Present: Contemporary Responses to Classical Sources*, ed. Daniel Frank and Aaron Segal (New York: Routledge, 2017), 126–37, 127. On the expansion of the dictum mentioned here (which originally referred only to idolaters in the land of Israel), see Jacob Katz, "The Vicissitudes of Three Apologetic Statements" *Zion* 23 (1959): 186–193 (Hebrew).

10 The literature on Me'iri is vast. It is sufficient here to recommend Alon Goshen-Gottstein's treatment and the sources he cites and discusses in *Same God, Other God* (New York: Palgrave Macmillan, 2016), 107–131, and, in addition, Gerald Blidstein, "Menachem Meiri's Attitude towards Gentiles—Apologetics or Worldview?" *Zion* 51 (1985): 153–166 (Hebrew), Moshe Halbertal, "'Ones Possessed of Religion': Religious Tolerance in the Teaching of the Meiri," *Me'orot* 1 no. 1 (2000): 1–24, and Gedaliah Oren, "R. Menahem Ha-Meiri's Attitude toward the 'Other,'" *Da'at* 60 (2007): 29–49 (Hebrew).

11 Me'iri ignores Christians who behave brutally. One can make the reasonable argument that since some Christians behave morally and some immorally, Christianity is not the decisive factor in their behavior, whatever they themselves might think. A similar argument must be made with respect to brutal and immoral Jews.

12 This is the overall thesis of my *Must a Jew Believe Anything?* In the context of idolatry, see Moshe Halbertal and Avishai Margalit, *Idolatry* (Cambridge, MA: Harvard University

with his attempt to "theologify" Judaism (an attempt that, to my mind, has had unfortunate consequences). Me'iri, on the other hand, replaces a theological criterion with a moral criterion. It is not my place here to decide who is more "correct," Maimonides or Me'iri, only to point out that both views are found in the tradition. Personally, I have argued (in *Must a Jew Believe Anything?*) against Maimonides's attempt to turn Judaism into a "synagogue of true believers," but that issue need not detain us at this point—we simply need to be aware of what he is doing.

With respect to the first of these questions, the issue should be quite simple; the Talmud teaches us that contemporary idolaters are not really idolaters, since the evil impulse of idolatry has been extirpated from the cosmos. But, and there is always a but, that is not the way halakhah works. Relatively isolated aggadic statements such as the one about the extirpation of the idolatrous impulse are often ignored or explained away (unless they involve discrimination against women, in which case they are made core values of Judaism, dating back to Sinai, as it were), but "hard-core" halakhah is not so easy to ignore, especially when it makes cultural and historical sense.

A propos Me'iri, a huge amount of energy has been invested in arguing that he did not really mean what he wrote. On the face of it, this has involved generous portions of special pleading and disingenuous argumentation.[13] I will not involve myself in that argument here; instead, I refer the reader to what I take to be convincing refutations of these attempts.[14]

Further, as discussed above, the vast majority of medieval and early modern decisors in Ashkenaz found a middle path, originally charted by the

---

Press, 1992), 31. For Maimonides, heresy is the opposite of knowledge, not the opposite of belief. Contrasting Maimonides's relatively benign view of the nature of Muslim practice (such as throwing stones at the Kaba in Mecca), with his condemnation of Christianity without reference to its rituals, sharpens my point here. On Maimonides's exoneration of Islam from the charge of idolatry, see his Responsum to Ovadiah the Proselyte, cited and discussed in Diamond, *Converts, Heretics, and Lepers*, 11–31 and above, chapter 4.

13 The earliest example of this with which I am familiar is an article by J. David Bleich, "Divine Unity in Maimonides, the Tosafists, and Me'iri," in *Neoplatonism and Jewish Thought*, ed. Lenn Goodman (Albany: SUNY Press, 1992), 237–254. It might be argued that since Meiri was largely unknown to the halakhic tradition until only recently, that there is no reason for halakhic decisors to factor his views into their positions. Nevertheless, many of the rabbis who reject Christianity as idolatry belong to the (allegedly) more modern camp (as opposed to the Haredi world that has a hard time integrating Meiri into its outlook). Thus, they *could* use Mei'iri as a precedent vis-à-vis Christianity. They *choose* not to.

14 See above, note 10.

Tosafists: Christianity is *avodah zarah* when practiced by Jews, but not when practiced by Gentiles.[15]

What appears to follow from all this is that contemporary rabbinic figures who condemn Christianity as idolatry are not *forced* to do so; they *choose* to do so. Why? It seems to me that the answer is obvious. By any measure, Christianity is closer to Judaism than is Buddhism. Christianity has a personal God, thinks of itself as monotheist, and acknowledges the sanctity of Tanakh. In North America, at least, Buddhism appears to be a greater challenge to Jewish continuity than does Xianity: there are certainly far more JUBUs (Jewish Buddhists) than Jews for Jesus. Despite all that, in the Jewish community, the former usually arouse no more than a tolerant smile, while Jews for Jesus arouse great anger. Why? The reason appears to be clear: how many Jews were murdered in the name of Buddha as opposed to those murdered in the name of Jesus? Further, Buddhism does not present itself as the fulfillment of Judaism, and Buddhists do not claim to be *verus Israel*.

3. CHRISTIANITY/IDOLATRY—MAIMONIDES

I trust that most of you reading this book (at least those of you who have not yet torn their hair out) will find this explanation convincing. However, halakhah does not work in this fashion. Precedent must be found for halakhic decisions. As it turns out, there is a very clear precedent for the claim that Christianity is idolatry in the writings of the greatest halakhist of all time, Maimonides. All the sources I have found which claim that Christianity is idolatry begin their analyses with Maimonides.[16]

Thus, even though it was Maimonides, the Andalusian, who convicted Christianity of idolatry, his decision was widely (but not universally) adopted in an Ashkenazi Europe whose Jews suffered great persecution in Christendom, and who were familiar, to one degree or another, with aspects of Christianity.[17]

While I cannot claim to have made an exhaustive survey of every rabbinic authority who condemns Christianity as idolatry, I have certainly examined quite a few. I have yet to find an exception to the following statement: Maimonides is the halakhic authority upon whom all others base their claim that

---

15 See above, chapter 6.
16 For an exhaustive survey for places in which Maimonides treats of Christianity, see Dror Fixler and Gil Nadal, "Are Christians Today Idolaters?" *Tehumin* 22 (2002): 68–78 (Hebrew).
17 Here is a good place to inform readers that Maimonides himself knew more about Christianity than is often thought to be the case. See Lasker, "Rashi and Maimonides on Christianity."

Christianity is idolatry—and those who deny that Christianity is idolatry are forced to contend with Maimonides.[18] Maimonides, however, does not explain his position at all.[19] He simply repeatedly states that Christianity is idolatry and accepts the halakhic consequences of that view (including forbidding the conducting of business with Christians three days before Sundays—their idolatrous holiday—using wine touched by Christians, entering their places of worship, etc.),[20] but he never explains why he condemns Christianity as idolatry.

It is, of course, not hard to understand why he would do so: the *doctrines* of incarnation, trinity, and virgin birth are enough in themselves to explain why Maimonides (and not only Maimonides) would likely view Christianity as out-and-out idolatry. That he was probably aware of Christian *practices* such as image worship, veneration of relics, and so forth, only makes it easier to understand why he would condemn Christianity as *avodah zarah*.

There are, however, a number of texts from which one can deduce the reasons for Maimonides's opposition to Christianity. I propose to examine them, one by one, in the order in which Maimonides wrote them. These texts are not part of the standard yeshiva syllabus and are often ignored by halakhists.

4. OBJECTION

At this point it is necessary to note a possible objection to the line of argument I am developing here. According to my argument, halakhists after Maimonides ignored his own reasons for his positions, and treated them as technical precedents without reference to why he arrived at them himself. (This parallels my arguments in *Dogma* and in *Must a Jew Believe Anything?*, to the effect that Maimonides's principles of faith were accepted—to the extent they *were* accepted—shorn of their philosophical basis.) Might it not be countered that in his halakhic writings Maimonides does precisely what I accuse subsequent halakhists of doing, namely, deciding halakhah technically according to accepted rules, with no reference to the philosophic basis that (possibly) motivated the halakhic opinions adopted? This is a large issue, and here I can only deal with it schematically.

---

18 Maimonides does not view Christianity solely through the lens of idolatry. He saw Christianity as part of God's plan to prepare the world for the coming of the (true) messiah; see "Laws of Kings," xi. 4 (in the uncensored texts), quoted above, chapter 6.
19 As noted in Fixler and Nidal, "Are Christians Today Idolaters?": 70, 71.
20 Like many people I know, I was raised with the clear understanding that it was forbidden to enter a church.

First, unlike in "standard" halakhah, in the two cases here mentioned (the principles of faith, the status of Christianity), Maimonides breaks new ground and is not simply applying standard decision procedures (*kelalei ha-psak*). It therefore makes excellent sense for halakhists also to wonder why he arrived at his positions.[21] Second, it is not the case that Maimonides's halakhah is divorced from his philosophy: witness the first four chapters of *Mishneh Torah* ("Laws of the Foundations of the Torah," i–iv); the final paragraphs of each of the fourteen volumes of the *Mishneh Torah*;[22] the evidence adduced by Marc Shapiro for the influence of philosophy/science on Maimonides's halakhot concerning what we would call superstition;[23] and generally the investigations of David Hartman and Isadore Twersky on the interplay of law and philosophy in Maimonides's writings.[24] Furthermore, I have argued at great length in my book *Maimonides's Confrontation with Mysticism* that many of Maimonides's philosophical *and* halakhic positions reflect his opposition to what I there call "proto-Kabbalah." I further show there that Maimonides, on philosophical grounds, adopted a form of halakhic nominalism.[25] His philosophy definitely affected his halakhah, and there is no reason to think that such would not be the case with respect to his views on Christianity.

---

21 But, in fact, they do not, at least so far as I could determine. It is not much use to examine those of his commentators who searched for his precedents, since printed editions of the *Mishneh Torah* generally have "idolaters" (*aku"m*—worshipers of stars and constellations) where Maimonides wrote "Christians." Those copyists and printers who replaced "Christians" with *aku"m* apparently thought that Christianity was *avodah zarah*.

22 The subject of Kellner and Gillis, *Maimonides the Universalist*.

23 *Studies in Maimonides and His Interpreters* (Scranton: University of Scranton Press, 2008).

24 David Hartman, *Maimonides: Torah and Philosophic Quest* (Philadelphia: Jewish Publication Society, 1976) and Isadore Twersky, *Introduction to the Code of Maimonides*, chapter 6, "Law and Philosophy."

25 See Yochanan Silman, *Bein "Lalekhet be-Derakhav" O Lishmo'a be-Kolo"* [Halakhic Instructions—as Guiding Principles or as Commands] (Alon Shvut: Herzog College, 2012) (Hebrew); "Commandments and Transgressions in Halakhah—Obedience and Rebellion, or Repair and Destruction?," *Dine Israel* 16 (1991): 183–201; "Halakhic Determinations of a Nominalistic and Realistic Nature: Legal and Philosophical Considerations," *Dine Israel* 12 (1986): 249–266; and *Kol Gadol ve-Lo Yasaf: Torat Yisrael Bein Shelemut ve*-Hishtalmust (Jerusalem: Magnes, 1999)—all in Hebrew—and "Introduction to the Philosophical Analysis of the Normative-Ontological Tension in the Halakha," *Da'at* 31 (1993): v–xx. The reading of Maimonides which Silman and I present has recently been given extensive grounding in a wide variety of texts in Yohai Makbili, "Consciousness and Community: Ritual Impurity and Purity in Maimonides's Thought" (PhD diss., University of Haifa, 2018; Hebrew). The nominalist understanding of halakhah has been traced back to rabbinic sources in Christine F. Hayes, *What's Divine about Divine Law? Early Perspectives* (Princeton: Princeton University Press, 2015).

5. SO, WHAT IS IDOLATRY FOR MAIMONIDES?

In "Laws of Idolatry," ii. 1 Maimonides explains that the essential definition of *avodah zarah* is the worship of any entity other than God. It behooves us therefore to investigate what might count for Maimonides as an entity other than God for purposes of worship. Before beginning a survey of such texts, I will cite one text from near the end of the *Guide of the Perplexed* (iii. 51; Pines, 620) to set the scene for our discussion (and, by the by, to help us understand what Maimonides means by perfect worship):

> So I'll return to this chapter's theme: having come to know God as I've described, gaining the strength to focus on Him alone. This is the special worship of those who apprehend reality. The more they focus on Him and on abiding in His presence the more profound their worship. But one who has all sort of notions about God and has much to say about Him without real knowledge, pursuing some fantasy or someone's dogma, is not just outside the palace and far removed from it but, in my view, does not really speak or think of God at all. For what he speaks of and fancies corresponds to nothing whatever. It's a figment of his imagination, as I explained.

Thus, worship of an entity which is not one and unique in every sense of the term, to which corporeality attaches in any sense of the term, an entity susceptible to passions, an entity which can be changed or swayed, an entity which can love (the Jewish people), an entity which has needs—such worship is *avodah zarah* according to Maimonides.[26] On this account, there are very few Orthodox Jews who are not worshipers of *avodah zarah*.

Technically speaking, for Maimonides *avodah zarah* means worshiping any created thing, even if the worshiper knows that behind or above the worshiped entity, there exists God the Creator ("Laws Concerning Idolatry," ii. 1). However, Maimonides also treats idolatry generally as denial of the "great principle" upon which all depends ("Idolatry," ii. 6 and "Laws of the Foundations of the Torah," i. 6—the nature of that "great principle" will be treated below).

---

26 While Maimonides devotes much attention to the obligation to love God, I have seen only one place where he mentions God's love of any of His creatures (drawn to my attention by Zev Harvey): "Laws of Idolatry" i. 3, near the end. This is quite remarkable in light of the prevalence of expressions of God's love for His people in the Jewish liturgy, not to mention in the blessings of the Shema. Maimonides was consistent in denying to God any human affections.

Beyond that, Maimonides holds belief in God's corporeality to be worse than idolatry (*Guide* i. 36) (since such belief denies God's unity).[27] He also expands the notion of idolatry to include magical practices, such as the use of talismans, the belief in spirits that can be caused to descend and affect us, demons, desert ghouls, and other such phenomena (*Guide* iii. 29; Pines, 517–518).

6. MAIMONIDEAN MONOTHEISM

Let us now turn to our survey. In his commentary to the Mishnah Maimonides famously presents his thirteen foundations of faith. He puts them forward as dogmas in the strictest sense of the term.[28] The first five all relate to God:

- The first foundation is the existence of the Creator, may He be praised. … He is self-sufficient.
- The second foundation is God's unity, may He be exalted; to wit, that this One, Who is the cause of [the existence of] everything is one. … Rather, He, may He be exalted, is one with a oneness for which there is no comparison at all.
- The third foundation is the denial of corporeality to Him; to wit that this One is neither a body nor a force within a body. None of the characteristics of a body appertains to Him, either by His essence or as an accident thereof.
- The fourth foundation is God's precedence;[29] to wit, that this one who has just been described is He who precedes everything absolutely. No other being has precedence with respect to Him.
- The fifth foundation is that He, may He be exalted, is He whom it is proper to worship and to praise; and [that it is also proper] to promulgate praise of Him and obedience to Him. This may not be done for any being other than Him in reality. … Do not, furthermore, seize upon intermediaries in order to reach Him but direct your thoughts towards Him, may He be exalted, and turn away from that which is other than

---

27 Harry Wolfson, "Maimonides on the Unity and Incorporeality of God," *JQR* 56 (1965): 112–136, and *Guide* ii. 31: idolatry is forbidden in order to protect God's unity (Pines, 539)
28 See his statement at the end of the principles (*Must a Jew Believe Anything?*, 173–174) and my analysis of that text in chapter 4 of that book.
29 In the original version of this foundation, Maimonides spoke only of God's logical precedence to the cosmos (the view of Aristotle); later in his life, he added a sentence explicitly referring to creation. For details, see Kellner, *Dogma*, 54–61.

He. This fifth foundation is the prohibition against idolatry and there are many verses in the Torah prohibiting it.[30]

The upshot of these five dogmas is that God is absolutely one, unique, incorporeal, creator of the cosmos (and as such wholly unlike creation), and, crucially for our purposes, to be worshiped directly, without intermediaries. Prayers may not be addressed to angels (as in the Friday eve hymn "Shalom Aleichem"),[31] to sefirot,[32] and certainly may not be addressed to God via various types of rabbis, rebbes, miracle workers, and the like.[33]

In his *Mishneh Torah* Maimonides restates his principles and in so doing adds to our understanding of his notion of idolatry. The first of these places is indirect, but very important. It is the very opening of the work as a whole:

> The foundation of all foundations and the pillar of all sciences[34] is to realize that there is a First Being who brought every existing thing into being. All existing things, whether celestial, terrestrial, or belonging to an intermediate class, exist only through His true Existence. If it could be supposed that He did not exist, it would follow that nothing else could possibly exist. If, however, it were supposed that all other beings were non-existent, He alone would still exist. Their non-existence would not involve His non-existence. For all beings are in need of Him; but He, blessed be He, *is not in need of them nor of any of them*.[35]

God's existence is necessary; that of all created things, contingent. By definition, therefore, God is not and cannot be in need of anything outside of God.

---

30 I cite the translation as brought in *Must a Jew Believe Anything?*, 164ff.
31 Technically speaking, there is no prayer to angels in this hymn, but they are beseeched for blessings, which is no better in Maimonides's view.
32 Moshe Idel describes sefirot as "manifestations that are either part of the divine structure, or directly related to the divine essence, serving as its vessels or instruments." See his *Kabbalah: New Perspectives* (New Haven: Yale University Press, 1988), 112. Unless taken as entirely metaphorical (which is not the way it is generally taken in kabbalistic texts), the doctrine of sefirot must undermine God's unity, even without reference to the question of whether or not prayers be addressed to them. For more on this, see Tzahi Weiss, "Prayers to Angels and the Early Sefirotic Literature," *Jewish Studies Quarterly* 27 (2020): 22–35.
33 For striking examples of this sort of behavior, see Joel Marcus, "The Once and Future Messiah in Early Christianity and Chabad," *New Testament Studies* 46 (2000): 381–401.
34 For a very detailed exposition of this text, see Kellner, *Gam Hem*, chapters 2–5. The word "science," of course, means something different for us than it did for Maimonides.
35 I cite here and below the translation of Moses Hyamson (New York: Feldheim, 1974), with emendations (and emphasis added).

Worshipping a god for whom the commandments of the Torah are a need (*mizvot tzorekh gavoha*)[36] is to worship an entity other than God, that is, to engage in *avodah zarah*.

Maimonides continues:

> This being is the God of the Universe, the Lord of all the Earth. And He it is, who controls the sphere with a power that is without end or limit; with a power that is never intermitted. For the sphere is always revolving; and it is impossible for it to revolve without someone making it revolve. God, blessed be He, it is, who, without hand or body, causes it to revolve. Knowing this thing is an affirmative precept, as it is said *I am the Lord, thy God* (Exod. 20:2; Deut. 5:6). And whoever permits the thought to enter his mind that there is another deity besides this God, violates a prohibition; as it is said *Thou shalt have no other gods before me* (Exod. 20:3; Deut. 5:7), and denies the essence of Religion—this doctrine being the great principle on which everything depends.[37]

It is very important to understand the upshot of this paragraph: the first commandment of the 613 commandments of the Torah is to know something. And what is that thing? That God is Lord of all the earth. And how do we know it? On the basis of an argument relying upon the notion of an uncreated universe (as Maimonides makes clear in *Guide of the Perplexed* i. 71). The God Who is to be worshiped without intermediaries, is the God Whose existence must be *known* on the basis of a philosophical argument. Any other object of worship is not God, but an imagining, and, once again, *avodah zarah*.[38]

---

36 See Morris Faierstein, "God's Need for the Commandments' in Medieval Kabbalah," *Conservative Judaism* 36 (1982): 45–59. For further background on this, see Kellner, "Tabernacle, Sacrifices, and Judaism: Maimonides vs. Nahmanides," The Torah.com, March 2020, https://www.thetorah.com/article/tabernacle-sacrifices-and-judaism-maimonides-vs-nahmanides.

37 Hebrew: *ve-kofer ba-ikkar, she-zehu ha-ikkar ha-gadol she-hakol talui bo*. Note well how Maimonides converts the expression *kofer be-ikkar* from disassociating oneself from the Jewish community (as in the wicked son of the Passover Haggadah), to a theological stance. See *Must a Jew Believe Anything?*, 41n27.

38 Let it be noted that in *Guide* i. 34 (Pines, 75–76) Maimonides may have modified this conclusion somewhat. There he distinguishes between fulfilling the first commandment and satisfying the first principle of faith (knowing correctly that God exists) on the one hand, and avoiding idolatry on the second. In that passage, one can fail to know God properly without being an out-and-out idolater. However, even there, God is to be known through a study of creation (that is, physics). See the text cited from *Guide* i. 34 below.

Further on, Maimonides states:

> Since it has been demonstrated that He is not a body, it is clear that none of the accidents of matter can be attributed to Him. ... Nor does He change, for there is nought in Him that would effect a change in Him. He does not die, nor has He life like that of an animal body. Folly is not an attribute of His Being, nor wisdom, like that of a wise man; neither passion nor frivolity; neither joy nor melancholy; neither silence nor speech like that of human beings. And so the sages have said, "Above, there is neither sitting nor standing, neither rigidity nor relaxation."

Change cannot affect a purely incorporeal entity, especially one that is perfect in every possible way. That being so, God cannot change in any way whatsoever. Furthermore, a changeable god is not perfect as he is, and is therefore not God. To have emotions is to change, to be *moved*.[39] A god subject to emotions like joy and melancholy is not God, as is a god who can be swayed by prayer or repentance. A true God is not one the inner workings of which can be aided, as it were, by human actions (be such actions prayer or the fulfillment of the commandments of the Torah). A god subject to theurgy is not God, but the object of *avodah zarah*.[40]

The fourth of the five parts into which the first volume of the *Mishneh Torah* is divided is 'Laws Concerning Idolatry." Maimonides opens that part with a long historical disquisition on the origins of idolatry—in effect, a natural history of idolatry. This is necessitated by the fact that it is difficult to understand how idolatry arose: after all, the first humans according to the biblical account (Adam and Eve) were certainly not idolaters—so where did it come from?[41] Maimonides presents idolatry here as the outcome of a philosophical mistake. This has an important consequence for our purposes: *avodah zarah* is mistaken worship, not foreign or alien worship (although such worship is

---

39 Note well: attributing personality traits to God is no better than attributing corporeality to Him (ibid. i. 53; Pines, 119–120).
40 On theurgy in Kabbalah, which Moshe Idel defines as "operations intended to influence the Divinity, mostly in its own inner state or dynamics, but sometimes also in its relationship to man," see his *Kabbalah: New Perspectives* (New Haven: Yale University Press, 1988), 173–199. The quotation above is from p. 157. Maimonides seeks a God above all things human, especially emotion. Note: the English term "emotion" (being *moved*), like the medieval Hebrew *hitpa'alut* and the modern Hebrew *hitragshut*, all refer to responses to outside stimuli.
41 For the text, see above in chapter 1 and, for a detailed analysis of it, *Confrontation*, 77–79.

definitely foreign and alien). Thus, one who worships a god conceived incorrectly is performing *avodah zarah*.

Moving on in the *Mishneh Torah*, in "Laws Concerning Repentance," iii. 6, Maimonides writes that "The following have no portion in the world to come, but are cut off and perish, and for their great wickedness and sinfulness are condemned forever and ever." In paragraph 7 he specifies one of the groups of people here mentioned include *minim*:

> [H]e who says that there is no God and that the world has no ruler; he who says that there is a ruling power but that it is vested in two or more persons; he who says that there is one Ruler, but that He has a body and has form; he who denies that He alone is the First Cause and Rock of the universe; likewise he who renders worship to anyone beside Him, to serve as a mediator between the human being and the Lord of the universe. Whoever belongs to any of these five classes is termed a sectarian.[42]

On this text, as we noted above (chapter 3), Maimonides's acerbic critic, R. Abraham ben David (Rabad), writes:

> Why has he called such a person [he who says that there is one Ruler, but that He has a body and has form] a sectarian? There are many people greater than, and superior to him, who adhere to such a belief on the basis of what they have seen in verses of Scripture, and even more in the words of the aggadot which corrupt right opinion about religious matters.

As I stated above, I do not believe that Rabad was affirming the corporeality of God (after all, those who do believe in divine corporeality are *misled* by Torah verses and aggadot "which corrupt right opinion about religious matters"); rather he was affirming that one is allowed to be mistaken about that issue. But for Maimonides, God's corporeality is an issue about which no one is permitted to remain mistaken, not even "little children, women, and the dull and

---

42 Hyamson, *Book of Knowledge*, 84b. Hannah Kasher subjects the terms in this paragraph to detailed analysis in *Al ha-Minim*. Note well, please, that Maimonides's discussion in this text relates to positions that it is forbidden to hold *publicly* (following the Mishnah in Sanh. X.1, he introduces the various forbidden positions with the term *ha-omer*, "one who says"). For discussion, see Kellner, "Must We Have Heretics?," *Conversations* 1 (2008): 6–10, https://www.jewishideas.org/article/must-we-have-heretics.

Christianity | 151

deficient" (*Guide* i. 35; Pines, 81).⁴³ The important point for our purposes here is that Rabad recognizes that Maimonides does not allow for inadvertence (*shegagah*) with respect to theological matters. A sincere mistake about God is still a mistake and constitutes heresy. It follows that worship of a god about which one is objectively mistaken is *avodah zarah*.⁴⁴

The points we have made so far are all based on texts drawn from Maimonides's commentary on the Mishnah and his *Mishneh Torah*. Emphasis on the rejection of *avodah zarah* as divergences from philosophical orthodoxy, as it were, is even more clear-cut in the *Guide of the Perplexed*. Let us examine a few passages in the *Guide*:

> For nothing exists but God and His creations—everything besides God; and there's no way of knowing Him but through His creations. They are the evidence for His existence and what we should believe—what should be affirmed or denied of Him. That means one must study the world and learn all about its true nature, explore every field to gather the sure and solid premises to support our theological inquiries. ... With cosmology and natural science, I don't think you'll have trouble seeing how vital such knowledge of the world is to understanding the real and not fanciful workings of God's rule. ... Anyone aspiring to human fulfillment must train in logic first, then in mathematics in due sequence, then in the natural sciences, and then in theology. (i. 34; Pines, 74)

The upshot of this passage is that if a person worships God without studying God's creation (which, for Maimonides means the study of physics (*ma'aseh*

---

43 Let it be noted that Maimonides, unlike almost all other medieval figures (Jewish, Christian, or Muslim), held women to be fully human, fully created in the image of God. See Kellner, "Misogyny." As mentioned above, I maintain that Maimonides's misogyny is halakhic, not philosophical. Hannah Kasher has recently addressed this issue: see above, chapter 6, footnote 83.

44 In his statement at the end of "Thirteen Principles" Maimonides defines his principles as dogmas in the strict sense of the term: beliefs taught by the highest religious authority (in this case, the Torah itself), acceptance of which is both a necessary and sufficient condition for both being part of the community of Israel and for achieving a share in the world to come. We have already seen that Rabad clearly understood (and rejected) the implication that there is no possibility of *shegagah*, inadvertence, playing an exculpatory role here. For discussion, see Kellner, "What is Heresy?," reprinted in *Studies in Jewish Philosophy: Collected Essays of the Academy for Jewish Philosophy, 1980–85*, ed. Norbert Samuelson (Lanham, University Press of America, 1987): 191–214.

bereshit) and metaphysics (*ma'aseh merkavah*),⁴⁵ then the object of that worship is not God, but a figment of the worshiper's imagination. In other words, such worship is *avodah zarah* in the strictest sense of the term. The worship of anyone who approaches God without understanding God's creation to one degree or another, or who only knows God through traditional Jewish texts, or who only knows God thanks to mystical illumination (as it were) is false, alien worship, *avodah zarah*.⁴⁶

In chapter i. 35, Maimonides emphasizes that the God who is to be worshiped is indeed the unmoved mover, not only in the Aristotelian sense of an uncaused cause, but in the sense of Abraham Joshua Heschel's (anti-Maimonidean) claim that God is the "most moved mover":⁴⁷

> Don't think that all the caveats in these early chapters about how dark and deep this subject is—how hard to fathom and how rightly kept from the multitude—apply to God's incorporeality and impassivity. ... God is not a body and cannot be affected. For affections are changes, and He is untouched by change.

For our purposes, the important points made here are that God is wholly impassive, untouched by change and impervious to all attempts to move God, not only in the physical sense (which is obvious) but in the emotional sense as well. Maimonides connects this imperviousness to being affected to God's incorporeality, which is itself a function of God's absolute unity. Thus, the worship of someone who believes that the commandments of the Torah fulfill a divine need is, once again, *avodah zarah* in the strictest sense—worship of an

---

45 Maimonides consistently identifies *ma'aseh bereshit* with physics and *ma'aseh merkavah* with metaphysics. See, for example, his commentary on Mishnah Hagigah ii.1, the ends of chapters 2 and 4 in "Laws of the Foundations of the Torah," the introduction to the *Guide* (Pines, 8–9), and the introduction to part 3 of the *Guide* (Pines, 415–416).

46 Eugene Korn (personal communication) objects: "Could not one have accurate belief (i.e. without scientific or philosophical reasons) of the true God without going thru these disciplines? That would not be *avodah zarah*." To suggest that is to ignore the important distinction in Maimonides between belief and knowledge. See my article cited above in footnote 44.

47 For the source of this expression, see Robert D. MacFadden, "Rabbi Abraham Joshua Heschel Dead," *New York Times*, December 24, 1972, https://www.nytimes.com/1972/12/24/archives/rabbi-abraham-joshua-heschel-dead.html. As long as I have mentioned Heschel, whom Maimonides would certainly have considered an idolater, see Eliezer Berkovits, "Dr. A. J. Heschel's Theology of Pathos," *Tradition* 6 (1964): 67–104.

entity that is not God. Similarly, the worship of someone who believes that the Tabernacle in the desert and the Temple in Jerusalem were constructed out of divine need is, once again, *avodah zarah* in the strictest sense of the term—worship of an entity that is not God.[48]

In *Guide* i. 36 Maimonides takes up the issue of God's impassiveness again and anticipates later discussions concerning the metaphorical sense in which the Torah attributes pleasure, displeasure, and anger to God.[49] Maimonides also emphasizes the importance of knowing God correctly, claiming that philosophical error about God is worse than idolatry:

> What then of one whose misbelief attaches to God Himself, who believes Him other than He is, denies His existence, or takes Him to be dual or corporeal, passive, or in any way lacking? He is doubtless worse than a pagan who takes idols for intermediaries or claims they can cause good or ill. Be

---

48 See the following—to me amazing—passage in Nahmanides (on Exod. 29: 46):

> But Rabbi Abraham ibn Ezra explained [the verse to mean that] the purpose of My bringing them forth from the land of Egypt was only that I might dwell in their midst, and that this was the fulfilment of [the promise to Moses], *you shall serve God upon this mountain* [Exod. 3:12]. He explained it well, and if it is so, there is in this matter a great secret. For in the plain sense of things it would appear that [the dwelling of] of the Divine Glory [*ha-shekhinah*] in Israel was to fulfil a need below, but it is not so. It fulfilled a need above as in the meaning of Scripture, *Israel, in whom I will be glorified* [Is. 49:3]. And Joshua said, [*For when the Canaanites ... hear of it ... and cut off our name from the earth,*] *and what wilt Thou do for Thy great name?* [Josh. 7:9]. There are many verses which express this thought: *He hath desired it* [i.e., Zion] *for His habitation* [Ps. 132:13]; *Here I dwell, for I have desired it* [ibid. 14]. And it is further written, *and I will remember the land* [Lev. 26:42].

Charles B. Chavel, trans., *Ramban: Commentary on the Torah—Exodus* (New York: Shilo, 1973), 506–507 (emended). See further Nathan Laufer, *Rendevous with God: Revealing the Meaning of the Jewish Holidays and Their Mysterious Rituals* (Jerusalem: Maggid, 2016), 206. According to the picture presented here, God desires to live in the world generally, but He wants to dwell in one place more than in all others: among *Am Yisrael* (the Jewish people), in *Eretz Yisrael* (the Land of Israel), in the Temple. The verse explains that owing to this desire on God's part, there was a need to redeem the Israelites from Egypt, for God could not dwell in their midst so long as they were still enslaved and mired in the forty-ninth level of impurity. Further on this, see Kellner on Maimonides and Nahmanides on the tabernacle (above, note 36). On many issues, Nahmanides seems to go out of his way to reject Maimonidean positions. For important examples, see Schwartz, "From Theurgy to Magic: 165–213.

49 See Hannah Kasher, "The Myth of 'God's Anger' in the *Guide of the Perplexed*," *Eshel Beersheva* 4 (1996): 95–115 (Hebrew).

advised, then, if you be such, that when you believe God to be corporeal or subject to any physical state, you have "roused His jealousy and anger, kindled His wrath," become a worse "enemy and foe," far more "hateful to God" than an idolater.

Mistakes about a topic as important as God cannot be allowed, and there is no room for inadvertence, *shegagah*: "If it occurs to you that a corporealist is to be excused because he was brought up as such or was naive or undiscerning, you must hold the same for the idolater: He too worships as he does out of ignorance or tradition: 'They follow the ways of their forebears (Hullin 13a).'" As in the *Mishneh Torah*, Maimonides teaches us here that when it comes to theology, teachings about God, honest mistakes are not exculpatory.[50]

As noted above, in his terms Maimonides had many reasons for condemning Christianity as *avodah zarah*. But, as also noted above, post-Maimonidean rabbis (and certainly those today) did not have to follow him in that condemnation: they *chose* and *choose* to do so. However, as argued throughout this chapter, this comes at great expense: consistent halakhic Maimondeans who condemn Christianity as idolatry should also condemn as idolatry much of the Judaism which they and their neighbors practice.

7. WHAT TO DO?

What precisely is going on here? Maimonides went to great lengths to protect Jews from idolatry, the greatest of sins. In pursuit of this aim, he depopulated the heavens, disenchanted the universe, and sought to lighten the burden of religious observance (as in *Guide* iii. 47). He battled against astrology and magic, denied their efficacy, and railed against those (such as Nahmanides after him) who maintained that magic was forbidden *because* of its efficacy.[51] At the same time, he also created Jewish orthodoxy in the strictest sense of the term, introducing the heresy hunting which is so popular a pastime in the Orthodox world (witness the recent battles against "open Orthodoxy" in North America and against non-Orthodox streams of Judaism in the Israeli Knesset).[52] Consistent with his understanding of Judaism primarily in terms

---

50 On *Guide* i. 36, see the detailed discussion in Hannah Kasher, "Between the Idolater and the Believer in God's Corporeality," *Da'at* 61 (2007): 73–82 (Hebrew).
51 "Laws of Idolatry," chapter 11, end.
52 Arguing against all this is the thrust of my *Must a Jew Believe Anything?*

of truth, he felt forced to reject as idolatrous Christianity, with is triune god, its incarnationism, its claim that the messiah has come and that we are already living in a redeemed world.

However, as we have seen in this chapter, calling Christianity idolatry on Maimonidean grounds is to force one to reject as idolatry much the Judaism of the last 1,000 years.

A number of paths lie before the intellectually honest and consistent rabbinic decisor:

- One can ignore Maimonides, erase close to 1,000 years of rabbinic *psak* on Christianity, ignore the Talmudic claim that idolatry no longer really exists, ignore Me'iri, ignore the Tosafists, and find new reasons to condemn Christianity as idolatry.
- One can accept Maimonides and reject most of contemporary Judaism (especially in the Orthodox world) as idolatrous.
- One can admit that for all his greatness, Maimonides's Judaism is simply too abstract, too abstruse, too demanding for actual flesh and blood Jews. Maimonidean Judaism must be taken as an ideal to be aimed at, but not as a criterion by which to judge whether fellow Jews are actually Jewish.
- One can say that the whole issue is irrelevant today and look for new ways to disagree with fellow Jews and with fellow monotheists, and with fellow humans who may not be monotheists at all but who are, withal, decent human beings.

No one who has read this far will be surprised to discover that I prefer the last two options over the first two.

8. POSTSCRIPT: WHAT ARE WE TO DO WITH MAIMONIDES?

I would like to flesh out the point I made just above, to wit: one can admit that, for all his greatness, Maimonides's Judaism is simply too abstract, too abstruse, too demanding, and too discomforting for most actual Jews. Maimonidean Judaism must be taken as an ideal to be aimed at, but not as a criterion by which to judge whether fellow Jews are actually Jewish.

Thus, I agree with David Berger that in strict Maimonidean terms Habad is heresy, but disagree with him in that I reject the practical consequences of that view. Similarly, I do not accept the consequences of what I have shown here: that in strict Maimonidean terms almost all Jews today who think they worship God are actually guilty of *avodah zarah*. I do not believe that almost all Jews are worshipers of *avodah zarah*, and are in principle no different from Christians or polytheists. What does that say about my attitude towards Maimonides?

The simplest thing to do is to say that Maimonides was an interesting historical personage, but hardly one to be taken today as anyone's rebbe. In a certain sense, that is obviously the case: no rational thinker can accept Maimonides's physics and metaphysics as adequate accounts of the world.[53] However, this is no solution for those of us for whom Maimonides makes it possible to be Jewish in the cosmos as science teaches us to know it. This view of the universe is very different from the way in which it is described in the first chapters of Genesis. This is no solution for those of us for whom Maimonides makes it possible to live with a Judaism freed of the "hyper-realism," magic, irrationalism, and downright racism of so much of today's Kabbalistically inflected Judaism.[54] This is also no solution for those of us for whom Maimonides makes it possible to practice a Judaism characterized by universalism, rationalism, and the study of God's created cosmos as an integral part of Jewish practice and, indeed, worship. For such Jews, Maimonides is simply indispensable.

A number of approaches suggest themselves for other kinds of Jews. They can ignore what Maimonides actually wrote in favor of what they would have liked him to have written.[55] They can reinterpret him to make him unobjectionable (to them).[56] Hardly an approach available, I assume, to most of the readers of this volume.

Honesty demands that I admit that I pick and choose among Maimonides's positions. As noted, I do not accept his science. I wrote a whole book against his introduction of theological orthodoxy into Judaism. I certainly do

---

53 See Menachem Kellner, "Maimonides's Allegiances to Torah and Science," *Torah u-Madda Journal* 7 (1997): 88–104, reprinted in my *Science in the Bet Midrash*, 217–231. For the surprising number of contemporary Jewish authorities who reject heliocentrism, see Jeremy Brown, *New Heavens and a New Earth: The Jewish Reception of Copernican Thought* (Oxford: Oxford University Press, 2013), 255–273.
54 On "hyper-realism" see Y. Tzvi Langerman, "Science and the *Kuzari*," *Science in Context* 10 (1997): 495. On racism in many (but not all) Kabbalistic texts, see above, chapter 1, note 28.
55 See, for example, Kellner, "Farteitcht un Farbessert."
56 This is the burden of the essays collected in Diamond and Kellner, *Reinventing Maimonides*.

not identify with his intellectual elitism.⁵⁷ As is clear from this chapter, I reject his understanding of *avodah zarah*.

Does that make me any the less a Maimonidean? On the contrary, accepting Maimonides's teachings uncritically would perhaps be the least Maimonidean thing I could do. Maimonides was not searching for *hasidim* (blindly fervent followers). It is his example, not his teachings, which should be our lodestar. His is the example of an extremely learned Jew (to put it mildly) who is devoted to Torah and to the people of Israel (in the narrow and also in the messianic sense of the term "Israel"); who is unwilling to close his eyes to the simple teaching of Torah that all human beings are equally made in the image of God; who is unwilling to turn off his brain; and who is unwilling to give in to the siren song of magic and irrationalism.⁵⁸

---

57   On Jolene S. Kellner's annoyance with Maimonides's elitism, see above, chapter 6, footnote 80. On his elitism, see Kellner, *Confrontation*, 15–17 and Rynhold and Harris, *Nietzsche, Soloveitchik, and Contemporary Jewish Philosophy*, 268–277. Maimonides's elitism was intellectual, not social: there is much evidence that he suffered fools, if not gladly, at least patiently. See, for example, his account of his daily schedule in his famous letter to Samuel ibn Tibbon, translator of the *Guide of the Perplexed* into Hebrew, and, for another example, Paul Fenton, "A Meeting with Maimonides," *Bulletin of the School of Oriental and African Studies* 45 (1982): 1–5. The letter to ibn Tibbon may be found in Y. Sheilat, *Iggerot ha-Rambam* (Jerusalem: Ma'aliyot, 2007), 530–554 and in English in Leon D. Stitskin, *Letters of Maimonides* (New York: Yeshiva University Press, 1977), 130–136.

58   Full disclosure: I am a signatory to "Dabru Emet—A Jewish Statement on Christians and Christianity," *New York Times*, September 23, 2000. Further full disclosure: upon our aliyah in 1980, my wife and I were surprised to discover that the line "they bow down to vanity and emptiness" which had been censored from the *aleinu* prayer had been reintroduced in the prayer books used in our community (Rinat Yisrael). We chose not to say those words, then, and now.

Conclusion

Maimonides opens his *Guide of the Perplexed* with a letter to his student Joseph ben Judah,[1] who had come to study with Maimonides, but was unable to remain in Egypt to continue his lessons. Maimonides then sent Joseph the chapters of the *Guide*, chapter by chapter.[2] In his letter, Maimonides explains that Joseph had written to him from Alexandria, and that Maimonides then sensed, he writes, that Joseph was

> ready for some of the mysteries of Scripture to be opened up to you and to discover what mature readers should find there. I dropped a few hints and glimmers and saw you asking for more. You wanted me to clarify certain points of theology, to tell you what the *Mutakallimūn* were after and whether their methods are cogent—or, if not, how to class them.

Maimonides continues:

> I saw you had touched on these subjects with others but were still perplexed and puzzled, your fine soul *seeking good answers* (Ecclesiastes 12:10), but I was reining you in, urging you to take one step at a time and get a firm grip on the truth, not just stumble into certitude. As long as you were here, whenever some verse came up, or some passage from the Sages that hinted at an out of the way idea, I explained it to you freely. But when God decreed our parting and you moved on, memories of our sessions revived an old plan of mine: Your absence spurred me to set down this work, written for you and others like you, no matter how few. It is laid out in separate chapters that will all reach you in sequence where you are as I write them. Farewell.[3]

---

1 On Joseph and his relationship with Maimonides, see Davidson, *Moses Maimonides*, 330–332, 472–475, and 520–524.
2 On Maimonides's method of writing, see Y. Tzvi Langermann, "*Fusul Musa*: On Maimonides's Method of Composition," *Maimonidean Studies* 5 (2008): 325–344.
3 Pines, 4–5.

The *Guide*, therefore, was written for Joseph ben Judah and people like him. Who exactly are those people? Maimonides offers an answer to that question in the actual introduction to the book (Pines, 5–6). There he lays out the nature of the perplexed individual for whom the book is meant to be a guide.

He writes:

> My goal is not to make this work transparent all through to the masses or to intellectual beginners. Nor is it my object to instruct those who study the Torah only for its law.[4] The object of this work, throughout, as of any other of its sort, is a sound grasp of the Torah. But here the aim is to instruct a person who is religious, morally and spiritually mature, settled of mind, and committed to the Torah's truth, who has engaged in philosophical studies and grasped their import. Human reason draws such a person invitingly to its domain, but he is troubled by the surface sense of certain biblical expressions. Resisting what he still takes (or was taught) to be the meaning of its multivalent, metaphorical, or ambiguous words, he hangs back, baffled and perplexed.

Here we learn that the book is not aimed at those whom Maimonides will call (in *Guide* iii. 51) practitioners and scholars of the legalistic side of the Torah. It is aimed, rather, at those whom we would today call fully observant and committed Jews who have gone beyond standard rabbinic studies and engaged in science and understand its importance. Such a person is perplexed by the apparent contradictions between Torah, as it was taught to him, and science as it was understood in Maimonides's time.

Such a perplexed person is faced with two options:

> Should he follow his reason, reject what he took those terms to say and think he's shed core biblical precepts? Or should he hold fast to what he took those words to mean and fight reason's sway, dig in his heels and resist, but feeling injured, as though it had sullied his faith, retaining his fanciful beliefs but fearful and uneasy, deeply anxious and troubled constantly.

Neither option is acceptable. Following reason means rejecting the Torah as it was taught to him. Following Torah as it was taught to him and rejecting science

---

4   Compare *Guide*, iii. 27 on the aims of the Torah.

leaves him profoundly unsettled. Maimonides's solution will be to show that Torah itself does not actually teach what it was ordinarily thought to teach.

The perplexed Jew today is in many senses in much worse shape than were Maimonides's student and those like him. Today's perplexities include a great deal more than the apparent contradiction between science and Torah. They also include contradictions between the morality of the Torah and our convictions that genocide is never justified, that slavery is evil, that women are fully human and fully Jewish, that homosexuality is not an abomination, and that every single human being is created in the image of God and is the object of divine concern. All this, and leaving aside questions of history, archeology, and biblical criticism.

Judaism has wrestled with many of these problems since the close of the Mishnah almost 2,000 years ago.[5] In my own lifetime the changes, even in Orthodoxy, have been and continue to be dramatic. There is, however, much work still to be done. That is the point of this book.

Too many Jews believe that Judaism calls upon them to affirm that the election of Israel means the disparagement of non-Jews; that converts are in some sense second-class Jews; that we cannot be true to the Torah without denigrating Jews who disagree with us, not to mention non-Jews; that Jews who disagree with us, not to mention non-Jews, are to be tolerated but not fully respected; and that Christianity is a form of idolatry, with all that implies.

In each of the chapters of this book, I have taken issue with positions which were once universally held by Jews and which today are still held in certain sectors of the community. My object was not to deny that Jewish texts and traditions teach views which I have here called particularist and which I find objectionable. Denying that would involve ripping out of our history huge swathes of Bible, Mishnah, Talmud, medieval and contemporary rabbinic authorities, and many, many Jews whom I love and with whom I interact on a regular basis.

Denying these texts and traditions is to say, in effect, that most if not all tannaim, amoraim, and geonim, individuals like Judah Halevi, Rashi, Nahmanides, Kabbalists, and Hasidim and early modern and contemporary yeshiva heads and rabbis have all misunderstood Judaism. That is what Maimonides did. He said, If you think that God is in any sense corporeal, that God has any human emotions, that God rewards the righteous and punishes the wicked literally *midah ke-neged midah* (tit for tat), that divine providence governs every act

---

5   See Kellner, "And Yet, the Texts Remain" and the sources cited there.

of every human being (or at least that of Jews), then you simply misunderstand Torah.

Maimonides could do that because he was first and foremost Rambam, about whom it is often said, "From Moses to Moses, none arose like Moses." I am neither Rambam nor Maimonides (to say the least) but, as has also often been remarked, even a dwarf standing on the shoulders of a giant sees further than the giant.[6] I am not sure how much further than Maimonides I can actually see, but I do have the advantage (perhaps) of living in a world dramatically different from his. As such, I am faced by many perplexities that he could not have foreseen. Faced with these perplexities, I could affirm that true Judaism is fundamentally universalist and condemn as deviant the many examples of particularism we have seen throughout this book. That, in effect, is the road taken by Hermann Cohen and classical Reform Judaism. Alternatively, I could reject as concessions to contemporary "week-kneed liberalism" many of the positions adopted in this book. That, in the end, is the road taken by many Jews in wide swathes of contemporary Orthodoxy. It is an accusation that has been thrown at me more times than I care to count.

Both approaches are historically false. The Jewish tradition has always had both universalist and particularist elements.[7] My point in this book has been to show that individuals who *choose* to emphasize the universalist elements of Jewish tradition can often find support in positions held by Maimonides or implied by his explicit positions (the implications of which he may or may not have been aware).

I would like to think that people who choose to emphasize Judaism's universalist tendencies, or, alternatively who choose to emphasize its particularist bent, do so out of the conviction that they are representing the Jewish tradition as it always was, or at least as it should be. The situation becomes more complicated for individuals who admit that Judaism has a history. And it is even more complicated for individuals who have come to realize that few of our choices are

---

6 On this motif generally, see Robert K. Merton, *On the Shoulders of Giants: A Shandean Postscript* (New York: Free Press, 1965). In Jewish contexts, see Kellner, *Maimonides on the "Decline of the Generations"*; Ephraim Kanarfogel, "Progress and Tradition in Medieval Ashkenaz," *Jewish History* 14 (2000): 287–315; Jeffrey Woolf, "Between Diffidence and Initiative: Ashkenazic Legal Decision-Making in the Late Middle Ages (1350–1500)," *Journal of Jewish Studies* 52 (2001): 85–97; and, in great detail, Abraham Melamed, *Al Kitfei Anakim: Toldot ha-Pulmus Bein Aharonim be-Rishonim be-Hagut ha-Yehudit Bimei ha-Benayim u-Ve-Reshit ha-Et ha-Hadashah* (Ramat-Gan: Bar Ilan University Press, 2003).

7 See Kellner, "On Universalism and Particularism in Judaism."

binary—that all of them are consequences of a dizzying array of earlier choices, family, socialization, ideals, social background, understanding of history, and many other factors.

While acknowledging that no normal human being can actually achieve a "view from nowhere,"[8] scholars strive for the greatest possible objectivity when writing as scholars. The book before you is not a scholarly treatise (even if based on much scholarship). It is written by a Jew, for Jews. It is also apologetic (in the classic sense of the term)—I defend a specific view of Judaism as an insider, not as an outsider writing, as it were, as a person from Mars (or from Porlock, for that matter). I have written an apology, but not a polemic: one can defend a point of view while striving to present alternative positions in the best possible light.[9]

Rabbi Yizhak Shailat, a rosh yeshiva in an institution clearly influenced by its head, the late Rabbi Dr Nachum Rabinovich, has spent much of his career studying, editing, and translating works by Maimonides. His respect for Maimonides is great, but, it would seem, his affection for Judah Halevi is greater. He wrote a very interesting book comparing the two thinkers: *Bein ha-Kuzari la-Rambam* (Between the Kuzari and Maimonides).[10] Using a clever play on words, Shailat contrasts Maimonides's emphasis on *re'ayah* (proof) with Halevi's emphasis on *re'iyah* (vision or seeing). In Hebrew, the two words have the same letters—without vowel points, they are indistinguishable. However, the difference between these two approaches is vast. Halevi bases his Judaism on the shared *experience* of the Jewish *people* at Sinai. Maimonides bases his Judaism on the *conviction* of an *individual* philosopher named Abraham.

One is tempted to say that ideally Halevi's God is experienced; Maimonides's God is discovered through the examination of the cosmos. Halevi's God is presented; Maimonides's God is deduced.

I can only speak for myself, but I am confident that I also speak for many others: Tevye could talk *to* God; we can talk *about* God. It would seem that Tevye's God was Halevian; for many of us, our God is Maimonidean.[11] Were

---

8   See Thomas Nagel, *The View from Nowhere* (Oxford: Oxford University Press, 1986).
9   This is easy for me with respect to Judah Halevi, more difficult for me with many aspects of Kabbalistically inflected Judaism, and impossible for me with respect to books such as *Torat Ha-Melekh*.
10 Rabbi Yizhak Shailat, *Bein ha-Kuzari la-Rambam* [Between the Kuzari and Maimonides] (Jerusalem: Hoza'at Shailat, 2011). The title is of interest: it compares Halevi's *book* with Maimonides. I am not sure what to make of that.
11 Compare Hartman, *Israelis and the Jewish Tradition*.

that indeed the case, it would seem that the choice of Maimonidean Judaism over Halevian Judaism should be a "slam sunk" for Jews who live, not next to modernity, but in it.

Is that the case? Hardly. Maimonidean Judaism is indeed austere and demanding, and, it appears, far outside the mainstream of traditional understandings of Torah. Over the centuries those rabbis who were willing to admit that what Maimonides wrote is what he actually thought responded by saying, as it were, "It's Greek to me!" Thus, for example, in his commentary on *Guide* iii. 51 Shem Tov ben Joseph ibn Shem Tov (Iberia, fifteenth century) wrote:

> Many rabbinic scholars said that Maimonides did not write this chapter and if he did write it, it ought to be hidden away or, most appropriately, burned. For how could he say that those who know physics are on a higher level than those who engage in religion, and even more that they are with the ruler in the inner chamber, for on this basis the scholars who are engaged with physics and metaphysics have achieved a higher level than those engaged with Torah!

Asking contemporary Jews to practice a Judaism which in effect downplays the significance of prayer and commandments, which denies that Jews in and of themselves are in any way special, which rejects traditional views of reward and punishment, and so forth, is to ask of them a lot. Is it too much? For Jews who are content to live next to modernity, but not in it, who are content to adopt the fruits of modern technology without confronting the science on which it is based, Maimonidean Judaism really is asking too much.

For many, living next to modernity, but not in it, is simply too high a price to pay. Like Joseph ben Judah, such a person will be "fearful and uneasy, deeply anxious and troubled constantly." Such people are comforted by the model of Maimonides. The author of a commentary on the Mishnah, the author of the *Mishneh Torah*, the author of hundreds of responsa, the leader of his community, lived in his modernity, not next to it. He serves as model for the many Jews today who refuse to give up on Torah but seek to lead their Jewish lives in the contemporary world, not only next to it.

Moreover, portraying Maimonides as only a somber intellectual elitist who calls upon Jews, in effect, to enter into a relationship with an idea, not with a person, is to misrepresent Maimonides. Without the benefit of reading Pierre

Hadot,[12] Maimonides knew that the philosophical life was meant to be transformative. The philosopher at the beginning of the *Guide* was indeed a pure intellectualist. The philosopher at the end of the *Guide* has come to understand that his or her role in life is not only to know and understand, but—following Jeremiah 9:23—to realize that the ultimate goal is doing grace, justice, righteousness in the earth (*hesed mishpat u-zedaka ba-aretz*), as Maimonides himself emphasizes at the very end of the *Guide*.[13]

---

12 Pierre Hadot, *Philosophy as a Way of Life* (Oxford: Blackwell, 1995).
13 I have argued for this reading of Maimonides in a number of places, among them, *Maimonides on Human Perfection* (Atlanta: Scholars Press, 1990), and in "Is Maimonides's Ideal Person Austerely Rationalist?" *American Catholic Philosophical Quarterly* 76 (2002): 125–143; reprinted in Kellner, *Science in the Bet Midrash: Studies in Maimonides*, 63–80.

Bibliography

WORKS BY MAIMONIDES

The Book of Holiness. Translated by Louis I. Rabinowitz and Philip Grossman. New Haven: Yale University Press, 1965.

The Book of Judges. Translated by A. M Hershman. New Haven: Yale University Press, 1949.

The Book of Knowledge. Translated by Moses Hyamson. New York: Feldheim, 1974.

The Book of Divine Commandments (Sefer ha-Mitzvoth of Moses Maimonides). Translated by Charles B. Chavel. 2 vols. London: Soncino, 1967.

Epistle to Yemen. In *Epistles of Maimonides: Crisis and Leadership*, translated and edited by Abraham Halkin, with discussion by David Hartman, 91–131. Philadelphia: Jewish Publication Society 1985; also translated in Lerner, Ralph. *Maimonides's Empire of Light: Popular Enlightenment in an Age of Belief*. Chicago: University of Chicago Press 2000.

Essay on Resurrection. In *Epistles of Maimonides: Crisis and Leadership*, translated and edited by Abraham Halkin, with discussion by David Hartman, 209–233. Philadelphia: Jewish Publication Society, 1985.

Guide of the Perplexed (Dalalat al-h.a'irin, Moreh nevukhim). Translated by Lenn Evan Goodman and Phillip Lieberman. Stanford: Stanford University Press, forthcoming; Shlomo Pines's English translation—Chicago: University of Chicago Press, 1963; Joseph Kafih's Hebrew translation—Jerusalem: Mossad ha-Rav Kook, 1972; Michael Schwarz's Hebrew translation in 2 vols.—Ramat Aviv: Tel Aviv University Press, 2002.

"Introduction to His Commentary on the Tractate Avot." In *Ethical Writings of Maimonides*, translated by Raymond Weiss and Charles Butterworth. New York: Dover, 1983.

Letters. In *Iggerot ha-Rambam* (The Letters and Essays of Moses Maimonides). Translated into Hebrew by Isaac Sheilat. 2 vols. Ma'aleh Adumim: Shailat Publishing, 1987; J. Kafih's Hebrew translation—Jerusalem: Mossad ha-Rav Kook, 1972.

Letters of Maimonides. Translated by Leon D. Stitskin. New York: Yeshiva University Press, 1977.

Mishneh Torah le-ha-Rambam, Mahadurat Mofet. Edited by Yohai Makbili. Haifa: Or Veshua, 2008.

Responsa. Translated and edited by J. Blau. Teshuvot ha-Rambam. 4 vols. Jerusalem: Mekize Nirdamin, 1957 (vol. 1), 1960 (vol. 2), 1961 (vol. 3), 1986 (vol. 4, published by Rubin Mass for Mekize Nirdamin).

SECONDARY WORKS

Ahituv, Yosef. "State and Army According to the Torah: Realism and Mysticism in the Circles of Merkaz Ha-Rav." In *Dat u-Medinah ba-Hagut ha-Yehudit be-Me'ah ha-Esrim*, edited by Aviezer Ravitzky. Jerusalem: Israel Democracy Institute, 2005. Hebrew.

Almog, Shmuel, and Michael Heyd, eds. *Ra'ayon Ha-Behirah Be-Yisrael U-Ve-Amim*. Jerusalem: Merkaz Zalman Shazar, 1991.

Altmann, Alexander. "The God of Religion, the God of Metaphysics, and Wittgenstein's 'Language Games.'" *Zeitschrift für Religions- und Geistesgeschichte* 39 (1987): 289–306.

———. "Judah Halevi's Theory of Climates." *Aleph* 5 (2005): 215–246.

———. *Moses Mendelssohn: A Biographical Study*. Tuscaloosa: University of Alabama Press, 1973.

———. *Tolerance and the Jewish Tradition: The Robert Waley Cohen Memorial Lecture*. London: The Council of Christians and Jews, 1957.

Amital, Yehudah. "Yaakov Was Reciting the Shema." Etzion.org.il. Accessed February 9, 2021. https://www.etzion.org.il/en/yaakov-was-reciting-shema.

Angel, Marc. *Loving Truth and Peace: The Grand Religious Worldview of Rabbi Benzion Uziel*. Northvale: Jason Aronson, 1999.

Anonymous, *Sha'arei Geulah*. New York: Kehat, 1992.

Aran, Gideon. "The Father, the Son, and the Holy Land: The Spiritual Authorities of Jewish-Zionist Fundamentalism in Israel." In *Spokesmen for the Despised: Fundamentalist Leaders of the Middle East*, edited by R. S. Appleby, 294–327. Chicago: University of Chicago Press, 1997.

Arkush, Allan. "From Diaspora Nationalism to Radical Diasporism." *Modern Judaism* 29 (2009): 326–350.

Aviner, Shlomo. *Commentary on the Kuzari, Part 1*. Bet El: Sifriyat Hava, n.d. Hebrew.

———. *Ma'ayanei Ha-Yeshuah*, no. 403, 28 Sivan, 5769.

———. *Me-Hayil el Hayil*. Jerusalem: Sifriat Hava, 1998.

———. "Why Should We Be a Nation?" Havabooks.co.il. Accessed February 9, 2021. http://www.havabooks.co.il/article_ID.asp?id=632. Hebrew.

Balk, Hanan. "The Soul of a Jew and the Soul of a Non-Jew: An Inconvenient Truth and the Search for an Alternative." *Hakirah—The Flatbush Journal of Jewish Law and Thought* 16 (2013): 47–76.

Bamberger, Bernard. *Proselytism in the Talmudic Period*. Cincinnati: Hebrew Union College Press, 1939.

Batnitzky, Leora. *How Judaism Became a Religion: An Introduction to Modern Jewish Thought*. Princeton: Princeton University Press, 2011.

Benamozegh, Elijah. *Israel and Humanity*. Translated by Maxwell Luria. Mahwah: Paulist Press, 1995.

Ben-Johanan, Karma. "Wreaking Judgment on Mount Esau: Christianity in R. Kook's Thought." *Jewish Quarterly Review* 106 (2016): 76–100.

Ben-Rafael, Eliezer. *Jewish Identities: Fifty Intellectuals Answer Ben-Gurion*. Leiden: Brill, 2002.

Benson, Ophelia and Jeremy Stangroom. *Why Truth Matters*. London: Continuum, 2006).

Berger, David. *The Rebbe, the Messiah, and the Scandal of Orthodox Indifference*. London: Littman Library of Jewish Civilization, 2001.

———. Review of *Must a Jew Believe Anything?*, by Menachem Kellner. *Tradition* 33 (1999): 81–89.
Berkovits, Eliezer. "Dr. A. J. Heschel's Theology of Pathos." *Tradition* 6 (1964): 67–104.
Berman, Joshua. *Ani Maamin: Biblical Criticism, Historical Truth, and the Thirteen Principles of Faith*. Jerusalem: Magid, 2020.
Blass, Yehonatan Simhah. "Contributions from Evangelicals and the Prohibition of Expressing Thanks to Priests." *Tehumin* 34 (Sivan 5774 [June 2014]): 214–221. Hebrew.
Bleich, J. David. "Divine Unity in Maimonides, the Tosafists, and Me'iri." In *Neoplatonism and Jewish Thought*, edited by Lenn Goodman, 237–254. Albany: SUNY Press, 1992.
Blidstein, Gerald (Ya'akov). "A Note on Rabbinic Missionizing." *Journal of Theological Studies* 47 (1996): 528–31.
———. "The 'Other' in Maimonidean Law." *Jewish History* 18 (2004): 173–95.
———. "R. Menahem Ha-Me'iri: Aspects of an Intellectual Profile." *Journal of Jewish Thought & Philosophy* 5 (1995): 63–79.
Blidstein, Ya'akov (Gerald). "Maimonides's Attitude towards Karaites." *Tehumin* 8 (1988): 501–510. Hebrew.
———. "Menachem Meiri's Attitude towards Gentiles—Apologetics or Worldview?" *Zion* 51 (1985): 153–166. Hebrew
———. "The Status of Islam in Maimonidean Halakhah." In *Rav-Tarbutiut Be-Medinah Demokratit U-Yehudit*, edited by Avi Sagi, Menachem Mautner, and Ronen Shamir, 465–476. Tel Aviv: Ramot, 1998. Hebrew.
Boyarin, Daniel. *Judaism: The Genealogy of a Modern Notion*. New Brunswick: Rutgers University Press, 2018.
Brague, Remi. "Athens, Jerusalem, Mecca: Leo Strauss's 'Muslim' Understanding of Greek Philosophy." *Poetics Today* 19 (1998): 235–59.
Brill, Alan. *Judaism and Other Religions. Models of Understanding*. New York: Palgrave Macmillan, 2010.
Brown, Jeremy. *New Heavens and a New Earth: The Jewish Reception of Copernican Thought*. Oxford: Oxford University Press, 2013.
Cohen, Gerson. "Esau as Symbol in Early Medieval Thought." In *Jewish Medieval and Renaissance Studies*, edited by Alexander Altmann, 19–48. Cambridge, MA: Harvard University Press, 1967.
Cohen, Hermann. *Religion of Reason out of the Sources of Judaism*. Translated by Simon Kaplan. New York: Frederick Ungar, 1972.
Cohen, Naomi G. "Rabbi Meir, a Descendant of Anatolian Proselytes: New Light on His Name and the Historical Kernel of the Nero Legend in Gittin 56a." *Journal of Jewish Studies* 23 (1972): 51–59.
Cohen, Shaye J. D. *The Beginnings of Jewishness: Boundaries, Varieties, Uncertainties*. Berkeley: University of California Press, 1999.
Crescas, Hasdai. *Or Ha-Shem*. Jerusalem: Sifrei Ramot, 1990. Translated by Roslyn Weiss. Oxford: Oxford University Press, 2018.
Davidson, Herbert A. *Moses Maimonides: The Man and His Works*. Oxford: Oxford University Press, 2005.
Dehan, Alon. *Go'el Aharon: Mishnato ha-Meshihit shel Rabbi Menachem Mendel Schneerson*. Tel Aviv: Contento de Semrik, 2004.

Deutscher, Isaac. *The Non-Jewish Jew and Other Essays*. Oxford: Oxford University Press, 1968.
Diamond, James. *Converts, Heretics, and Lepers: Maimonides and the Outsider*. Notre Dame: University of Notre Dame Press, 2007.
———. "Exegetical Idealization: Hermann Cohen's Religion of Reason out of the Sources of Maimonides." *Journal of Jewish Thought and Philosophy* 18 (2010): 49–73.
———. "King David of the Sages: Rabbinic Rehabilitation or Ironic Parody?" *Prooftexts* 27 (2007): 373–426.
———. *Maimonides and the Hermeneutics of Concealment*. Albany: SUNY Press, 2002.
Diamond, James, and Menachem Kellner. *Reinventing Maimonides in Contemporary Jewish Thought*. London: Littman Library of Jewish Civilization, 2019.
Ellenson, David. "The Orthodox Rabbinate and Apostasy in Nineteenth-Century Germany and Hungary." In *Tradition in Transition*, 732–758. Lanham: University Press of America, 1989.
———. "Rabbi Hayim David Halevi on Christians and Christianity: An Analysis of Selected Legal Writings of an Israeli Authority." In *Transforming Relations: Essays on Jews and Christians. … In Honor of Michael A. Signer*, edited by Franklin Harkin, 340–361. Notre Dame: Notre Dame University Press, 2010.
———. "Traditional Reactions to Modern Jewish Reform: The Paradigm of German Orthodoxy." In *History of Jewish Philosophy*, edited by Daniel H. Frank and Oliver Leaman, 651–673. London: Routledge, 1996.
Epstein, Baruch Halevi. *Baruch She-Amar*. Tel Aviv: Am Olam, n.d.
Faierstein, Morris. "God's Need for the Commandments' in Medieval Kabbalah." *Conservative Judaism* 36 (1982): 45–59.
Farber, Zev. "Torah Min ha-Shamayim: A Guide to the Four Questions." TheTorah.com. Accessed February 9, 2021. http://thetorah.com/torah-four-questions/.
Faur, Jose. *Homo Mysticus: A Guide to Maimonides's Guide for the Perplexed*. Syracuse: Syracuse University Press, 1999.
Feldmann-Kaye, Miriam. *Jewish Theology for a Postmodern Age*. London: Littman Library of Jewish Civilization, 2019.
Fenton, Paul. "A Meeting with Maimonides." *Bulletin of the School of Oriental and African Studies* 45 (1982): 1–5.
Ferziger, Adam. *Beyond Sectarianism: The Realignment of American Orthodox Judaism*. Detroit: Wayne State University Press, 2015.
———. "From Demonic Deviant to Drowning Brother: Reform Judaism in the Eyes of American Orthodoxy." *Jewish Social Studies: History, Culture, Society* 15 (2009): 56–88.
———. "Religion for the Secular: The New Israeli Rabbinate." *Journal of Modern Jewish Studies* 7 (2008): 67–90.
———. "The Role of Reform in Israeli Orthodoxy." In *Between Jewish Tradition and Modernity*, edited by Michael Meyer and David Myers, 51–66. Detroit: Wayne State University Press, 2014).
Fischer, Shlomo. "Radical Religious Zionism from the Collective to the Individual." In *Kabbalah and Contemporary Spiritual Revival*, edited by Boaz Huss, 285–309. Beersheva: Ben-Gurion University Press, 2011.
———. "Self-Expression and Democracy in Radical Religious Zionist Ideology." PhD diss., Hebrew University of Jerusalem, 2007. Hebrew.

Fixler, Dror, and Gil Nadal. "Are Christians Today Idolaters?" *Tehumin* 22 (2002): 68–78. Hebrew.
Freudenthal, Gad. "The Biological Foundations of Intellectual Elitism: Maimonides vs. Al-Farabi." *Maimonidean Studies* 5 (2008): 293–324.
Friedman, Mordechai Akiva. *Ha-Rambam, ha-Mashiah be-Teiman ve-ha-Shemad* [Maimonides, the Yemenite Messiah, and Forced Conversion]. Jerusalem: Makhon Ben-Zvi, 2002.
Frimer, Dov. "Israel, the Noahide Laws and Maimonides: Jewish-Gentile Legal Relations in Maimonidean Thought." In *The Legacy of Maimonides: Religion, Reason, and Community*, edited by Yamin Levy and Shalom Carmy, 96–110. New York: Yashar Books, 2006.
Funkenstein, Amos. "'Scripture Speaks the Language of Man': The Uses and Abuses of the Medieval Principle of Accommodation." *Philosophes Medievaux* 26 (1986): 92–101.
Garb, Jonathan. "The Conversion of the Jews: Identity as Ontology in Modern Kabbalah." *Proceedings of the International Conference on Religious Responses to Modernity*. Jerusalem and Berlin: Israel Academy of Sciences and Humanities/Berlin Brandenberg Academy of Sciences, forthcoming.
Gellman, Jerome. "The God of the Jews and the Jewish God." In *The Routledge Companion to Theism*, edited by Victoria S. Harrison et al., 38–53. N.p.: Routledge Handbooks Online, 2012.
———. *God's Kindness Has Overwhelmed Us*. Boston: Academic Studies Press, 2013.
———. "Jewish Mysticism and Morality—Kabbalah and its Ontological Dualities." *Archiv fuer Religionsgeschichte* 9 (2008): 23–35.
———. *This Was from God: A Contemporary Theology of Torah and History*. Boston: Academic Studies Press, 2016.
Gibbon, Edward. *The History of the Decline and Fall of the Roman Empire*. Abr. ed. London: Penguin Books, 2000.
Goldin, Joshua L. "On the Limits of Non-Literal Interpretation of Scripture from an Orthodox Perspective." *Torah u-Madda Journal* 10 (2001): 37–59.
Goodman, Lenn Evan. *God of Abraham*. New York: Oxford University Press, 1996.
Goodman, Martin, et al. *Toleration within Judaism*. London: The Littman Library of Jewish Civilization, 2013.
Goshen-Gottstein, Alon. *Same God, Other God*. New York: Palgrave Macmillan, 2016.
Grossman, Avraham. *Rashi*. Oxford: Littman Library of Jewish Civilization, 2012.
Hadot, Pierre. *Philosophy as a Way of Life*. Oxford: Blackwell, 1995.
Haim ben Isaac of Volozhin. *Nefesh ha-Hayyim*. N.p.: Bnai Brak, 2009.
Halbertal, Moshe, and Avishai Margalit, *Idolatry*. Cambridge, MA: Harvard University Press, 1992.
———. *Maimonides*. Princeton: Princeton University Press, 2014.
———. "'One Possessed of Religion': Religious Tolerance in the Teaching of the Meiri." *The Edah Journal* 1 (2000): 1–24.
Halevi, Judah. *Kuzari*. Translated by Barry Kogan. New Haven: Yale University Press, forthcoming.
Halkin, Hillel. Review of *How to Fight Antisemitism*, by Bari Weiss. *New York Times*, September 10, 2019. https://www.nytimes.com/2019/09/10/books/review/how-to-fight-anti-semitism-bari-weiss.html.
Hallamish, Moshe. "The Kabbalists' Attitude to the Nations of the World." In *Joseph Baruch Sermonetta Memorial Volume*, edited by Aviezer Ravitsky, 289–312. Jerusalem: Hebrew University, 1998. Jerusalem Studies in Jewish Thought 14. Hebrew.

Hammer, Reuven. *Akiva: Life, Legend, Legacy*. Lincoln: University of Nebraska Press, 2015.

Hardy, Henry. "Isaiah Berlin: Against Dogma." *Times Literary Supplement*, January 31, 2020. https://www.the-tls.co.uk/articles/isaiah-berlin-against-dogma/.

Hartman, David. *Israelis and the Jewish Tradition: An Ancient People Debating Its Future*. New Haven: Yale University Press, 2000.

——. *Maimonides: Torah and Philosophic Quest*. Philadelphia: Jewish Publication Society, 1976.

Harvey, Warren Zev. "Averroes, Maimonides, and the Virtuous State." In *Iyyunim Bi-Sugyot Filosofiyot Likhvod Shelomoh Pines*, 19–31. Jerusalem: Israel Academy of Sciences, 1992. Hebrew.

——. *Physics and Metaphysics in Hasdai Crescas*. Amsterdam: Gieben, 1998.

——. "The Question of God's Incorporeality in Maimonides, Rabad, Crescas, and Spinoza." In *Minhah le-Sarah*, edited by S. Rosenberg et al., 63–78. Jerusalem: Magnes, 1994. Hebrew.

——. "Two Jewish Approaches to Evil in History." In *The Impact of the Holocaust on Jewish Thought*, edited by Steven Katz, 194–201. New York: New York University Press, 2007.

Hayes, Christine. "The Complicated Goy in Classic Rabbinic Sources." In *Perceiving the Other in Ancient Judaism and Early Christianity*, edited by Michal Bar-Asher Siegal et al. Tuebingen: Mohr Siebeck, forthcoming.

——. *Gentile Impurities and Jewish Identities: Intermarriage and Conversion from the Bible to the Talmud*. Oxford: Oxford University Press, 2002.

——. "The 'Other' in Rabbinic Literature." In *The Cambridge Companion to the Talmud and Rabbinic Literature*, edited by C. Fonrobert and M. Jaffee, 243–269. Cambridge: Cambridge University Press, 2007.

——. "The Torah Was Not Given to Ministering Angels: Rabbinic Aspirationalism." In *Talmudic Transgressions: Engaging the Work of Daniel Boyarin*, edited by Charlotte Fonrobert et al., 123–160. Supplements to the Journal for the Study of Judaism 181. Leiden: Brill, 2017.

——. *What's Divine About Divine Law? Early Perspectives*. Princeton: Princeton University Press, 2015.

Heilman, Samuel. *Sliding to the Right: The Contest for the Future of American Jewish Orthodoxy*. Berkeley: University of California Press, 2006.

Held, Shai. "What Zvi Yehudah Kook Wrought: The Theopolitical Radicalization of Religous Zionism." In *Rethinking the Messianic Idea in Judaism*, edited by Michael Morgan and Steven Weitzman, 229–255. Bloomington: Indiana University Press, 2015.

Henshke, David. "On the Question of Unity in Maimonides's Thought." *Da'at* 37 (1996): 37–52. Hebrew.

Herberg, Will. *Protestant—Catholic—Jew: An Essay in Religious Sociology*. Chicago: University of Chicago Press, 1955.

Herzog, Isaac. "The Rights of Minorities According to Halakhah." *Tehumin* 2 (1981): 169–199. Hebrew.

Heschel, Abraham Joshua. "No Religion is an Island." *Union Seminary Quarterly Review* 21 (1966): 117–134.

Higger, Michael. *Massekhet Semahot*. Jerusalem: Makor, 1970.

Hirshman, Marc (Menachem). "Election and Rejection in the Midrash." *Jewish Studies Quarterly* 16 (2009): 71–82.

———. "Rabbinic Universalism in the Second and Third Centuries." *Harvard Theological Review* 93 (2000): 101–115.

———. *Torah Lekhol Ba'ei Olam: Zerem Universali Be-Sifrut Ha-Tana'im Ve-Yahaso Le-Hokhmat He-Amim.* Tel Aviv: Ha-Kibbutz ha-Meuhad, 1999.

Hoch, Liron and Menachem Kellner. "'The Voice Is the Voice of Jacob, But the Hands Are the Hands of Esau': Isaac Abravanel between Judah Halevi and Moses Maimonides." *Jewish History* 26 (2012): 61–83.

Holtz, Barry. *Rabbi Akiva: Sage of the Talmud.* New Haven: Yale University Press, 2017.

Hyman, Aharon. *Toledot ha-Tannaim ve-ha Amoraim.* 3 vols. London: n.p., 1910.

Idel, Moshe. *Kabbalah: New Perspectives.* New Haven: Yale University Press, 1988.

Inbari, Motti. *Jewish Fundamentalism and the Temple Mount: Who Will Build the Third Temple?* Albany: SUNY Press, 2009.

———. *Messianic Religious Zionism Confronts Israeli Territorial Compromises.* Cambridge: Cambridge University Press, 2012.

Ivry, Alfred "The Image of Moses in Maimonides's Thought." In *Rambam: Shamranut, Mekoriut, Mahapkhanut,* edited by Aviezer Ravitzky, 481–499. Jerusalem: Merkaz Zalman Shazar, 2008). Hebrew.

Jospe, Raphael. "Affirming Chosenness and Pluralism. Ritual Exclusivity vs. Spiritual Inclusivity." Forthcoming.

———. "Moses Mendelssohn: A Medieval Modernist." In *Sepharad in Ashkenaz: Medieval Knowledge and Eighteenth-Century Enlightened Jewish Discourse,* edited by Andrea Schatz, Irene Zwiep, and Resianne Fontaine, 107–140. Amsterdam: Royal Netherlands Academy of Arts and Sciences, 2007.

Loewe, Judah Leib ben Bezalel (Maharal). *Derekh ha-Hayyim, Gur Aryeh, Nezah Yisrael, Tiferet Yisrael.* http://responsa-orum.co.il/www/?page_id=322&lang=en.

Judt, Tony. *Postwar: A History of Europe since 1945.* London: William Heinemann, 2005.

———. *When the Facts Change.* London: William Heinemann, 2014.

Kaminsky, Joel. "Did Election Imply the Mistreatment of Non-Israelites?" *Harvard Theological Review* 96 (2003): 397–425.

———. "A Light to the Nations: Was There Mission or Conversion in the Hebrew Bible?" *Jewish Studies Quarterly* 16 (2009): 6–22.

———. *Yet I Loved Jacob: Reclaiming the Biblical Concept of Election.* Nashville: Abingdon, 2007.

Kaminsky, Joel, and Anne Stewart. "God of All the World: Universalism and Developing Monotheism in Isaiah 40–66." *Harvard Theological Review* 99 (2006): 139–163.

Kanievsky, Chaim. *Kiryat Melekh.* http://responsa-forum.co.il/www/?page_id=322&lang=en.

Kaplan, Lawrence. "Maimonides on the Singularity of the Jewish People." *Da'at* 15 (1985): v–xxvii.

Kaplan, Mordecai. *Judaism as a Civilization: Towards the Reconstruction of American Jewish Life.* New York: Thomas Yoseloff, 1934.

———. *Know How to Answer: A Guide to Reconstructionism.* New York: Jewish Reconstructionist Foundation, 1951.

Kasher, Hannah. *Al ha-Minim, ha-kofrim, ve-ha-Epikorsim be-Mishnat ha-Rambam.* Tel Aviv: Ha-Kibbutz ha-Me'uhad, 2011.

———. "Between the Idolater and the Believer in God's Corporeality." *Da'at* 61 (2007): 73–82. Hebrew.

———. *Elyon Al Kol ha-Goyyim: Tsiyyunei Derekh ba-Philosophiah ha-Yehudit be-Sugiyat ha-Am ha-Nivhar*. Tel Aviv: Idra, 2018.

———. "Maimonides's Interpretation of the Story of the Divine Revelation in the Cleft of the Rock." *Da'at* 35 (1995): 29–66. Hebrew.

———. "Maimonides on the Intellects of Women and Gentiles." In *Interpreting Maimonides*, edited by Charles Manekin and Daniel Davie, 46–64. Cambridge: Cambridge University Press, 2018.

———. "Maimonides's View of Circumcision as a Factor Uniting the Jewish and Muslim Communities." In *Studies in Muslim-Jewish Relations*, edited by Ronald L. Nettler, 103–108. Luxembourg: Harwood Academic Publishers, 1995.

———. Review of *Gam Hem Keruyim Adam: Ha-Nokhri Be-Einei ha-Rambam*, by Menachem Kellner. *Iyyun* 65 (2016): 400–404. Hebrew.

———. "The Myth of 'God's Anger' in the *Guide of the Perplexed*." *Eshel Beersheva* 4 (1996): 95–115. Hebrew.

———. "Three Punishments Which Are One, According to Maimonides." *Sidra* 14 (1988): 39–58. Hebrew.

Katz, Jacob. *Exclusivism and Tolerance*. New York: Schocken, 1962.

———. "The Vicissitudes of Three Apologetic Statements." *Zion* 23–24 (1958–1959): 174–93. Hebrew.

Kellner, Menachem. "And Yet, the Texts Remain: The Problem of the Command to Destroy the Canaanites." In *The Gift of the Land and the Fate of the Canaanites in Jewish Thought*, edited by Katell Berthelot, Menachem Hirshman, and Josef David, 153–179. Oxford: Oxford University Press, 2014).

———. "'The Beautiful Captive and Maimonides's Attitude towards Gentiles." In *Essays for a Jewish Lifetime: The Burton D. Morris Jubilee Volume*, edited by Menachem Butler and Marian E. Frankston. New York: Hakirah Press, forthcoming.

———. "Chosenness, Not Chauvinism: Maimonides on the Chosen People." In *A People Apart: Chosenness and Ritual in Jewish Philosophical Thought*, edited by Daniel H. Frank, 51–75. Albany: SUNY Press, 1993.

———. "The Convert as the Most Jewish of Jews? On the Centrality of Belief (the Opposite of Heresy) in Maimonidean Judaism." *Jewish Thought/Mahshevet Yisrael* (Ben Gurion University Annual) 1 (2019): 33–52.

———. *Dogma in Medieval Jewish Thought*. Oxford: Littman Library of Jewish Civilization and Oxford University Press, 1986.

———. "*Farteitcht un Farbessert* (On 'Correcting' Maimonides)." *Me'orot* 6, no. 2 (2007). http://library.yctorah.org/files/2016/07/Kellner-on-Rambam-FINAL.pdf.

———. *Gam Hem Keruyim Adam: Ha-Nokhri Be-Einei ha-Rambam*. Ramat Gan: Bar Ilan University Press, 2016.

———. "Maimonides's Allegiances to Torah and Science." *Torah u-Madda Journal* 7 (1997): 88–104; repr. in Kellner, Menachem. *Science in the Bet Midrash: Studies in Maimonides*, 217–231. Boston: Academic Studies Press, 2009.

———. *Maimonides's Confrontation with Mysticism*. Oxford: Littman Library of Jewish Civilization, 2006.

———. *Maimonides on the "Decline of the Generations" and the Nature of Rabbinic Authority*. Albany: SUNY Press, 1996.

———. *Maimonides on Human Perfection*. Atlanta: Scholars Press, 1990.
———. *Maimonides on Judaism and the Jewish People*. Albany: SUNY Press, 1991.
———. "Maimonides's Moses: Torah, History, Cosmos." In *Moshe Avi ha-Nevi'im: Demuto Bere'i he-hagut le-Doroteha*, edited by Moshe Hallamish et al., 151–177. Ramat Gan: Bar Ilan University Press, 2011. Hebrew.
———. "Maimonides on the Science of the *Mishneh Torah*: Provisional or Permanent?" *AJS Review* 18 (1993): 169–194.
———. "Maimonides's *True Religion*—for Jews, or All Humanity?" *Me'orot* 7, no. 1 (2008): 1–24. https://www.academia.edu/36128107/Menachem_Kellner_Maimonides_True_Religion_for_Jews_or_All_Humanity_Me_orot_Edah_Journal_vol._7_no._1_2008_1-24.
———. "Misogyny: Gersonides vs. Maimonides." In *Torah in the Observatory: Gersonides, Maimonides, Song of Songs*, 283–304. Boston: Academic Studies Press, 2010.
———. "Monotheism as a Continuing Ethical Challenge to Jews." In *Monotheism and Ethics: Historical and Contemporary Intersections among Judaism, Christianity, and Islam*, edited by Y. Tzvi Langermann, 75–86. Leiden: Brill, 2012.
———. *Must a Jew Believe Anything?* 2nd ed. Oxford: Littman Library of Jewish Civilization, 2006.
———. "Must We Have Heretics?" *Conversations* 1 (2008): 6–10.
———. "A New and Unanticipated Textual Witness to the Reading, 'All Who Kills a Single Person—it is as if He Destroyed an Entire World.'" *Tarbiz* 57 (2007): 565–566. Hebrew.
———. "On Universalism and Particularism in Judaism." *Da'at* 36 (1996): v–xv.
———. "Rashi and Maimonides on Torah and the Cosmos." In *Between Rashi and Maimonides: Themes in Medieval Jewish Thought, Literature and Exegesis*, edited by Ephraim Kanarfogel and Moshe Sokolow, 23–58. New York: Yeshiva University Press, 2010.
———. *Science in the Bet Midrash: Studies in Maimonides*. Boston: Academic Studies Press, 2009.
———. "Steven Schwarzschild, Moses Maimonides, and 'Jewish Non-Jews.'" In *Moses Maimonides (1138–1204): His Religious, Scientific, and Philosophical Wirkungsgeschichte in Different Cultural Contexts*, edited by Goerg K. Hasselhoff and Oftried Fraise, 587–606. Wuerzburg: Ergon, 2004.
———. Tabernacle, Sacrifices, and Judaism: Maimonides vs. Nahmanides." TheTorah.com. Accessed February 11, 2021. https://www.thetorah.com/article/tabernacle-sacrifices-and-judaism-maimonides-vs-nahmanides.
———. "Thinking Idolatry With/Against Maimonides—The Case of Christianity." In *Thinking Idolatry Today*, edited by Alon Goshen-Gottstein. Boston: Academic Studies Press, forthcoming.
———. "Tolerance." In "Key Concepts in Interreligious Discourses," edited by Georges Tamer et al. Berlin/Boston: Walter de Gruyter, forthcoming.
———. "What is Heresy?" In *Studies in Jewish Philosophy: Collected Essays of the Academy for Jewish Philosophy, 1980–85*, edited by N. Samuelson, 191–214. Lanham: University Press of America, 1987.
———. "We Are Not Alone." In *Radical Responsibility: Celebrating the Thought of Chief Rabbi Lord Jonathan Sacks*, edited by Michael J. Harris, Daniel Rynhold, and Tamra Wright, 139–154. Jerusalem: Magid Books, 2012.
Kellner, Menachem, and David Gillis. *Maimonides the Universalist: The Ethical Horizons of Mishneh Torah*. Liverpool: Littman Library of Jewish Civilization, 2020.

Kellner, Menachem, and Jolene Kellner, "Respectful Disagreement: A Response to Raphael Jospe." In *Jewish Theology and World Religions*, edited by Alon Goshen-Gottstein and Eugene Korn, 123–133. Oxford: Littman Library of Jewish Civilization, 2012.

Kimelman, Reuven. "Judaism and Pluralism." *Modern Judaism* 7 (1987): 131–150.

———."Lekhah Dodi" ve-Kabbalat Shabbat: Ha-Mashma'ut ha-Mistit. Jerusalem: Magnes, 2003.

———. "My Response to Alon Goshen-Gottstein's 'Luther the Anti-Semite': A Contemporary Jewish Perspective." *Contemporary Jewry* 40 (2020): 85–107.

———. "Rabbis Joseph B. Soloveitchik and Abraham Joshua Heschel on Jewish-Christian Relations." *Me'orot* 4 (2004): 1–21.

———. Review of *For the Sake of Heaven and Earth: The New Encounter between Judaism and Christianity*, by Irving Greenberg. *Modern Judaism* 27 (2007): 103–125.

———. "U-N'Taneh Tokef as a Midrashic Poem." In *The Experience of Jewish Liturgy: Studies Dedicated to Menahem Schmelzer*, edited by Debra Reed Blank, 115–146. Leiden: Brill, 2011.

Klein-Braslavy, Sara. "The Philosophical Exegesis." In *Hebrew Bible/Old Testament: The History of Its Interpretation*, edited by Magne Saebo, 302–320. Goettingen: Vandenhoeck and Ruprecht, 2000.

Kobler, Franz. *Letters of Jews through the Ages*. New York: East and West Library, 1978.

Kochin, Michael. "Morality, Nature and Esotericism in Leo Strauss' *Persecution and the Art of Writing*." *Review of Politics* 64 (2002): 261–283.

Kook, Zvi Yehudah. *Yahadut ve-Nazrut*. Edited by Shlomo Aviner. Jerusalem: Sifriyat Hannah, 2001.

Korn, Eugene. "Extra Synagogam Sallus Est? Judaism and the Religious Other." In *Religious Perspectives on Religious Diversity*, edited by Robert McKim, 37–62. Leiden: Brill, 2016.

———. "Gentiles, the World to Come, and Judaism: The Odyssey of a Rabbinic Text." *Modern Judaism* 14 (1994): 265–87.

———. "Idolatry and the Covenantal Pluralism of Irving Greenberg." In *A Torah Giant: The Intellectual Legacy of Rabbi Dr. Irving (Yitz) Greenberg*, edited by Shmuly Yanklowitz, 59–70. Jerusalem: Urim Publications, 2018.

———. "The Man of Faith and Religious Dialogue: Revisiting 'Confrontation.'" *Modern Judaism* 25 (2005): 290–315.

———. "One God, Many Faiths: A Jewish Theology of Covenantal Pluralism." In *Two Faiths, One Covenant?*, edited by Eugene Korn and John Pawlikowsky, 147–154. Lanham: Rowman and Littlefield, 2005.

———. "The People Israel, Christianity, and the Covenantal Responsibility to History." In *Covenant and Hope*, edited by Robert W. Jensen and Eugene Korn, 145–172. Grand Rapids: Eerdmans, 2012.

———. "Religious Violence, Sacred Texts and Theological Values." In *Plowshares into Swords? Reflections on Religion and Violence*, edited by Robert W. Jensen and Eugene Korn. N.p.: Center for Jewish Christian Understanding and Cooperation, 2014. https://www.cjcuc.org/.

———. "Rethinking Christianity: Rabbinic Positions and Possibilities." In *Jewish Theology and World Religions*, edited by Alon Goshen-Gottstein and Eugene Korn, 189–216. London: Littman Library of Jewish Civilization, 2012.

Kraemer, Joel. *Maimonides: The Life and World of One of Civilization's Greatest Minds*. New York: Doubleday, 2008.

Kreisel, Howard. "Judah Halevi's Influence on Maimonides: A Preliminary Appraisal." *Maimonidean Studies* 2 (1991): 95–122.

———. "Maimonides on Divine Religion." In *Maimonides After 800 Years: Essays on Maimonides and His Influence*, edited by Jay Harris, 151–166. Cambridge, MA: Harvard University Press, 2007.

———. *Maimonides's Political Thought: Studies in Ethics, Law, and the Human Ideal*. Albany: SUNY Press, 1999.

Krinis, Ehud. *God's Chosen People: Judah Halevi's 'Kuzari' and the Shi'i Imam Doctrine*. Turnhout: Brepols, 2014.

Kymlicka, Will. "Two Models of Pluralism and Tolerance." In *Toleration: An Elusive Virtue*, edited by David Heyd, 81–105. Princeton: Princeton University Press, 1996.

Lachter, Hartley. "Israel as a Holy People in Medieval Kabbalah." In *Holiness in Jewish Thought*, edited by Alan Mittleman, 137–159. Oxford: Oxford University Press, 2018.

Langer, Ruth. "The Censorship of Aleinu in Ashkenaz and Its Aftermath." In *The Experience of Jewish Liturgy: Studies Dedicated to Menachem Schmeltzer*, edited by Debra Reed Blank, 147–166. Leiden: Brill, 2011.

———. "Jewish Liturgical Memory and the Non-Jew." In *Jewish Theology and World Religions*, edited by Alon Goshen-Gottstein and Eugene Korn, 167–186. Oxford: Littman Library of Jewish Civilization, 2012.

Langermann, Y. Tzvi. "*Fusul Musa*, on Maimonides's Method of Composition." *Maimonidean Studies* 5 (2008): 325–344.

———. "Science and the *Kuzari*." *Science in Context* 10 (1997): 495–522.

Lasker, Daniel J. *Jewish Philosophical Polemics against Christianity in the Middle Ages*. 2nd ed. Oxford: Littman Library of Jewish Civilization, 2007.

———. "Maimonides and the Karaites: From Critic to Cultural Hero." In *Maimonides Y Su Eoca*, edited by Carlos del Valle, 311–325. Madrid: Sociedad Estatal de Conmemoraciones Culturales, 2007.

———. "Popular Polemics and Philosophical Truth in the Medieval Jewish Critique of Christianity." *Journal of Jewish Thought and Philosophy* 8 (1999): 243–259.

———. "Proselyte Judaism, Christianity, and Islam in the Thought of Judah Halevi." *Jewish Quarterly Review*, 81 (1990): 75–91.

———. "R. Judah Halevi as Biblical Exegete in the *Kuzari*." In *Davar Davur Al Ofanav: Mehkarim Be-Parshanut Ha-Mikra Ve-Ha-Koran Bimei Ha-Benayim Mugashim Le-Haggai Ben-Shammai*, edited by S. Hopkins et al., 179–192. Jerusalem: Makhon Ben-Zvi, 2007. Hebrew.

———. "Rashi and Maimonides on Christianity." In *Between Rashi and Maimonides: Themes in Medieval Jewish Thought, Literature and Exegesis*, edited by Ephraim Kanarfogel and Moshe Sokolow, 3–21. New York: Yeshiva University Press, 2010.

———. "Tradition and Innovation in Maimonides's Attitude toward Other Religions." In *Maimonides after 800 Years: Essays on Maimonides and His Influence*, edited by Jay Harris, 167–182. Cambridge, MA: Harvard University Press, 2007.

Laufer, Nathan. *Rendevous with God: Revealing the Meaning of the Jewish Holidays and Their Mysterious Rituals*. Jerusalem: Magid, 2016.

Lawee, Eric. *Rashi's Commentary on the Torah: Canonization and Resistance in the Reception of a Jewish Classic*. Oxford: Oxford University Press, 2019.

Leibowitz, Nehama. *Studies in Shemot*. Jerusalem: World Zionist Organization, 1976.

Levenson, Jon. "Chosenness and Its Enemies." *Commentary* 126, no. 5 (December, 2008). https://www.commentarymagazine.com/articles/jon-levenson-2/chosenness-and-its-enemies/.

———. "The Universal Horizon of Biblical Particularism." In *Ethnicity and the Bible*, edited by Mark G. Brett, 143–169. Leiden: Brill, 1996.

Levinas, Emanuel. "Ideology and Idealism." In *Modern Jewish Ethics: Theory and Practice*, edited by Marvin Fox, 121–138. Columbus: Ohio State University Press, 1975.

Liebes, Yehudah. *Het'o shel Elisha*. Jerusalem: Akademon, 1990.

Linfield, Susie. *The Lion's Den: Zionism and the Left from Hannah Arendt to Noam Chomsky*. New Haven: Yale University Press, 2019.

Lobel, Diana. *Between Mysticism and Philosophy: Sufi Language of Religious Experience in Judah Ha-Levi's Kuzari*. Albany: SUNY Press, 2000.

———. "A Dwelling Place for the Shekhinah." *Jewish Quarterly Review* 90 (1999): 103–125.

Lorberbaum, Yair, and Haim Shapira. "Maimonides's Epistle on Martyrdom in the Light of Legal Philosophy." *Dine Israel* 25 (2008): 123–169.

Lubitch, Ronen. "The Righteous among the Nations of the Earth in the Thought of R. Hayyim David Halevi: Kabbalah and Natural Justice in the Question of the Attitude towards Gentiles." In *Yahadut Shel Ḥayyim: Iyyunim be-Yetsirato ha-Hagutit-Hilkhatit Shel ha-Rav Ḥayyim David Halevi*, edited by Zvi Zohar and Avi Sagi, 215–234. Jerusalem: Keter, 2007. Hebrew.

Luria, Maxwell, "Rabbi Eliyahu Benamozegh: Israel and Humanity." Jewishideas.org. Accessed February 10, 2021. https://www.jewishideas.org/article/rabbi-eliyahu-benamozegh-israel-and-humanity-0.

Maghen, Ze'ev. *John Lennon and the Jews: A Philosophical Rampage*. 2nd ed. Jerusalem: Toby Press, 2015.

Maimonides, Abraham. *Commentary on Genesis and Exodus*. Edited by S. D. Sasoon and E. Weisenberg. Hebrewbooks.org.

Makbili, Yohai. "Consciousness and Community: Ritual Impurity and Purity in Maimonides's Thought." PhD diss., University of Haifa, 2018. Hebrew.

Marcus, Joel. "The Once and Future Messiah in Early Christianity and Chabad." *New Testament Studies* 46 (2000): 381–401.

Mekhilta d'Rabbi Ishmael. http://responsa-orum.co.il/www/?page_id=322&lang=en.

Melamed, Abraham. *Al Kitfei Anakim: Toldot ha-Pulmus Bein Aharonim le-Rishonim he-Hagut ha-Yehudit Bimei ha-Benayim u-Ve-Reshit ha-Et ha-Hadashah*. Ramat-Gan: Bar Ilan University Press, 2003.

———. *Dat: me-Hok le-Emunah—Korotav Shel Minu'ah Mekhonen*. Tel Aviv: Ha-Kibbutz Ha-Me'uhad, 2014.

———. *The Image of the Black in Jewish Culture: A History of the Other*. London: Routledge, 2003.

———. "The Land of Israel and the Climatological Theory in Jewish Thought." In *Eretz Yisrael be-Hagut ha-Yehudit Bimei ha-Benayim*, edited by Moshe Hallamish and Aviezer Ravitzky, 52–79. Jerusalem: Yad Ben-Zvi, 1991. Hebrew.

Melamed, Eliezer. "Love and Respect for Lovers of Israel." *Ba-Sheva*, November 6, 2014. https://www.inn.co.il/News/News.aspx/277905. Hebrew.

Melamed, Yitzhak. "Idolatry and Its Premature Rabbinic Obituary." In *Jewish Philosophy Past and Present: Contemporary Responses to Classical Sources*, edited by Daniel Frank and Aaron Segal, 126–137. New York: Routledge, 2017.

Mendes-Flohr, Paul. "Israel: In Pursuit of Normalcy—Zionism's Ambivalence towards Israel's Election." In *Many Are Chosen: Divine Election and Western Nationalism*, edited by William R. Hutchison and H. Lehman, 201–224. Minneapolis: Fortress Press, 1994.

———. *Jewish Philosophy: An Obituary*. Occasional Papers 3: The Fourth Frank Green Lecture. Oxford: Oxford Centre for Hebrew and Jewish Studies, 1999. https://www.ochjs.ac.uk/wp-content/uploads/2011/09/4th-Frank-Green-Lecture-Jewish-Philosophy-An-Obituary.pdf.

Mendus, Susan. *Toleration and the Limits of Liberalism*. Atlantic Highlands: Humanities Press International, 1989.

Mirsky, Yehudah. *Rav Kook: Mystic in a Time of Revolution*. New Haven: Yale University Press, 2014.

Nahmanides, Moses (Ramban). *Commentary on the Torah—Exodus*. Translated by Charles B. Chavel. New York: Shilo, 1973.

Nehorai, Michael Zvi. "A Portion in the World to Come for the Righteous/Sages of the Nations." *Da'at* 50–52 (2003): 97–105. Hebrew.

———. "'Righteous Gentiles Have a Share in the World to Come.'" *Tarbiz* 61 (1992): 465–487. Hebrew.

Nelson, Cary. *Israel Denial: Anti-Zionism, Anti-Semitism, & the Faculty Campaign Against the Jewish State*. Bloomington: Indiana University Press, 2019.

Neudecker, Reinhard "'And You Shall Love Your Neighbor as Yourself—I Am the Lord' (Lev. 19:18) in Jewish Interpretation." *Biblica* 73, no. 4 (1992): 496–517.

Novak, David. *The Election of Israel: The Idea of the Chosen People*. Cambridge: Cambridge University Press, 1995.

———. *The Image of the Non-Jew in Judaism: An Historical and Constructive Study of the Noahide Laws*. New York: E. Mellen Press, 1983.

———. "Maimonides and Aquinas on Natural Law." In *Talking with Christians: Musings of a Jewish Theologian*, edited by David Novak, 67–88. Grand Rapids: Eerdmans, 2005.

———. Review of *Maimonides on Judaism and the Jewish People*, by Menachem Kellner. *Shofar* 11 (1992): 150–152.

Ophir, Adi, and Ishay Rosen-Zvi. *Goy: Israel's Multiple Others and the Birth of the Gentile*. Oxford: Oxford University Press, 2018.

Oren, Gedaliah. "R. Menahem Ha-Meiri's Attitude toward the 'Other.'" *Da'at* 60 (2007): 29–49. Hebrew.

Pinchot, Roy. "The Deeper Conflict between Maimonides and Ramban over the Sacrifices." *Tradition* 33 (1999): 24–33.

Rabinovitch, Nachum. *Melumedei Milhamah*. Ma'aleh Adumin: Ma'aliyot, 1992.

Ravitzky, Aviezer. "Introduction—the Binding of Isaac and the Covenant." In *Avraham Avi ha-Ma'aminim*, edited by M. Hallamish et al., 11–38. Ramat-Gan: Bar-Ilan University Press, 2002. Hebrew.

———. "On the Image of the Leader in Jewish Thought." In *Aharav: al Manhigut u-Manhigim*, edited by Hannah Amit, 45–57. Tel Aviv: Ministry of Defense, 2000.

———. "The Question of Tolerance in the Jewish Religious Tradition." In *Hazon Nahum: Studies in Jewish Law, Thought, and History Presented to Dr. Norman Lamm on the Occasion of His Seventieth Birthday*, edited by Yaakov Elman and Jeffrey S. Gurock, 359–391. New York: Yeshiva University Press, 1997.

———. "The Question of Tolerance: Between Pluralism and Paternalism." In *Ḥarut Al ha-Luḥot*, edited by Aviezer Ravitzky, 114–138. Tel Aviv: Am Oved, 1999. Hebrew.

Reiner, Rami "Le statut des prosélytes en Allemagne et en France du 11e au 13e siècle." *REJ* 167 (2008): 99–119.

———. "Tough Are Gerim: Conversion to Judaism in Medieval Europe." *Havruta* 1 (Spring 2008): 54–63.

Reines, Chaim. "The Self and Other in Rabbinic Ethics." In *Contemporary Jewish Ethics*, edited by Menachem Kellner, 162–174. New York: Sanhedrin Press, 1978.

Robbins, Bruce. "The Red Emigrant." *The Nation*, March 30, 2017. https://www.thenation.com/article/archive/the-red-emigrant/.

Robinson, James. "Maimonides, Samuel Ibn Tibbon, and the Construction of a Jewish Tradition of Philosophy." In *Maimonides after 800 Years: Essays on Maimonides and His Influence*, edited by Jay Harris, 291–306. Cambridge: Harvard University Press, 2007.

Rosenak, Avinoam. *Sedakim*. Tel Aviv: Resling, 2013.

Rosenzweig, Franz. Introduction to *Jüdische Schriften*, vol. 1, by H. Cohen, edited by B. Strauss. Berlin: n.p., 1924.

Rosner, Fred. "The Jewish Attitude toward Abortion." *Tradition* 10 (1968): 48–71. Repr. in *Contemporary Jewish Ethics*, edited by Menachem Kellner, 257–269, New York: Sanhedrin Press, 1978.

Ross, Tamar. *Expanding the Palace of Tora: Orthodoxy and Feminism*. Waltham: Brandeis University Press, 2004.

Roth, Leon. "Moralization and Demoralization in Jewish Ethics." In *Is There a Jewish Philosophy?*, edited by Leon Roth, 128–143. London: Littman Library of Jewish Civilization, 1999.

Rynhold, Daniel, and Michael J. Harris. *Nietzsche, Soloveitchik, and Contemporary Jewish Philosophy*. Cambridge: Cambridge University Press, 2018.

Sa'adia Gaon, *Book of Beliefs and Opinions*. Translated by Samuel Rosenblatt. New Haven: Yale University Press, 1948.

Sacks, Jonathan. "The Dignity of Difference: Exorcizing Plato's Ghost." In *The Dignity of Difference: How to Avoid the Clash of Civilizations*, 1–12. 2nd ed. New York and London: Continuum, 2003.

———. *The Politics of Hope*. London: Jonathan Cape, 1997.

Sagi, Raphael. *Radikalism Meshiḥi be-Medinat Yisrael: Perakim be-Sod ha-Tikkun ha-Meshiḥi bi-Haguto Shel ha-Rav Yizhak Ginsberg*. Tel Aviv: Gevanim, 2015.

Sagiv, Assaf. "George Steiner's Jewish Problem." *Azure* 15 (2003). Repr. in Alexander, Edward, and Paul Bogdanor, eds. *The Jewish Divide Over Israel: Accusers and Defenders*, 47–63. New Brunswick: Transaction, 2006; repr. again in Soeiro, Ricardo, ed. *Wounds of Possibility: Essays on George Steiner*, 194–213. Cambridge: Cambridge Scholars Publishing, 2012.

Sand, Shlomo. *The Invention of the Jewish People*. Translated by Yael Lotan. London: Verso, 2009.

Sandel, Michael J. *Liberalism and the Limits of Justice*. 2nd ed. Cambridge: Cambridge University Press, 1998.

Satherley, Tessa. "'The Simple Jew': The 'Price Tag' Phenomenon, Vigilantism, and Rabbi Yitzchak Ginsburgh's Political Kabbalah." *Melilah* 10 (2013): 57–91.

Schachter, Herschel. "Women Rabbis?" *Hakirah: The Flatbush Journal of Jewish Law and Thought* 11 (2011): 19–23.

Schaefer, Peter. *Mirror of His Beauty: Feminine Images of God from the Bible to the Early Kabbalah*. Princeton: Princeton University Press, 2002.

Schlossberg, Eliezer. "Maimonides's Attitude Towards Islam." *Pe'amim* 42 (1990): 38–60. Hebrew.

Schwartz, Dov. *Challenge and Crisis in Rabbi Kook's Circle*. Tel Aviv: Am Oved, 2001. Hebrew.

——. *Religion or Halakha: The Philosophy of Rabbi Joseph B. Soloveitchik*. Leiden: Brill, 2007.

——. "'From Theurgy to Magic': The Evolution of the Magical-Talismanic Justification of Sacrifice in the Circle of Nahmanides and His Interpreters." *Aleph* 1 (2001): 165–213.

Schwarzschild, Steven S. "The Democratic Socialism of Hermann Cohen." *HUCA* 27 (1965): 417–38.

——. "Do Noachites Have to Believe in Revelation? (A Passage in Dispute between Maimonides, Spinoza, Mendelssohn, and Herman Cohen) A Contribution to a Jewish View of Natural Law." In *The Pursuit of the Ideal: Jewish Writings of Steven Schwarzschild*, edited by Menachem Kellner, 29–59. Albany: SUNY Press, 1990.

——. "Franz Rosenzweig's Anecdotes about Hermann Cohen." In *Gegenwart in Rueblick*, edited by Herbert Strauss and Kurt Grossman, 209–218. Heidelberg: Stiehm, 1970. Repr. in Schwarzschild, Steven. *The Tragedy of Optimism: Writings on Hermann Cohen*, edited by George Kohler, 35–42. Albany: SUNY Press, 2018.

——. "The Messianic Doctrine in Contemporary Jewish Thought." In *Great Jewish Ideas*, edited by Abraham Millgram, 237–259. Washington, DC: B'nai B'rith Department of Adult Jewish Education, 1974.

——. "Moral Radicalism and 'Middlingness' in the Ethics of Maimonides." In *The Pursuit of the Ideal: Jewish Writings of Steven Schwarzschild*, edited by Menachem Kellner, 302–318, 137–161. Albany: SUNY Press, 1990.

——. "On Jewish Eschatology." In *The Pursuit of the Ideal: Jewish Writings of Steven Schwarzschild*, edited by Menachem Kellner, 209–228. Albany: SUNY Press, 1990.

——. *The Pursuit of the Ideal: Jewish Writings of Steven Schwarzschild*, edited by Menachem Kellner. Albany: SUNY Press, 1990.

Schwarzfuchs, Simon-Raymond. "Les lois royales de Maimonide." *Revue des etudes juives* 111 (1951–52): 63–86.

Seeman, Don. "God's Honor, Violence and the State." In *From Swords into Plowshares? Reflections on Religion and Violence*, edited by Robert W. Jenson and Eugene Korn. N.p: Center for Jewish-Christian Understanding and Cooperation, 2014. https://www.cjcuc.org/.

——. "Violence, Ethics, and Divine Honor in Modern Jewish Thought." *JAAR* 73 (2004): 1015–1048.

Seeskin, Kenneth. *Jewish Messianic Thoughts in an Age of Despair*. Cambridge: Cambridge University Press, 2012.

——. "Maimonides and Hermann Cohen on Messianism." *Maimonidean Studies* 5 (2008): 375–392.

——. *No Other Gods: The Modern Struggle against Idolatry*. New York: Berhman House, 1995.

———. "When Did the Bible Become Monotheist?" TheTorah.com. Accessed February 10, 2021. https://www.thetorah.com/article/when-did-the-bible-become-monotheistic.
Seforno, Ovadiah. Commentary to Exodus. http://responsa-forum.co.il/www/?s=Tiferet+Yisrael&lang=en.
Shapiro, David. *Studies in Jewish Thought*. Vol. 2. New York: Yeshiva University Press, 1981.
———. *Yesodei ha-Dat ha-Universalit Al Pi Mekorot ha-Yahduat*. New York: Bloch, 1936.
Shapiro, Marc. "Is It Permissible to Enter a Church? First Publication of a Responsum by Ha-Ga'on R. Eliezer Berkovitz on the Matter." *Milin Havivin* 4 (2011): 43–50.
———. "Is There an Obligation to Believe that R. Shimon bar Yochai Wrote the Zohar?" *Milin Havivin* 5 (2010–11): 1–20. Hebrew.
———. *The Limits of Orthodox Theology: Maimonides's Thirteen Principles Reappraised*. London: Littman Library of Jewish Civilization, 2004.
———. *Studies in Maimonides and His Interpreters*. Scranton: University of Scranton Press, 2008.
Silberstein, Laurence J. and Robert L. Cohn. *The Other in Jewish Thought and History: Constructions of Jewish Culture and Identity*. New York: New York University Pres, 1994.
Silman, Yochanan. *Bein Lalekhet be-Derakhav u-Lishmo'a be-Kolo*. Alon Shvut: Herzog College, 2012.
———. "Commandments and Transgressions in Halakhah—Obedience and Rebellion, or Repair and Destruction?" *Dine Israel*, 16 (1991): 183–201. Hebrew.
———. "Halakhic Determinations of a Nominalistic and Realistic Nature: Legal and Philosophical Considerations." *Dine Israel* 12 (1986): 249–266. Hebrew.
———. "Introduction to the Philosophical Analysis of the Normative-Ontological Tension in the Halakha." *Da'at* 31 (1993): v–xx.
———. *Kol Gadol ve-Lo Yasaf: Torat Yisrael Bein Shelemut ve-Hishtalmut*. Jerusalem: Magnes, 1999.
Simon, Ernst. "The Neighbor (*Re'a*) Whom We Shall Love." In *Modern Jewish Ethics: Theory and Practice*, edited by Marvin Fox, 29–56. Columbus: Ohio State University Press, 1975.
Sklare, David. "Are the Gentiles Obligated to Observe the Torah? The Discussion Concerning the Universality of the Torah in the East in the Tenth and Eleventh Centuries." In *Be'erot Yitzhak: Studies in Memory of Isadore Twersky*, edited by Jay Harris, 311–346. Cambridge, MA: Harvard University Press, 2005).
Smith, Anthony D. *Chosen Peoples*. Oxford: Oxford University Press, 2003.
Soloveitchik, Joseph Ber. "Confrontation." *Tradition* (1964): 5–29.
Stammler, Haggai. "Psychology of Nations: A Forgotten Field." *Moreshet* 15 (2015): 209–224. Hebrew.
Steiner, George. *Errata: An Examined Life*. New Haven: Yale University Press, 1998).
———. "Our Homeland, the Text." *Salmagundi* 66 (1985).
———. "We Are the Guests of Life and of Truth: Concerning the Capriciousness of Existence, the Wonder of the State of Israel and the Lost Nobility of the Jewish People (a Grateful Response of Acceptance to the Börne Prize)." *European Judaism* 36 (2003): 84–90.
Stern, Josef. "Maimonides's Parable of Circumcision." *Sevara* 2 (1991): 35–48.
Stone, Suzanne. "Tolerance versus Pluralism in Judaism." *Journal of Human Rights* 2 (2003): 105–117.
Sviri, Sara. "Spiritual Trends in Pre-Kabbalistic Judeo-Spanish Literature: The Cases of Bahya Ibn Paquda and Judah Halevi." *Donaire* 6 (1996): 78–84.

Tropper, Amram. *Ke-Homer Be-Yad Ha-Yozer: Ma'asei Hakhamim Be-Sifrut Hazal*. Jerusalem: Merkaz Zalman Shazar, 2011.

Turgeman, Asaf. "Typological Exegesis Concerning the Image of Esau in Rabbinic Midrash and in Medieval Exegesis." *Sha'anan* 18 (2009): 53–66. Hebrew.

Turkel, Eli. "Partial Bibliography of Works by and about Rabbi Joseph B. Soloveitchik zt"l." http://www.math.tau.ac.il/~turkel/engsol.html.

Twersky, Isadore. *Introduction to the Code of Maimonides*. New Haven: Yale University Press, 1980.

———. "Maimonides and Eretz Israel: Halakhic, Philosophic, and Historical Perspectives." In *Perspectives on Maimonides*, edited by Joel Kraemer, 257–290. Oxford: Littman Library of Jewish Civilization, 1991.

Urbach, Ephraim E. "'Whoever Saves One Soul ... [mSan 4:5]': The History of a Recension." In *Me-Olamam Shel Hakhamim: Kovets Mehkarim*, 561–577. Jerusalem: Magnes, 1988. Hebrew.

Weiss, Raymond L. *Maimonides's Ethics: The Encounter of Philosophic and Religious Morality*. Chicago: University of Chicago Press, 1991.

Weiss, Tzahi. "Prayers to Angels and the Early Sefirotic Literature." *Jewish Studies Quarterly* 27 (2020): 22–35.

Williams, Bernard. "Toleration. An Impossible Virtue?" In *Toleration: An Elusive Virtue*, edited by David Heyd, 18–27. Princeton: Princeton University Press, 1996.

Wolfson, Elliot. *Venturing Beyond: Law and Morality in Kabbalistic Mysticism*. Oxford: Oxford University Press, 2006.

Wolfson, Harry. "Maimonides on the Unity and Incorporeality of God." *JQR* 56 (1965): 112–136.

Yagur, Moshe. "*Zehut Datit u-Gevulot Kehilati'im be-Hevrat ha-Genizah (Me'ot 10–13): Gerim, Avadim, Mumarim*." PhD diss., Tel Aviv University, 2018.

Yahalom, Yosef. *Shirat Hayav shel Rav Yehudah Halevi*. Jerusalem: Magnes, 2008.

Zacuto, Abraham. *Sefer Yuhasin ha-Shalem*. Jerusalem: Yerid ha-Sefarim, 2004.

Zini, Eliyahu. *Hesed le-Umim Hatat*. Haifa: Yeshivat Or Vishua, 2018.

Zohar, Zvi. "Rabbi Uziel—Individual, Nation, Humanity." In *Ha-Rav Uziel: Hagut, Halakhah, ve-Historiah*, edited by Zvi Zohar et al., 75–102. Ramat-Gan: Bar-Ilan University Press, 2020. Hebrew.

Index

abortion, 109
Abraham (Bible), xiv–xv, 3, 10–17, 24–27, 33, 37–38, 43–44, 46, 50–53, 66, 75–80, 84, 91–92, 100–101, 103, 124, 129, 135
Abraham ben David, *see* Rabad
Abraham ibn Ezra, xiiin1, 153n48
Abravanel, Isaac, 18n47, 24–25
Adam (Bible), xvi, 24n66, 33, 70, 91, 149
Aher, *see* Elisha ben Abuyah
Akiva (Rabbi), xiv, 68–69, 96n43
Aleichem, Sholom, xvi
Alexander, Edward
    The Jewish Divide Over Israel, 62n47
Altmann, Alexander, 44
    Tolerance and the Jewish Tradition, 111n21
am segulah, 3, 43
Amalek (Bible), 7, 43–44, 93, 101
Amonites (Bible), 43, 101
amr al-ilahi, see inyan elohi
antisemitism, xv, 57, 87–88, 114n28, 132n89
anti-Zionism, xv, 57, 125n61
Ariel, Yaakov, 7
Ariel, Yisrael, 107n8
Aristotle, 13–14, 28, 32, 91n23, 146n29, 152
Ashi (Rav), 69
Asimov, Isaac
    Foundation, 88n12
assimilation, 15n41, 35, 39n29, 86, 88

atheism, 56–57, 63n51, 106n4, 125n61
Aviner, Shlomo, 2–8, 32n8, 53n28, 71n7, 138n5
avodah zarah, 110, 111, 116, 131, 137–139, 142–145, 148–157
    Maimonides on, 145–146

Bahya ben Asher, 96n43
BDS, 109
Benamozegh, Elijah, 115n33
Ben-Gurion, David, 38
Benjamin, Walter, 60n45
Ben-Simon, Yisrael, 70n7
Berger, David, 101n59, 131, 138n4, 155
Berlin, Isaiah, 87n7, 91n23
Bible
    Genesis
        1, 156
        1:1, 29
        4:3–6, 24n66
        4:26, 11
        5:7–11, 11
        7:21–22, 92n26
        8:20–21, 24n66
        9:6, 96n43
        11, 91
        12:1, 13, 46
        12:5, 25, 80
        17:1–4, 45n10, 92n29
        17:5, 78–79
        18, 100
        18:19, 15, 75

21:33, 12n33, 25
22:23, 24n66
25, 95n40
25:1–6, 33n10
25:22–23, 95n40
27:22, 95n40
27:27, 95n40
27:34, 95n40

Exodus
3:12, 153n48
3:15, 16n42
4:22, 32n7
12:2, 23, 29n2
12:3–13, 23
12:38, 101n55
15, xiv
15:22–26, 17
15:25, 23
15:26, 23
18:27, 101n55
19, 42n3
19:5, 88–89
19:6, 119n43
19:22, 10n28
20:2, 148
20:3, 148
20:13, 96n43
20:21, 20
22:20, 95n41
24:18, 25n68
25:8, 20
29:46, 153n48
31:18, 25n68
33, 128
33:13, 48
33:16, 48

Leviticus
1:2, 20
1:9, 18n48, 24n66
11:44, 37n24, 50n17
19:2, 37, 50n17
19:18, 95
20:26, 6n18
26:42, 16n42, 153n48

Numbers
10:29, 70
15:15, 77
19:2, 6n18

Deuteronomy
4:31–40, 45n10
5:6, 148
5:7, 148
6:5, 82
6:6, 79
7:6–8, 45
7:6–9, 92
7:7, 16n42
10:14–15, 45
10:15, 16n42
10:19, 95
14:1, 96n43
14:1–2, 46
16:1–11, 77n26
19:10, 95
21:13, 74
23:4, 101n56
23:4–8, 101
26:16–19, 46

Joshua
7:9, 153n48

I Samuel
1:11, 21
7:22–23, 21
15:22, 21

Isaiah
11:6–8, 64
11:6, 118
11:9, 63–64
12:3, 7
40–66, 94
41:8, 80
43:21, 3

44:5, 77
49:3, 153n48
56:3, 76
Jeremiah
   2:3, 30n2
   5:6, 118
   5:12, 22
   7, 18n47, 25
   7:9–10, 22
   9:22–23, 26
   9:23, 165
Hosea
   11:4, 73
Amos
   1:1–2, 46–47
   9:7, 47
   9:8, 47
Micah
   4:5, 106n4
Zephaniah
   3:9, 117, 120
Psalms
   34:9, 13n36
   50:7–9, 24
   111:6, 29n2
   132:13, 153n48
   139:21, 81
Proverbs
   4:2, 96n43
   8:22, 30n2
Ecclesiastes
   12:10, 159
Daniel
   11:14, 117
Bleich, J. David, 141n13
Blidstein, Ya'akov (Gerald), 28n1, 107n8
Bogdanor, Paul
   The Jewish Divide Over Israel, see
      Alexander
Boyarin, Daniel
   Judaism, xiiin1

Brill, Alan, 107n8, 115
Buddhism, 142

Cain (Bible), 24n66, 98
Canaan, 12, 29
cardinal sins, 110, 139
Cave of Makhpelah massacre, 8
Chabon, Michael, 86
Chavel, Charles, 38n24
chosen people, *see* election
Christianity, xiiin1, 2, 7, 30, 32–33,
   39–40, 80–81, 86, 96–97, 99, 107–
   111, 113–118, 120, 122–124, 126,
   129n79, 131–133, 135–157, 161
   Catholic, xv, 7n22, 106–107,
      109n16, 138n5
circumcision, 13, 16, 17, 25, 72
climatology, 31
Cohen, Hermann, xiv, 62n48, 64–66, 88,
   91n23, 104, 134n93, 162
conservatism, xii, xv, xvii, 19
converts, *see* proselytes
Crescas, Hasdai, 13–14
Cromwell, Oliver, 136

dat ha-emet, 118
David (Bible), 44, 68, 84
Deutscher, Isaac, 54, 56–59, 88n10
Diamond, James
   Converts, Heretics, and Lepers,
      74n19, 95n42, 141n12

Edels, Shlomo, 100n52
Einstein, Albert, 60
Election, 13–17, 42ff
   Deutscher on, 56–58
   Halevi on, 51–54
   Kaplan on, 54–56
   Maimonides on, 62–67
   Steiner on, 58–62
   In Bible, 44–47

188 | We Are Not Alone

In liturgy, 49–51
In rabbinic texts, 47–49
Eliezer (Rabbi), 69
Elijah ben Solomon Zalman, the Gaon of Vilna, 32n8
Elisha ben Abuyah (Rabbi), 85n1
Elitzur, Yosef, 8
 Torat ha-Melekh, see Shapira
Eliyahu, Mordecai, 7
Eliyahu, Shmuel, 7
Ellenson, David, 96n43, 113n26
Enlightenment, 9n26, 112
epistemological modesty, 129, 136
Epstein, Baruch Halevi
 Baruch She-Amar, 96n43
Esau (Bible), 33, 45, 91, 94n40
Exodus Rabbah, 15n41, 25n68

Fackenheim, Emil, 35, 86, 90, 126
feminism, xi–xiii
Fiddler on the Roof, 121–123
Flohr-Mendes, Paul, 135n96
Freud, Sigmund, xvi–xvii, 60, 112, 133

Gamliel, 69n5
Gaon, Sa'adia, xiii, 30, 122n53
 Beliefs and Doctrines, xiii
Gaza withdrawal, 2
Gellman, Jerome (Yehuda), 48n14, 112n23, 126
Genesis Rabbah, 12n32, 29, 129n75
Gentiles, xii, 1, 4–9, 15n40, 25–27, 34–35, 41, 70, 72, 74, 80, 82–84, 89n13, 101–102, 107n8, 115–116, 118n41, 142
Ger, 72, 94–95
Gibbon, Edward
 Decline and Fall, 135
Gillis, David, xiv
 Maimonides the Unversalist, see Kellner

Ginsburgh, Yizhak, 8–9
 Barukh ha-Gever, 8
God, image of, xii, xiv, xv, 9n26, 31, 35, 36, 39, 66, 68, 86, 96n43, 97–100, 103, 121, 131n83, 151n43, 157, 161
Goldberg, Zalman Nehemiah, 8–9
Goldstein, Barukh, 8
Goodman, Lenn Evan, 12n33
Goshen-Gottstein, Alon
 Same God, Other God, 140n10
Greenberg, Blu, 139

Habad, 89n13, 102, 114n28, 120n47, 138n4, 155
Hadot, Pierre, 164–165
Haidt, Jonathan
 The Righteous Mind, 132–133
Haim of Volozhin, 137
Habad, 89, 102, 114, 120, 131, 138, 155
Halbertal, Moshe
 Maimonides, 30n3, 79n29
Halevi, Judah, xiii n1, xv, 2–3, 5, 13–16, 21, 30–39, 43–45, 48n13, 50–53, 70–72, 76–77, 83, 89–94, 99n50, 102, 115, 120n47, 124, 133, 161, 163–164
 Kuzari, 2–3, 6n19, 13n36, 15–16, 21n59, 32–34, 45n11, 70–71, 77
Halkin, Abraham
 Crisis and Leadership, 16n42
Halkin, Hillel, 100n54
Hartman, David, 144
 Crisis and Leadership, see Halkin, Abraham
Harvey, Zev (Warren), 13–14, 64, 66n64, 95n41, 130n81, 145n26
Hasidism, xvi, 89, 131, 137, 161
Hayes, Christine, 53–54, 93–94
Hegel, Georg Wilhelm Friedrich, 4n10
Heidegger, Martin, 134

Heschel, Abraham Joshua, 122n55, 152
Hillel (Rabbi), 68
Hillerman, Tony, 50n14
Hinduism, 110, 138–139
Hirshman, Menachem, 49, 116n36
Hitler, Adolf, 35n16, 57, 86n5
Holocaust, xv, 5, 35, 57n36, 59–60, 86–87
homosexuality, 109, 161
Hutner, Isaac, 135n93

Ibn Khaldun, 31n6
idolatry, *see avodah zarah*
inyan elohi, 71
Isaac (Bible), 3, 12–13, 33, 38, 43–45, 51n21, 53, 77, 91–92, 100–101, 103, 129, 135
Ishmael (Bible), 13n36, 33, 43, 45, 91, 100
Islam, xiiin1, 2n2, 8, 17n43, 28n1, 30, 32–33, 39–40, 74n19, 80–81, 99, 107–111, 115, 118, 120, 122, 124, 131–133, 135–136, 141n12, 151n43 Shia, xv, 32n8, 52–53, 93n33
Israel, land of, xii, 9, 15, 33, 49, 79, 93, 101, 140, 153
Itamar attack, 8n24
Itturei Kohanim, 2
Iyyun, 37n20

Jacob (Bible), xiv, 3, 15, 33, 38, 42–43, 45, 47, 53, 77–78, 91–92, 101, 103, 135
Jesus, 33, 117, 136, 138, 142
Joseph ben Judah, 159–160, 164
Josephus, xvi
Jospe, Raphael, 52n25, 71n7, 112–114
Judah the Prince, 25, 68
Judaism, xiii
    Abrahamic, xiii–xv, 25–27, 66

Conservative, 102, 134n93
Orthodox, xi–xiii, xv, 1, 7, 35, 42n1, 80n35, 90, 96n43, 102, 105–106, 109, 111–114, 123, 131–132, 134n93, 137–139, 145, 151, 154–156, 161–162
Reconstructionist, 54
Reform, 102, 112–113, 134n93, 162
Judt, Tony, 57n37
    Postwar, 57n37

Kabbalah, xv–xvi, 3, 9–10, 32n8, 34, 52n23, 61, 66n64, 83n50, 89–90, 101–102, 119n43, 137, 144, 147n32, 149n40, 156, 161, 163n9
Kadish, Seth Avi, 117n39
Kafih, Joseph, 37–39, 71, 79n29
Kafka, Franz, 60n45
Kaminsky, Joel, 44, 93, 101
Kant, Immanuel, 66, 98, 103, 133
Kaplan, Mordecai, 35, 54–56
    Judaism as a Civilization, 54n32
    The Religion of Ethical Nationhood, 35, 55
Karaites, 32, 101
Kasher, Hannah, 17n43, 37n20, 71n10, 125n60, 130–131, 150–151
Katz, Jacob, 113
Kenobi, Obi-Wan, 35
Kellner, Jolene, 40, 102, 130, 132, 157
Kellner, Menachem
    Dogma in Medieval Jewish Thought, 143
    Gam Hem Keruyim Adam, xiv, 68n1, 71n10
    Maimonides on Judaism and the Jewish People, xiv, 15–16, 36, 82n45, 91n23, 119n43
    Maimonides the Universalist, xiv, 25–26, 65n60, 73n15

Maimonides's Confrontation with Mysticism, 144
Must a Jew Believe Anything?, 91n23, 101n59, 140–141, 143
Keturah (Bible), 33, 43–44, 91
Kimche, J. J., 60n45, 62n47
Kimelman, Reuven, 29n1, 102n60, 114, 119n43
King, Martin Luther, 65n58, 140
Kogan, Barry, 34n12
Kohler, George, 62n48
kol ba'ei olam, xiv, 4, 36, 51, 84
Kook, Abraham Isaac, xv, 4n10, 89, 126, 129n75, 138–139
Kook, Zvi Yehudah, 2n3, 4n10, 7n22, 139n5
Koran (Quran), 97, 99n51, 133
Korn, Eugene, 39n29, 63n51, 113, 116, 129, 152n46
Korobkin, Daniel, 33
Kreisel, Howard, 13n36
Krinis, Ehud, 52n22
Kuzari, see Halevi, Judah

Lasker, Daniel, 48n13, 71, 120n47, 129n79
Lawee, Eric, 96n43
Levinas, Emmanuel, 86n4
Levi-Strauss, Claude, 60n45
liberalism, xv–xvii, 31, 35, 65n59, 100n54, 108, 162
Lieberman, Phillip, 12n33
Linfield, Susie, 58
Lior, Dov, 8–9
Lot (Bible), 33, 44, 91, 100–101
Lubitch, Ronen, 3n7
Luxemburg, Rosa, 58

Maharal of Prague, 10n28, 52n23, 89–90
Maimonides, Abraham, 119n43
Maimonides, Moses, *passim*

Book of Commandments, 38n24, 79, 95n41
Epistle to Yemen, 16n42, 108n10
Guide of the Perplexed, xiv, 1, 12–13, 17–19, 22–27, 30–32, 52n26, 63–64, 72, 77n23, 90n21, 120, 127, 131, 145–146, 148, 151–154, 157n57, 159–160, 164–165
Mishneh Torah, xiv, 1, 20n55, 22n62, 25–27, 63–64, 68–69, 74n17, 79, 82, 84, 103, 116–119, 130, 144, 147, 149–151, 154, 164
Marah, xiv, 17, 18, 23–24
Marx, Karl, xvi, 56–58, 60n45
Meir (Rabbi), 68–69, 78
Me'iri, Menahem, 30, 140–141, 155
Mekhilta d'Rabbi Ishmael, 49n15
Mekhilta, 15n41
Melamed, Avraham, xiiin1, 138n5
The Image of the Black in Jewish Culture, 31n6
Melamed, Eliezer, 138n5
Mendelssohn, Moses, 112–113
Jerusalem, 112
messianism, xiv–xv, 4–5, 7, 19n51, 26, 33, 39, 51–52, 58, 61–67, 71, 83–86, 88–90, 94, 103–104, 108n10, 116–121, 126, 134, 143n18, 155, 157
Midrash Tanhuma, 29n2
Midrash Tehilim, 95n41
mipi ha-gevurah, 22
mishkan; see Tabernacle
Modern Orthodoxy, 1, 106n5
Mishna
Megillah, 53, 93
Hagigah, 152n45
Bava Metsia, 95n41
Sanhedrin, 81–82, 97, 124, 150n42
Avodah Zarah, 139n5
Avot, 9n26, 54n32, 96n43, 129

Yadayim, 101n56
Moabites (Bible), 43–44, 68, 84, 101
monotheism, 89, 100, 107, 120, 124–125, 134
    Maimonidean, 146–154
Moses (Bible), xiv, xvi, 5, 14, 16–17, 24–27, 29, 42n3, 48–49, 66, 69, 77, 116, 126–130, 153n48, 162
Moses de Leon, 32n8
mysticism, xv, 32n8, 82, 128n73, 152

Nahmanides, 15n40, 18n48, 24n66, 38n24, 52n23, 90n19, 137, 153–154, 161
nationalism, 28n1, 35, 55–58, 87–88
naturalism, 19, 65–67
Navajo, 14, 38
Neoplatonism, xv
New York Times, 100n54
Noah (Bible), 5n14, 10–11, 24n66, 33, 91, 115–116, 120–121
Noahides, 115–116
Novak, David, 51n22, 91n23
    The Image of the Non-Jew in Judaism, 115n32

Orwell, George
    Animal Farm, 71n10
Ovadiah the Proselyte, 13n33, 37, 74–77, 79, 95, 141n12

particularism, xiv–xv, 5, 10n28, 27–28, 31, 34–35, 54, 61, 86, 89–94, 96–97, 99–100, 108n14, 119–120–121, 124, 161–162
Passover Haggadah, 78n27, 148n37
Philo, xvi
Pines, Shlomo, 12n33
pluralism, 37, 40, 91n23, 95, 105, 112, 113–116, 121, 125, 132–134
Popper, Karl, 91n23

postmodernism, xv, 108
proselytes, 15, 35, 37, 44, 68–79, 81–84, 95, 121
    Halevi on, 70–71
    Maimonides on, 68–69, 72–84 *see also ger*
proselytization, 83–84

Rabad, 81n40, 130–131, 150–151
Rabbinical Council of America (RCA), 105–106, 109n16
Rabinovich, Nachum, 163
Rashi, 29–30, 78n27, 95n40, 101n55, 129n75, 161
rationalism, xv, 71n7, 156–157
re'a, 94, 96–97
Romanticism, xv, 4
Rosenzweig, Franz, 62n48, 135n96
Rosner, Fred, 109n16
Ross, Tamar, 126
Roth, Leon
    Is There a Jewish Philosophy?, 94n40

Sacks, Jonathan, 30–31, 34, 40, 87n7, 90
Sacrifices, 17–25
Sagiv, Assaf, 61n47
Samuel ibn Tibbon, 30, 157n57
Sand, Shlomo, 122n51
    The Invention of the Jewish People, 57n37
Sandel, Michael J.
    Liberalism and the Limits of Justice, 87n7
Sarah (Bible), 25, 43
Sartre, Jean-Paul, 133
Schachter, Hershel, 9n26, 71n10
Schechter, Solomon, 122n52
Schonfeld, Eli, 61n46
Schwarz, Michael, 71
Schwarzschild, Steven, 62n48, 64–66, 71n7, 91n23, 103–104, 133–134

secularism, 35n17, 58, 60n45, 62, 106n4, 111
Seeskin, Kenneth, 58n39, 66n62, 67n66, 88n11, 89n15, 138n3
Septimus, Bernard, 11n30
Sforno, Ovadia, 24
Shammai, 68
Shapira, Yizhak, 8
    Torat ha-Melekh, xiii, 7–9, 34–35, 163n9
Shapiro, Marc, 144
Sheilat, Yizhak, 163
    Bein ha-Kuzari la-Rambam, 163
    Iggerot ha-Rambam, 15n41
Shem Tov ben Joseph ibn Shem Tov, 164
Shim'on bar Yochai, xvi, 32n7
Shneur Zalman of Lyady, 89n13
Sifre Deuteronomy, 79–80
Simon, Ernst, 96n43
Smith, Anthony D. 28n1
Soeiro, Ricardo
    Wounds of Possibility, 62n47
Solomon (Bible), 44
Soloveitchik, Joseph B., 106, 134n93
Sperber, Daniel, xi–xii
Spinoza, Baruch, xvi, 60n45, 113n25, 133
Stalin, Joseph, 56
Steiner, George, 54, 58–61
Stewart, Anne, 94n35
Strauss, Leo, 65n57

Tabernacle, 18, 20n56, 153
Talmud
    Babylonian
        Berakhot
            7a, 48
            25b, 128n74
            27b, 69n5
        Shevi'it
            39a, 99n49

Shabbat
    17b, 36n19
    28b, 24n66
    86b, 7n21
    87b, 23
    156a, 14n36
Pesachim
    118a, 13n34
Yoma
    69b, 140n9
    71b, 69n3
Ta'anit
    4a, 129n75
Yevamot
    47a-b, 72
Nedarim
    32a, 14n36
Gittin
    57b, 69
Bava Metsia
    59b, 95n41
Sanhedrin
    37a, 100n52
    56b, 23
    59a, 80
    64a, 140n9
    102b, 140n9
Makkot
    23b, 22n63
Shevuot
    39a, 99n49
Avodah Zarah
    2b, 49
    17a–b, 140n9
    22b, 32n7
Hullin
    13a, 154
Tanhumah Terumah, 25n68
Temple, xvi, 5, 18, 20–22, 53, 93, 110, 140n9, 153
Thau, Tzvi, 7n22

toleration, paradox of 108, 110
Tradition, 109n16
Trotsky, Leo, 56, 58
Twersky, Isadore, 26n70, 52n23, 78n28, 90n19, 144
    Rabad of Posquieres, 130n82

universalism, xv, 26–27, 35, 39, 51, 54, 58, 65, 67, 85–86, 89–91, 94–95, 97, 99–100, 103–104, 108, 116–122, 124–125, 138n5, 156, 162
Uziel, Ben-Zion Meir Hai, 96n43

Wasserman, Elhanan, 125n61
Weiss, Bari, 100n54
Weiss, Roslyn, 14n36
Wittgenstein, Ludwig, 60n45, 136n98

yefat to'ar, 73–74
Yishmael (Rabbi), xiv
Yosef, Ovadiah, 8
Yosef, Ya'akov, 8

Zini, Eliyahu, 138n5
    Hesed le-Umim Hatat, 138n5
Zionism, 2, 57–58, 62n48, 132n89
    religious, xii, 2, 4n10, 9, 136
Zohar, xvi, 5n13, 15n40, 32n8, 83, 89n13

www.ingramcontent.com/pod-product-compliance
Lightning Source LLC
Chambersburg PA
CBHW071831230426
43672CB00013B/2819